Praise for
The Stirring of Soul in the W<

"A new voice.... Briskin clearly will become a major influence in the world of organizational consulting. Readers will put this book down refreshed, inspired, awed, and perhaps haunted by the gap between the way they've been living their organizational lives and the vision the book contains."

—Peter B. Vaill, author of *Managing as a Performing Art*
and *Learning as a Way of Being*

"An organizational consultant who is as deeply concerned about the human soul as he is about organizational development, Briskin closes the distance between the two concepts in a way that diminishes neither and augments both."

—*Library Journal*

"Briskin's insights, as a writer and consultant, reflect a deep understanding of how human beings interact in social systems. In *The Stirring of Soul in the Workplace,* he touches on dimensions of human nature which impact nearly everyone in a working environment, with stories and examples that make the meaning easily accessible. It is a timely work, as more business people at all levels in organizations seek to understand how personal and human values rightly should be reflected in the workplace."

—Stephen D. Arnold, Vice Chairman, George Lucas Educational Foundation,
and Partner, Polaris Venture Partners

"Similar to the way a spotlight illuminates what we were once blind to, Briskin brilliantly brings to full view the hidden maze of forces and dynamics that are destroying the life force within ourselves while fragmenting our organizations. He leads the reader on an adventure of discovery, hoping to stir our souls to action by guiding us to see what is invisible to others."

—Margaret R. O'Keefe Umanzio, Summer Executive Institute, Stanford University

---

"Accessible, insightful, intelligent, and well written, this may be the business book of the decade!"

—John Evans, Owner, Diesel, A Bookstore

"Briskin's effort to value the complexity and mystery and brutality of the workplace is a welcome relief from the usual mechanical answers of most of the things we read. This is an insightful and well-written book that values the complexity of the human being and the workplaces we have created. The book does a wonderful job of tracing the origins of the beliefs that dominate our institutions and, in doing this, offers hope and guidance on how real change may be possible. Briskin respects the intelligence of the reader by arguing against simple solutions and false promises. I strongly recommend this book."

—Peter Block, author of *Stewardship* and *The Empowered Manager*

"Briskin's ultimate question turns the more conventional concern, 'How can we change people?' into 'How can organizations better reflect the whole human being?' This reflective, contemplative book is a refreshing attempt to answer that."

—*Booklist*

"Briskin integrates the outer world of function with the inner soul of the person in an almost Zen-like fashion..."

—*Publishers Weekly,* Religion Book Line

"Briskin, whose work as a management consultant has exposed him to all sides of the corporate prism, adds to the enduring genre of workplace spirituality with a work rich in both history and vision... Since the future is uncertain, he says, look for answers in the present, in the dialogue that goes on between the inner and the outer. Listen close enough, and lasting truths will be revealed."

—*NAPRA Review*

"Briskin explores how to find work roles that bring a sense of wonder and passion..."

—*Orange County Register*

"*The Stirring of Soul in the Workplace* opens the long needed dialogue about how we are to work together in a world that no longer has any heroes, little room for loyalty or universal evil empires to strive against or pull down, and a global economy that can only be characterized as turbulent. As long as we had an acceptable reason to sacrifice some of our humanity in the workplace, few questioned being treated as a cog in a great machine. As long as we could see that the sacrifice guarded us and our families against another economic depression, world war, and that the organization we dedicated our work lives to would stand behind us, we said little. Now, however, there is no place to hide, no place to run to for security either as individuals or organizations. In short, the old rules, theories and structures no longer work. Briskin, thoughtfully and skillfully asks the questions all are asking but perhaps not yet voicing out loud. And thankfully, he opens a dialogue on how we might remember ourselves as individuals in organizations and as organizations."

—Ned Hamson, Editor, *The Journal for Quality and Participation*

"Briskin heralds the power and passion of soul as a necessary force field within the workplace. He challenges readers to express themselves more freely and to keep alert to the feeling states, rituals, power dynamics, and habits of organizational life. In the end, Briskin correctly argues that the soul can be stirred in the work arena through the spiritual practices of attention, being present, openness, and deep listening."

—Frederic A. Brussat, *Values & Visions* Reviews

"Briskin eloquently suggests that soul and self are inextricably linked to who we are both inside and outside the workplace.... Instead of sacrificing the well-being of the human soul for the goals of the organization, Briskin says that we must meld the two. We must be willing to shift between what organizations want of people and what humans need and desire."

—*Training & Development*

"Like few business books, *The Stirring of Soul in the Workplace,* hits on the essence of our work in corporate America. While spending our careers trying to help our companies make money and deliver goods, we must also attend to the ultimate purpose of our work— to make it as meaning-ful as possible. Briskin's book forces us to think hard about these twin goals. To some, it will suggest new practices; in all, it will inspire new thinking."

—David Murray, Editor-in-Chief,
Journal of Employee Communication Management

"This book will take the reader a step or two beyond Douglas MacGregor's "human side of enterprise." Open [the book] to any page and you'll find a stimulating story or idea."

—*Business Ethics Resource*

"Unlike most change management books, this powerful and provocative work addresses the complexities and paradoxes of corporate change. I have found it a useful tool in helping senior managers understand the need to honor the contradictions inherent in change and allow employees to personally reconcile the "shadow side" of change. Only after this recon-ciliation can employees bring their passion and energy into new, revital-ized roles. The book moves beyond the employee level and forces the orga-nization to probe deeply into its own soul to find what it really believes verses what it tells employees. I feel so strongly about the message that the book has inspired a training program and change strategy philosophy. I will continue to recommend this reading to our leaders because it is vital to the soul of our organization."

—Paul Leonetti, Director, Organizational Development,
Catholic Healthcare West

"I had the chill of recognition of my own workplace. Briskin uncovers what I encounter every day but don't know how to explain. The book is intensely practical and provides hope that progress can be made, not in spite of the wounds in our organizations, but because of them. This book meets me at the intersection of my heart and my performance review. The stories resonate, leaving me with a question to myself: when do I start doing something about it?"

—Terry South, Area General Manager, Showtime Networks

The Stirring of Soul in the Workplace is really about the journey to wholeness....his envisioned workplace is a metaphor for all groups, societies, and governments."

—*New Age Retailer*

"Business has discovered its soul in recent years—with uneven results. Sound treatments are available, but too much recent literature uses spiritual language to sugarcoat the hard realities of the business world. But in *The Stirring of Soul in the Workplace,* Alan Briskin takes us into those hard realities and reveals the creative potentials on the other side. Drawing on various wisdom traditions, Briskin identifies soul as our link to the shadow world, the source of our vitality, a center where opposites are joined, and our connection to the divine. He argues that classical management theory has defied the soul's imperative, yielding organizations that rob us of the very energies that make life possible. He shows how soul and organizations can be creatively joined, and how leaders can help that happen. He avoids technical "fixes" but offers something more lasting and powerful—insight and understanding. This is a splendid book, grounded in deep experience with organizations and with life. It's insights could help heal our souls, our structures, and our society."

—Parker Palmer, author of *The Active Life* and
To Know as We Are Known

The Stirring of Soul in the Workplace

. . . .

The Stirring of Soul
in the Workplace

· ·

Alan Briskin

Berrett-Koehler Publishers, Inc.
San Francisco

Berrett-Koehler Publishers, Inc.
450 Sansome Street, Suite 1200
San Francisco, CA 94111-3320
Tel.: (415) 288-0260   Fax: (415) 362-2512

ORDERING INFORMATION

Individual sales. Berrett-Koehler publications are available through most bookstores. They can also be ordered direct from Berrett-Koehler at the address above.

Quantity sales. Special discounts are available on quantity purchases by corporations, associations, and others. For details, contact the "Special Sales Department" at the Berrett-Koehler address above.

Orders for college textbook/course adoption use. Please contact Berrett-Koehler Publishers at the address above.

Orders by U.S. trade bookstores and wholesalers. Please contact Publishers Group West, 4065 Hollis Street, Box 8843, Emeryville, CA 94662. Tel.: (510) 658-3453; 1-800-788-3123. Fax: (510) 658-1834.

Printed in the United States of America.

 Printed on acid-free and recycled paper that is composed of 85% recovered fiber, including 15% postconsumer waste.

Library of Congress Cataloging-in-Publication Data

Briskin, Alan, 1954-
 The stirring of soul in the workplace / Alan Briskin.
  p. cm.
 "Originally published in hardcover in 1996 by Jossey-Bass Publishers. This paperback edition contains the complete text of the original"–T.p. verso
   Includes bibliographical references and index.
   ISBN 1-57675-040-X (alk. paper : pbk)
   1. Organizational change—Management.   2. Quality of work life.
   3. Psychology, Industrial.   I. Title.
HD58.8.B754 1998
658.4'06—dc20   97–53319
                    CIP

Paperback Edition

2001 00 99 98   10 9 8 7 6 5 4 3 2 1

*To my father, who taught in words and deeds that we should
never fear the truth.
And to my son, who teaches me daily that the search for truth
leads to further questions.*

. . . .

Contents

. . . .

Preface

No one who works today needs to be told that change in and out of the workplace is accelerating beyond our ability to grasp the implications of those changes. The future is uncertain. And during uncertain times, we search for what is truest about ourselves and what is most desirable about our relations with others. We ponder meaning. We also know, however, that uncertainty creates anxiety and sometimes desperate attempts to find something to believe in. Uncertainty engenders real opportunity as well as misleading choices, great leaders as well as false messiahs, and new ways of understanding the world alongside hollow maxims and deceptive promises. Understandably, we seek guides and guideposts to ease the anxiety of the journey. But we also need to depend on our own insight and imagination to cultivate, from our own experience, a way to move forward.

The Stirring of Soul in the Workplace is a reality check on management and the workplace: where we are, where we have been, and where we may be going. Although I am a management consultant, I am not writing from the perspective of making organizations more efficient or workers happier. Efficiency and harmony may be important goals, but they are not the only challenges we face. The challenge that runs like a thread through the chapters of this book is to keep alive the stirring of soul, a quality brought to life by grappling with the often ambiguous and contradictory aspects of our experience. In cultivating our own experience, we begin the process of acting as guides for ourselves and for each other. By struggling with ambiguity and contradictory impulses, we fan the flame of our own unique gifts and instincts.

But why talk about soul? Is there a danger in bringing a spiritual idea into the pragmatic world of work? While I was writing this book, a client working in corporate communications within a large conglomerate told me, "We're so busy moving people around, trying to meet our deadlines, trying to influence people to believe in what we're doing, that we just don't want to really look into anybody's eyes and see that they have souls. We should start with the premise that we have souls. But souls are difficult to manage. And even if we talked about people having souls, it would probably be from a corporate viewpoint." She said this last sentence with emphasis. Her point was not that a corporate viewpoint was inherently bad but that in the context of the current workplace, *soul* could easily be made into a slogan.

Her words, coming at a time of reflection in my life, helped remind me of my purpose and the challenge of writing about soul in organizations. I believe not only that we have souls, but that some of the qualities we associate with soul—meaning, memory, beauty, fragility, divinity, wildness, union—are fundamental aids for navigating into the future. But I also believe that soul is elusive and beyond our ability to harness it for only practical purposes. Her last sentences—"But souls are difficult to manage. And even if we talked about people having souls, it would probably be from a corporate viewpoint."—heightened my awareness and concern that our concept of soul is malleable, tempting us to accommodate soul to the outer world of practicality and immediate needs. Corporations and authors alike, we need to be cautious that the idea of soul not be used merely as an outer slogan for corporate inspiration, or even as an inner slogan, describing only our best intentions.

In the workplace, we have become polarized between managing the outer organization—work processes, organizational objectives, managerial structures—and the inner organization of people—emotional attitude, mental processes, cooperative spirit. Following a path with soul suggests an approach that borders both worlds but is not contained by them. In attending to experience and reflection on experience, we develop a heightened capacity to straddle these two worlds and discover something new.

The philosopher Jacob Needleman suggests that our capacity to recognize soul is at times hindered by a belief that the soul is a fixed entity. In contrast to this view, he offers an image of the soul as an emerging energy, activated and brought into being by our wrestling with the often contradictory nature of experience. In the workplace, where many different needs exist simultaneously, we birth the energy of soul by wrestling with our own experience of contradiction and forging a response from our deepest being.

But how does one begin? How can we bring the full force of our being to bear on the complexities of the workplace and the competing demands on our energies? Do we need to attend a workshop? Should we meditate? Should we find a guru?

I do not believe the answer lies in a program, a technique, or a mystical belief system. To listen to the soul's voice is to become more mindful, to pay attention to what is happening inside us and around us. The gathering of our attention awakens the energies of soul, and the patience to follow what we notice releases these energies within us.

The Soul in Organizations: A Bridge Between Two Worlds

My discussion of the soul borrows from an early insight that we cannot learn about the soul in isolation from group life. Organizations—religious, educational, business—are the context in which the *and* of "the individual and the group" takes place. Organizations are places where what is unique about the individual meets what is unique about social organization. Increasingly, organizations are where we spend the majority of our time and where the stirrings of the soul are often perceived as absent. To explore the challenge to the human soul in organizations is to build a bridge between the world of the personal, subjective, and even unconscious elements of individual experience and the world of organizations that demand rationality, efficiency, and personal sacrifice. For the individual, there is often no clear distinction between these worlds. We are both individuals and members of groups within organizations. We cannot leave behind who we are when we are inside organizations any more than we can shut out the organization when we are alone. We carry inside us all the time both the organization in our mind and the person we think we are. When there is a fit, we sense harmony and balance. When these two worlds collide, however, the individual feels torn and alone.

Social scientists have too often been seduced into finding ways to make individuals adapt to organizations. When organizations change, social scientists diagnose "resistance." They study principles of why people resist in order to "help" people resist less. They rarely explore the mystery of the *and* or ask what difference it makes if people function better in an environment not worth living in. To explore the role of the human soul in organizations, we must be willing to shift our viewpoint back and forth between what organizations want of people and what constitutes human complexity: the contradictory nature of human needs, desires, and experience.

To explore the human soul is not to abandon the importance of organizations in favor of the subjective and idiosyncratic tastes of individuals. We live in social organizations—families, communities, social clubs, workplaces—and it is in these groups that our souls are shaped and textured. Being open to the demands of relationship, whether with a single human being or within a group, provides an extraordinary opportunity. When conflict arises between the individual and the group, there is an opportunity to learn more about what our souls are made of.

Organizations and the Whole Human Being

The Stirring of Soul in the Workplace is drawn from my experience in organizations and from reflections on that experience over the past twenty years. For half of that time, I have been an organizational consultant, working with individuals and groups learning to create more effective organizations in the face of change, disruption, and sometimes turmoil. But the book originated in my earlier work with disturbed adolescents in residential homes and with inmates in a state correctional institution. In those confined spaces, the darker aspects of the soul were free to flare up; the less rational and less socialized parts of ourselves were less restrained, more visible. I learned about an *underworld* of soul, feelings of abandonment, rage, guilt, despair, and shame. I learned something in those years about the limitations of managing others. For years after my work in these institutions, I dreamed about the children and men I worked with and saw traces of their spirit in the faces of others in the outside world. I came to believe that genuine change is never a function of dominance, or even of education, but of empathy and common ground.

My early experience within institutions propelled me into a study of the origins of institutions. My question was not *how can we change people* but instead *how can organizations better reflect the whole human being?* How, I wondered, can our experience within organizations be the basis for how we shape change? How can we account for the different parts of ourselves, the upper realm of rational behavior and the underworld of passions and emotions? These two worlds meet all the time in organizations, though we may often be unaware of their connection. If we design organizations only with the upper world in mind, we are less able to account for the tremors that are set off from below. And even more relevant to organizations today, when we are cut off from the deeper regions of soul, we lose the energies that give rise to the imagination and passions necessary for creativity and adaptation to a changing world. *The Stirring of Soul in the Workplace* is a look at how we have fragmented work and people from the deeper regions of soul and what we may still be able to do about it.

Why Should We Care (and Read) About Soul in Organizations?

For everyone who has gone through various management fads and prescriptions, this book is meant as a retreat. It is for those who feel the need to reflect on how we have come to our current workplaces. What human price did we pay for the organizations we created? How does rapid change not only make us work harder but with less ability to be mindful of what we are doing? How can our own experience within an organization be valued and valuable during times of uncertainty? What role can insight and imagination play in becoming more effective?

I hope this book can serve as an alternative to the flood of management books offering to fix it, shift your paradigm, and get you home for dinner. It is also an alternative to the ceaseless flow of self-help books that promise you salvation regardless of the environment you work in. This book should be of interest to those who value reflection and imagination as prerequisite to a genuine capacity to act in organizations. I have written it for leaders managing change efforts, managers coping with the new demands of the workplace, consultants pondering their role in helping organizations develop, and individuals who seek a way of joining their own spiritual path with the realities and expectations of the workplace.

The Contents of this Book and the Journey of the Soul

The Stirring of Soul in the Workplace is organized into three parts. Part One, Perceiving the Soul, explores the idea of soul. How do we think about soul? What is its relevance today? What were some of the ancient origins of soul beliefs? In the first chapter, I write about soul as an interaction of the many different parts of ourselves, both an upper world of conscious intention and an underworld of feelings, fantasies, and imagination. And I point to how these questions remain alive in organizations today. Chapter Two is about the struggle we face when we acknowledge an underworld of shadows, contradictory impulses, and secrets we keep even from ourselves. In organizations, the recognition of shadow in collective behavior as well as in ourselves becomes a fundamental skill in navigating during times of turbulence and change. Chapter Three is a tale about the origins of institutional attempts to manage irrational behavior and social maladjustment. In exploring facets of the soul that had to be repressed, I present challenges for all of us to comprehend the loss of soul and the effects of surveillance, the uses of social conformity, and the desire for control over human behavior. In organizations today, the echo of these practices can still be heard, even amidst calls for self-regulation, self-managing teams, and employee empowerment.

Part Two, Chasing the Dream of Order, addresses the challenges to the soul in past organizational practices and in today's workplace. Part Two presents the problems we face in designing a workplace more reflective of the whole human being. It tells of the underworld of organizational structures, techniques, and philosophies for managing the human soul. Chapter Four is a story about the mechanization of the workplace and how individual experience became subordinate to the emerging technologies of the industrialized workplace. It is an account of material progress and the growing efficiency of production amidst fragmentation and standardization of how work was to be accomplished. Chapter Five is a retelling of the story of Frederick W. Taylor, an engineer honored and vilified for his ideas about creating a science of management. In Taylor's life and ideas are lessons about efficiency and control that we still debate today as we try to comprehend the science of reengineering and the complexities of managing change. In Chapter Six, I focus on the legacies of efficiency as they relate to human endurance, the meaning of work, and the challenge to value reflection as a skill for managing the contradictory experience of the workplace. Chapter Seven is a chronicle of how organizations attempt to reformulate motivational strategies and personal incentives in order to balance the needs of productivity with the needs for motivating the workforce. We are presented with the challenge to the soul to distinguish between the illusion of greater involvement and genuine efforts to face the conflicting realities of workplace demands.

Part Three, Journeying Toward Meaning, Coherence, and Wholeness, is about the question "So what?" In Chapter Eight, I explore a new way of looking at organizational role that suggests it can be a psychological stance one *takes* rather than a position one is *given*. In taking up a role, we must make use of the skill of experience and reflect on what truly matters, to the individual, to the organization, and to the larger community we serve. The ability to comprehend and respect an *organization in the mind* becomes a central premise for navigating the changing arrangements of the workplace. In Chapter Nine, I stress the need to think creatively about human systems, both the upper world of organizational structure and the underworld of human emotion and fantasy, because only then can we recognize patterns and act from within the stance of our role. Chapter Ten returns to the challenge to the soul in negotiating the journey from within the workplace. I talk about a need to respect uncertainty, an inclination for dialogue, and a regard for paradox and for the interconnectivity of all life.

The Stirring of Soul in the Workplace is about management and the workplace. But it is also about our trials as individuals to account for all of ourselves. The journey of the soul is indirect, circular, and metaphorical, imbued with a richness and confusion evoking our deepest longings and most profound fears. I have written this book partly for others, to leave them a record of my own journey to understand the invisible cry of the soul and the challenges we face. And partly I have written it for myself, to exorcise a responsibility I felt to put into words what seemed at times only ghostly intuitions. You may find that this book at times evokes your own ghosts and intuitions about organizations and your place within them. My hope is that the book will support your journey and offer some guideposts for traveling a path that has soul.

The Importance of Telling Stories

I learned about the soul as a child at the kitchen table, with my family telling stories to each other, jokes, fables, religious anecdotes, how it looked when a neighbor's kid slipped on the ice, or how it sounded when an argument broke out on the bus. Everyone got in on it, no matter how many times the same story was told or how long it took. We had time to listen, to interrupt, to yell over each other's voices. My mother had the most novel approach. She would tell a joke or sometimes a poignant story, and in the midst of our laughing or reflecting she would ask why it was funny or what about her story was so important. We never ceased to be amazed that she was earnest and wanted to know why, not to test us but to be sure that she wasn't missing something. My brother, my sister, and I would then take turns explaining what was funny or important. We each learned something new, not the least of which was that we all understood the jokes and stories differently.

I learned that the soul is expressed not only with people you care about but across the entire spectrum of humanity. I learned that it is not the number of times you hear a story that is important but the degree to which you let it into your heart. And I learned to appreciate, beyond the kitchen table where I received my early education, that stories shape the way we learn how to approach the world. If the stories speak to the struggles and hopes of our own experience, they give us confidence in our future, no matter how dark or even tragic the tale. But if the stories we tell each other do not reflect the experiences we have, then we stop believing both the stories and our own hearts.

I write about the soul in much the same fashion as I learned about the soul at my kitchen table: with stories and with speculation about what they might mean. My stories and comments are meant as an invitation for readers to reflect on their own experience, hoping that through reflection new truths and new ways of imagining the future will be revealed.

Appreciation

Though writing is a solitary activity, many friends supported me, offering counsel, appropriate caution, and comfort. I could not imagine attempting, let alone finishing, this work without them. Often, just when I feared I had reached the edges of my understanding or lacked the stamina to continue, I was guided by their insights and encouragements to finish what I started and leave off the moaning and wailing.

Glenn Tobe and Kate Regan coached, advised, and when necessary prodded me with their perspective and wisdom throughout all the stages of the manuscript. Their enthusiasm for the ideas in the book continually stirred my thinking and reminded me of the reasons I took up this project. In addition, my writing group colleagues in the Duck Club—Bill Bergquist, David Bradford, Susan Harris, and Peg Umanzio—engaged my thoughts, challenged my clarity, and badgered me to action as only those who share common passions can do. Susan Kelly, Nancy Barber, Nurya Love Lindberg, and my editorial collaborator, Sheryl Fullerton, aided me at critical stages of the manuscript's development. When I was at a loss for a structure to contain divergent ideas or for language to best communicate an idea or story, these four were there. Also, Nancy Raulston offered critical research assistance when deadlines loomed. I am also most appreciative of Sarah Polster, editor at Jossey-Bass, for taking the risk that this book could be brought to fruition and for her stalwart guidance along the way.

I am indebted to members of The Grubb Institute, whose deep reflections on roles and systems strongly influenced my approach to writing Chapters Eight and Nine. Papers on these subjects are available from the institute in its publication *Professional Management*. My thanks to Barry Evans, George McCauley, S.J., and J. Randall Nichols, who mentored me during my internship at the institute. I further want to thank Jill Janov and John Evans for reading the first full draft of this manuscript and offering feedback both gracious and wise.

Along the way, there have been many friends and colleagues who offered the thoughts and stories that have found their way into this work. I want to thank them, while offering my apologies to those I have not named: John Brett, Carol Briskin, Jules Briskin, Rick Brown, Cindy Buckle, Jeanne Cherbeneau, Lisa and Rufus Cole, Arthur Colman, Adam Cornford, Anna Ewins, Carolyn Firmin, Jan Felicitas, Gary Ferrini, Rachel Flaith, Diane Foster, Jim Herold, Amy Honigman, Paul Johnson, Barbara and Marty Kaplan, Mario Leal, Lanz Lowen, Barbara Bunn McCullough, Mern O'Brien, Perviz Randeria, Ralph Reed, Alison Reid, Saul Siegel, Toby Simons, Karen Young, and Arnold Zippel. I especially want to thank my clients, whose openness to delving into their own experience and offering perceptions of their workplace gave substance and meaning to the ideas I was exploring. They taught me to respect that in each of us lies an answer to those willing to find the question.

I want to thank my mother, who often seems to capture what is unspoken. When I worried that some might find my book disturbing, she recalled Mark Twain's comment that he wasn't sure which kinds of books he admired more: those that put him to sleep at night or those that kept him awake. What was important, she counseled me, was that I tell my story as best I can.

Finally, I want to thank my wife, Jane, and son, Alex, who accompanied me through the trials and demands of writing. They stuck with me, grounding me in the realities of family and the nurturance of caring for each other. I appreciate their patience, tolerance, and insistence that we are in this together.

Oakland, California   Alan Briskin
June, 1996

Part One

· ·

Perceiving the Soul

The Wilderness Within

Ancient Views of the Soul

*The journey is difficult, immense, at times impossible,
yet that will not deter some of us from attempting
it. . . . I can at best report only from my own wilderness. The important thing is that each man possess
such a wilderness and that he consider what marvels
are to be observed there.*

Loren Eiseley, The Immense Journey

A ndy is in his mid-thirties. He graduated with an M.B.A. from a prestigious university and sees himself as particularly skilled in transition management. He describes himself as comfortable with ambiguity and positive in his outlook on managing change—confident that he can help others with the difficult task of organizational transition.

When a reengineering was announced in his organization, he welcomed the opportunity for himself and his organization, which he saw as too insular and too reluctant to change. Told that an entire layer of senior administrators would be removed, he remained optimistic even though he was in one of the positions likely to be terminated. "Everyone was walking around with their heads down and filled with gloom," he said of his peers, "but I'm feeling upbeat about the changes. Sure, there'll be pain, but I'm not a victim. If I stay with the organization, that'll be fine, and if I don't, that's OK too."

Note: All vignette characters in this book are composites and are not meant to indicate specific individuals; all are identified pseudonymously.

In the next six months, a great deal changed. He found his ideals shattered, first by disquieting minor inconsistencies and later by a feeling of assault on his personal integrity and dignity. He was one of the few administrators among his peers who had not been terminated during the reorganization, but now that seemed a detail to him.

During the course of the transition, an outside consulting firm was hired to evaluate senior managers for potential new roles in the company. Andy's colleagues, subordinates, and superiors were asked to assess his value to the new organization. He was informed, almost by chance in a hallway, that their findings had been communicated to the CEO, who would be reviewing Andy's future in the organization. Andy was told when and where to report for the review. He was also told that a second consulting firm, hired to support employees being terminated, would be available following the interview.

The interview did not go well. There were high hopes for him in the organization, the CEO said, but nothing was mentioned about where Andy would be going or what he might be doing. The feedback on his performance was cursory, with the CEO stating that the consultants' interviews were confidential and therefore could not be discussed. The CEO did mention, however, that Andy didn't seem to be managing the transition very well. He seemed moody and not handling change in a particularly positive manner. The CEO referred obliquely to reports that at times Andy was perceived as losing control. He said that change was painful for everyone, but at Andy's level the expectation was that people should be able to cope. The CEO held out the hope that whatever Andy's new assignment, it would be an opportunity for him to grow and develop.

Andy felt convicted on charges he could not determine, let alone refute. He felt that he was supposed to be pleased with the interview, but what he actually felt was that he was being told he was a reclamation project. His performance ratings during the years of service to the organization had never been anything but positive.

Somehow, and without explanation, he had become a problem that needed to be fixed.

Andy found himself in crisis, a crisis that echoed deep within him. The certainty he had felt about himself was shaken. The self-confident, forward-looking individual he knew himself to be now gave way to new aspects of his personality that seemed foreign and uncomfortable. Something was stirred up within him, feelings and emotions that he had trouble recognizing as his own.

The soul, as I use the word in this book, stands for the *multiplicity of selves* within each of us; their interactions and struggles are the threads that weave the self together. In tension with this interior complexity are the constant pressures, from within and without, to foreclose the mystery of our many selves. Understandably, we fear that the unknown may be dangerous. But to care for our soul—a timeless struggle made more urgent by modern society—we must combat those forces that would reduce us to just a singular self. The soul represents the mysterious, multifaceted dimension of our personality, never fully known, yet a source of vital influence.

How does such a way of looking at soul become relevant to and reflect our experience in the workplace? How can we bring more of ourselves into the workplace and into our own awareness? When is it we are most likely to confront different parts of ourselves and the organizations we work in?

For Andy, the rupture of his singular self led to a period of deep reflection. He felt as if veil after veil of illusion had been lifted from his sight, as if all he had done to rationalize his image of himself and his image of the organization had suddenly shifted. Where he had seen only individual pain, now he saw patterns of behavior that hurt people. Where he had accepted pain as necessary and inevitable during change, now he saw examples of abuse that were unnecessary and damaging. And more critically, he saw a different picture of himself emerging.

He was not only the strong, willful individual who had previously focused his attention outward, analyzing how others coped and viewing his role as helping others to cope better. Now, feeling vulnerable, he noticed more how much he held back, even from himself, his emotional reactions to events. He became aware that his instinct to analyze others was a protective mechanism, motivated as much by a sense of others' being dangerous as by a wish to help people cope better. And he saw that even his supposed strength at coolly analyzing situations was at times also an urgent attempt to distance emotions.

He described this new awareness of himself as revitalizing, as if he were a diver discovering new treasures beneath the surface of his previous awareness. He specifically discounted these discoveries as major insights; instead he saw that he had been aware of these things before, but never with the same attention and significance. What he found so revitalizing was not the discoveries themselves, but the depth of self that he had not known was waiting there for him. Before, he had been so enamored with his intellectual skills of figuring out and fixing problems that he had never perceived a need to plunge into the murky and shifting recesses of his own mind. Now he laughed at his image of himself as being comfortable with ambiguity; he was actually terrified of it. He had just never considered ambiguity as something that might last long enough to disturb him.

Andy began to express a new kind of confidence, though tentatively. A curtain had been pulled back, revealing his past and hinting at a new possibility for his future; options existed where before there had been linear direction. He saw that his personality had not been shaped entirely by conscious will and effort but rather by what the world threw at him. He had responded to events outside his control and then, after the fact, said he had chosen rational responses. He was not a victim, but neither did he always control events or his responses to them. Andy found this revelation liberating because he had carried into his adult life a terrible burden that he *could* control events, if only he could figure out the right thing to do.

Andy saw the irony that the CEO's hurtful feedback triggered a personal journey that might not have happened if all had gone well. He was at a loss for words to describe his sadness at the thought that this period of reflection might not have occurred. He imagined himself looking into a mirror and seeing a face appear that had not been there before—and disappearing just as suddenly. The joy at seeing this face was life affirming, but the notion that he might never have glimpsed it was disturbing, filling him with feelings of loss. He thought, however, that he had no intention of thanking the CEO.

Andy did not use the word *soul* to describe his experience. Yet his "double vision," the face he knew and the other face that appeared for an instant in the mirror, had the quality of multiplicity that is an aspect of soul. Andy was not describing just an insight into his personality. He was describing a mystery, a self he was but dimly aware of, one that had darker features and that contradicted essential aspects of his conscious personality. Yet his experience was of a person finding a relative long thought dead or never born. How could he be whole without this other person? How could he see the world differently, more contoured, and with greater dimension, if not through the eyes of this other face? There were few people he could talk to about this experience, he said. Who would believe him?

In the modern organizations that have developed over the past 150 years of the industrial revolution, there has emerged a concept of an *individual* personality, shaped by the necessities of work and the internal control individuals are required to have over themselves. This view has created a schism within the psyche of individuals, a fundamental polarization between wanting more control and a desire to experience ourselves as part of a mystery that is beyond our control. We seem often at cross purposes with ourselves, preaching the virtue of control and practicing its opposite.

The soul as multiplicity implies a dimension to the self much greater than what we know about ourselves consciously. Thomas

Moore talks of a soul infinite in capacity, full of mystery, and contradictory in its designs over our life. Oscar Wilde, who wrote about the soul from his prison cell, said that only the shallow know themselves: if you know yourself, you have not touched the depths. But to know something of these depths, we first must be able to see in new ways.

Seeing with Soul

I was once in a photography class in Yosemite Valley. Other amateur photographers and I hoped to capture some of the beauty and grandeur of the granite rock faces and flowing waterfalls with our high-tech photographic gear. There was only one problem. It was raining so heavily that there was virtually nothing to see. Clouds covered the mountains, the fields and streams were gray, the movement of the water was almost invisible in the pelting rain. Our cameras were useless; one well-placed drop of rain could short-circuit the electronic brain, making the camera fire repeatedly or shut down entirely. Our instructor, an old hand at the idiosyncrasies of nature photography, cautioned us to remain aware of the constantly shifting light and the changing shapes of the mountains wreathed by the clouds. She encouraged us to see with a "third eye," to practice *seeing* with heightened awareness. Art, she reminded us, does not reproduce the visible. Art renders visible.

So I was staring at El Capitan with my third eye, only it felt like my two eyes and a headache. There was nothing much to see; the granite rock was almost completely invisible, the trees and streams flat in the dull gray overcast of the day. I was mostly engaged in an internal conversation with myself about not becoming frustrated. "What does it mean to render visible?" I asked myself.

When my attention returned to the mountain, I saw that something was happening. The rain had lessened by degrees, and suddenly feelings within me began to stir. Pulling out my camera, I framed different sections of the mountain with my lens. I saw something otherworldly, something I could not have seen were I staring numbly at the scenery. I got an image in my mind of the trees in partial silhouette staring at the mountain in awe, their sharp triangular shapes huddled together below the mysterious outcropping of rock that hovered above them. I now understood that to render visible is to see through the visible into a world that becomes animated with imagination.

Seeing through and beyond is essential in our work as well. We cannot know ourselves, or the workplaces we are part of, in any depth unless we engage the full breadth of our humanity, vitality, and understanding.

The elusive nature of knowing how to see with the soul requires a certain stillness and attentiveness. Stillness creates an opening in the surface world of things. Attentiveness leads us out from the thicket of thoughts, events, and beliefs that snare us. How could I see through the flat gray landscape of an overcast day if I was snared by my frustration with technology, my disappointment with the weather, and my confusion with mystical abstractions calling me to see with a third eye? The instructor's comment to watch the light was both a concrete suggestion and a metaphor for finding a way below my conscious thoughts and beyond the limits of my vision. Attending to the light brought a hidden awareness to the surface that rendered visible not just a landscape of trees and cloud and rock but one of mood and emotion and fantasy.

So it was with Andy in the story that opens this chapter. He knew himself too well. There was no mystery to his responses. Through his frustration, he learned that any reasonable person reviewing a common body of facts would not, as he believed, come to a conclusion similar to his. Frustration taught Andy, as it taught me, to sense greater depth and complexity and to open to mystery. The challenge of finding soul in organizations, as in life, is to embrace not only what we see, hear, and understand but also to attend to what we don't know, what we cannot see at first glance or hear on first listening.

The soul in its multiplicity is an idea directly contradicting the literal, rational, unitary interpretation of events so common in organizations. The soul speaks in the language of metaphor, fantasy, and emotion. I watched clouds taking on different shapes and colors with each subtle shift in the wind and nuance of light; that is exactly how the unconscious feels to me when I pay attention to it in myself. My thoughts, moods, fantasies, and emotions are constantly shifting, rearranging, coming in and out of focus. What is real for the soul is different from what is real for the objective manager who assumes a reality that can be discovered through external facts and reasoned argument. Below the surface of reason is an unconscious wilderness animated by feelings of awe and danger.

We need an approach to soul that respects its own complex language, that allows us to see its stirrings in the workplace and in our own hearts. Soul reminds us of what has been forgotten and disowned. We bring more of ourselves into the workplace when we remember what we have come to achieve and what struggles we must face.

The soul's vitality as an idea lies in its capacity for renewal, a conception born in the depth of human imaginings about the limitations and infinite potentialities of being human. The philosopher Friedrich Nietzsche, who decried that God was dead, insisted that we should keep soul alive, for it is "one of the oldest and most venerable of hypotheses" (Thiele, 1990, p. 52). Why is this so? What is it about the soul as a symbol that it can remain open to new forms of interpretation, yet still represent a timeless attribute of beauty, human fragility, and the longing for meaning? How does one approach the soul?

Ancient Wisdom About the Soul

As far back as we can trace, concepts of the soul have been diverse, with multiple meanings in varied contexts. The word *soul* is used so frequently today that it has become something of a projection screen from which we each can envision our own particular meaning. Soul is a concept used in religion, literature, philosophy, poetics, psychology, politics, and now increasingly in the world of management and the workplace. The *Soul of Business* by Tom Chappell has become a best-seller, Bolman and Deal write about *Leading with Soul,* and Tom Peters uses the word *soul* repeatedly in his books on the changing workplace. But soul is an ancient idea, central to traditions in both the East and the West.

The soul as an ancient hypothesis seems to touch at least four core themes vital to human health and resilience. The first, linked with early Greek writings, is that soul is associated with the underworld, a place of depth and shadowy realities. The underworld is what gives us dimension and connection to unconscious facets of ourselves.

The second, evident in Greek and Hebrew stories, is that soul is associated with our vitality, the source of animation, essence, and renewal.

Third, soul is a place of union among opposites, the joining of spirit and matter, the light and dark aspects of the whole person. This theme is found in Hebrew as well as Taoist philosophy.

Fourth, soul contains a spark of the divine, a bridge to the qualities of a supreme being or a cosmic aspect to consciousness. Gnostic myths portray this theme vividly.

These themes overlap and move off in uncountable directions. Each theme relates to creation myths or stories about the origin of the soul and the responsibilities associated with having souls. No tradition holds exclusive rights to knowing what stirs soul into being. What is common among the themes is that soulmaking is an odyssey of self-discovery that connects us to the world and to our duties in this life. To approach the soul means to go deeper, down into a place in which past and future blur, where what we strive for and what drives us can be glimpsed.

The Greek Idea of the Soul

The Greek word for soul, *psyche,* also meant *butterfly.* This suggests to us both a certain gentleness and a consideration of the soul's

ability to take flight. If we approach the soul with too rigid a definition, we risk caging its essentially "wild" nature. If we approach
soul with objective reason, we risk pinning its wings to study it.
And if we sentimentalize it, making it only a concept for our best
intentions, then we risk it flying away from our benevolent net. To
approach the soul with respect and rigor, we must be prepared to
appreciate its capacity for metamorphosis, its contradictory nature,
its habits of taking flight and remaining still. We must be prepared
to follow its path as it has appeared in ancient traditions and as it
still appears in our day-to-day lives.

In ancient Greek literature, *The Odyssey* is a vivid portrayal of
what it means to go down into the depths of an underworld.
Odysseus, Homer's protagonist, is told by Circe that he must consult the shades (disembodied souls) in the land of the dead if he is
to continue his journey. In Hades, he meets his dead mother, whom
he wishes to embrace:

> Three times I started toward her, and my heart was
> urgent to hold her, and three times she fluttered out of
> my hands like a shadow or a dream, and the sorrow
> sharpened at the heart within me, and so I spoke to her
> and addressed her in winged words, saying: "Mother, why
> will you not wait for me, when I am trying to hold you,
> so that even in Hades with our arms embracing we can
> both take the satisfaction of dismal mourning? Or are
> you nothing but an image that proud Persephone sent
> my way, to make me grieve all the more for sorrow?"
>
> So I spoke, and my queenly mother answered me
> quickly: "Oh my child, ill fated beyond all other mortals,
> this is not Persephone, daughter of Zeus, beguiling you,
> but it is only what happens, when they die, to all mor-
> tals. The sinews no longer hold the flesh and the bones
> together, and once the spirit has left the white bones, all
> the rest of the body is made subject to the fire's strong

fury, but the soul flitters out like a dream and flies away"
[Knox, 1993, p. 158].

Homer's image of the soul, slipping and fluttering away from the
body, gave way in Greek art to the portrayal of the soul as a butterfly, and later as a beautiful young girl with wings. The soul hypothesis of this ancient Greek story is that of an essence that can fly
away from the limbs, out through the mouth, the chest, or a wound
in the body. Ironically, the origins of the Greek soul hypothesis
reflect less a psychological or moral concept of the soul than an
attempt at physical description of it.

This ancient Greek story is more, however, than a physical
description of the soul after it leaves the body. It stimulates our
imagination, offering a picture of an underworld that lies beneath
our journey, our personal odyssey. Odysseus is forced to consult the
souls of the dead prophets and make offerings to shades from his
past and from recent battles. Without these offerings, the dead will
not speak the truth. Odysseus must listen to their prophesies, even
though he may not fully understand them, and he must mobilize
all his strength. His mother wonders how he even came to Hades:
"My child, how did you come here beneath the fog and darkness
and still alive? All this is hard for the living to look on" (Knox,
1993, p. 157).

At times we too have to consult parts of ourselves that are difficult to hold onto. We too are disrupted from our goals, obliged to
make an offering of our time in order to pay attention to realities
we may have resisted. We too wonder, "How did I get here? How,
amidst the confusion and darkness, can I see what I need?" The
meaning of Odysseus's journey to the underworld still echoes in our
individual and collective imagination, carried forward by modern
interpreters of ancient myth and in the works of twentieth-century
depth psychologists such as Sigmund Freud and Carl Jung. Jung
wrote: "The dread and resistance which every natural human being
experiences, when it comes to delving too deeply into himself is,

at bottom, the fear of the journey to Hades" (Jung, [1953] 1968, p. 336).

The underworld is where the deeper part of our soul resides, where the shades of our collective past and our multiple selves still live. Sometimes we are obliged, like Odysseus, to confront these shadowy selves, but the cost of refusing to go there can be severe. When the conscious mind attends only to what lies at the surface, the deeper parts of our soul no longer animate us, no longer offer us counsel, prophecies, and warnings. The butterfly takes wing.

Lessons from the Greek Idea of the Soul

From the Greek myths we have come to understand the soul as the source of vitality, physical presence, and animation. The Latin root, *anima,* meaning breath or soul, is the source of our English word *animation.* When we lose our souls, metaphorically, we lose our animation, our natural rhythms—including the most natural of all our instincts, the flow of our breath. We hold tightly, we try to stay in control, but we are no longer "animated" by our deeper self.

Observe any meeting or group encounter where something significant is left unsaid. There is that moment when we notice a deadening in the conversation. We might say the meeting is empty or even soulless. What is often meant is the absence of any vigor, any physical presence of the people participating. At these moments, we fear the journey to Hades, far below the surface of the situation, where danger lurks in the form of a spontaneous eruption of the truth or the expression of a strong emotion. For it is in this underworld that we repress from consciousness what we both yearn for and fear.

To shut out the underworld, to constrain the unconscious, is to foreclose the individual and collective odyssey that we must undertake to wrest meaning from the commonplace and mundane. If we attend to only the surface of reason, staying in control, trying to make sense, we often find ourselves frustrated with the outcome. The bridge to the underworld follows a meandering course, not unlike the soul that meanders from the body in death or sleep. The hypothesis that we have souls, and that they can leave us, reminds us that awareness is not solely in the realm of our surface consciousness. To remain animated, physically present in our bodies, aware of what is happening around us, we must stay alert to what is happening inside us and to us.

I learned this the hard way, in a conference designed to bring out the relevance of unconscious processes in groups. I was still in graduate school and one of my instructors, an African American woman, was the conference director. She inspired fear and respect from the conference participants. In leading a session of the whole group, she seemed deadly serious and annoyed with the quality of our interpretations about our group's behavior. The more we participants in the conference tried to make sense of events, the more I found myself empty and numb. Finally, at a point of uncomfortable silence that seemed to last forever, her assistant director commented that it was important to attend to our fantasies.

I immediately took a breath and sensed the tension in my shoulders and neck. From out of nowhere (or from out of the underworld), I had an image of the director as secretly enjoying our discomfort. I spoke out, reporting my *fantasy*. I said I thought she was so turned on by our struggling that in the evening between sessions she probably snuck out to a local blues club and danced the night away in pink hot pants. The mood of the room was so still as I spoke that my immediate thought on finishing was that I could kiss my graduate degree goodbye. From out of this stillness, however, came gales of laughter. The severe expression of the director melted and she looked down at the floor, stifling a laugh. The energy in the room shifted, the sense of an oppressive weight was lifted.

The soul is expressed in images, metaphor, and stories. We had come to the conference to struggle with the effects of unconscious behavior, and here I was pointing out a contradiction: that our very ineffectiveness was a demonstration of our capability. Our struggle was in some fashion a gift to the director. I had given the group an image and a story of the director that made an *undersense*, that got underneath our unspoken fear of disappointing her. The image of this stern woman dancing in hot pants permitted some relief from the oppressive nature of our reasonable—but superficial—explanations of group behavior.

I am sure there are a variety of explanations for the laughter, but for me there was another valuable lesson in this episode. I learned something about what it was like to find myself in an underworld of fog and darkness. I had allowed myself to listen for activity in my unconscious, and to let it animate my actions. The fantasy of the director in hot pants blended both my irreverence for what was happening and my respect for her. It felt, however, as if I had announced a discovery from below, a discovery not completely of my making although one having my unique stamp. I discovered that the soul that resides below can be both personal and an expression of the group's consciousness.

The Ancient Hebrew Idea of the Soul

The underworld is not the exclusive domain of the soul. Soul also stands for the grittiness and earthiness of the human spirit. In Hebrew scripture, the soul hypothesis begins with the creation story of how a divine being gathered up the dust of the earth and made a human being from lifeless matter. Many of us know this story from childhood, a religious story about the first creation of a human being, as opposed to a scientific explanation of how humans evolved. What may be less known is that this story can also be understood as one of the earliest and earthiest of the soul hypotheses, one proposing that body and spirit are inseparable.

The King James translation of the Bible describes the creation of the first human being as follows: "And the Lord God formed man of the dust of the ground, and breathed into his nostrils the breath of life; and man became a living soul." The living soul is an outcome of matter animated by spirit. In other English translations, living soul is defined simply as human being. But isn't the soul something inside the human being? How could something supposedly inside the body be synonymous with a human being?

The answer lies in the Hebrew words distinguishing "dust of the ground," "breath of life," and "living soul." In Hebrew, the word for the phrase "dust of the ground" is *adamah*. Adam gains his name from the root of this word, literally meaning *earth*. The soul's earthiness, its grounding in the realities of matter, is suggested by this early relationship between Adam and *adamah*. Here the soul, in contrast to a butterfly that takes flight, is associated with the muck, the impurities, the richness, and the grittiness of the earth.

The second term, "breath of life," in Hebrew is *ruach*. God gathered the earth together and breathed into its shape *ruach*, Hebrew for breath or wind, but also rendered in English as *spirit*. In other words, God breathes spirit into lifeless matter, and the result is a living soul. Spirit—as distinct from soul—is the wind of a divine inspiration. Spirit comes from higher up and descends into the body. The metaphor suggests that for the spirit nature to have reality, it must be embodied, it must join with the physical nature. Soul is in the middle, holding together spirit and body, lofty inspiration and physical limitation.

Nephesh is the Hebrew word for "living soul." Among its many meanings, it suggests a human being animated by breath. For the ancient Hebrews, soul suggested neither body nor mind, but rather the totality of instinct, emotion, and thought. In contrast to Greek ideas that influenced later Jewish and Christian theology, the living soul did not have a continued existence after the death of the body. It ceased to exist when the physical body died.

Soul is a gift of divinity, but it is also something closer to life, connected to the mundane and everyday. The living soul of Hebrew scripture is not something inside or outside, but rather a term that weds divinity with humanity, spirit with body, and the beating of the human heart with sacred inspiration. By *not* distinguishing the soul as exclusively the realm of mind as opposed to body, or feeling as opposed to thought, or higher as opposed to lower, the soul hypothesis of the ancient Hebrews avoids the dualities that will come later with the institutionalization of philosophy and religion. The living soul hints at a mysterious union of opposites: being human includes both the base textures of the earth and the ethereal nature of the heavens. This is a soul of both appetite and vision.

The living soul has meaning today as a metaphor for coping with the contradictions and limitations of modern life. The soul that is made up of the earth does not move away from failure, disillusionment, or inferiority. This soul is comfortable with instinct, unperturbed by the desires, needs, and longings of the body. For this soul, the struggle amidst contradictory urgings is not simply tolerated but acknowledged as necessary. This soul knows that it must extract a deeper meaning from the ongoing feast of possibilities that lie before it. In living, there are times of fierce combat within ourselves, times that demand heroic efforts to mediate contradictory impulses within ourselves. The living soul expresses appreciation and respect for the multiplicity of drives, instincts, and emotions that at times oppose reason and virtue. Nietzsche, who had a unique feeling for this heroic aspect of the living soul, wrote that "struggle is the perpetual food of the soul, and it knows well enough how to exact the sweetness from it" (Thiele, 1990, p. 11).

The body that is brought to life by the wind of spirit can also appreciate striving for greater awareness and higher values and seeking greater consciousness. Spirit suggests a transcendence of the mundane, a capacity to see far off into other worlds and into other dimensions. Creativity can be an outcome of feeling the wind of inspiration move through us. Teamwork can be a function of group inspiration. The body that is quickened by spirit is capable of extending beyond itself because it is comfortable with intuition, imagination, and metaphor.

The soul of the ancient Hebrew hypothesis holds together the middle, what is heavier and darker than spirit alone because it has body but also what is lighter and less predictable than matter devoid of spirit. Soul suggests that matter and spirit need each other. Spirit, without being embodied, has no substance, while matter that has lost touch with spirit's breath becomes an inanimate body, corrupted and shallow.

Lessons from the Hebrew Idea of the Soul

In organizations today, soul can no longer hold the middle between the material and the spiritual world. Instead, there is too often a polarization between cries for spirit on the one hand and recognition of the harder, harsher realities of what really matters in the business world. The consequences are that the spiritual and the material have been split off from one another. The search for spirit has become a thin and airy call for abstract workplace virtues such as teamwork, responsibility, accountability, and inspired leadership. The material world is now associated with fierce competition that leads to the corruption of the corporate body. In *Care of the Soul*, Thomas Moore emphasizes this point by suggesting that polarization intensifies the pathological aspects of both the material and the spiritual. The more compulsively materialist we become, the more desperate and neurotic we become in our search for spiritual fulfillment.

This was illustrated to me in a recent walk through a local bookstore. On the shelves marked *Business* were titles such as *Den of Thieves* and *Liars Poker* (tales of greed on Wall Street), *Free Fall* and *Too Big to Fall* (on the demise of Eastern Airlines and Olympia & York), *True Greed* and *Barbarians at the Gate* (on the takeover of RJR Nabisco), *False Profits* and *Rude Awakening* (on corruption and mismanagement at BCCI and General Motors), as well as general titles such as *Crashes and Panics*, *The Morning After*, and *Capitalist Fools*. These titles evoke the most materialistic and corrupt passions of the soul: greed and arrogance, fear and dominance, foolishness and dishonesty. Turning my head only slightly, I observed a second list of titles under the heading *Management*. If I had not known better, I would have wondered if someone was playing a joke on me.

These titles were uniformly idealistic and spiritual in the sense of being abstract and lofty in their aspirations. They touched on leadership, ethics, teamwork, and global responsibility to community and ecology. The titles included *Stewardship* and *Alchemy of a Leader, The Wisdom of Teams* and *The Corporate Coach, Principle Centered Leadership* and *The Healing Manager*. If I were simply innocent, I might have wondered how Business could be so ruthless and demeaning while Management could be so kindly and visionary. But I am not so innocent. I recognize here what I face daily in my practice as an organizational consultant. The demands of the workplace can be absolutely ruthless and crushing, while the dreams of the people in the same workplaces can be inspiring.

The ancient Hebrew passage reminds us that soul holds the middle between the most corrupt passions and the loftiest of ideals. We cannot compartmentalize these attributes as neatly as a bookstore can categorize titles under Business and Management. We are the whole story, both the passions and the visionary ideals. Forgetting this simple lesson adds to the polarization of the spiritual from the material. People are not simply good or bad, sacred vessels or physical commodities. When spirit loses its depth and substance, when it does not descend into the realities of the body, then we can say it has no soul. And when the body no longer seeks the struggle brought about by vision and ideals, then we might also say that the coarseness of life is no longer leavened by spirit, breathed fresh each day into a living soul.

The polarization of the spiritual and material is so much a matter of course that we often cannot easily see how it colors our day-to-day lives. Tom, a manager in a corporate communications department of a large apparel company, thought he had found a balance between his spiritual needs and his corporate identity. He worked for a company that was well known for its charitable contributions, had won numerous awards for its philanthropic activities, and was rated highly by progressive investment money managers. The community-mindedness of the firm was one of its

chief marketing assets. The spirit of the company's corporate giving matched well with Tom's own interest in spiritual pursuits and
social responsibility; he meditated regularly, volunteered his time
in community activities, and took an active interest in Buddhist
philosophy.

During his time with the company, however, something changed.
He became aware of a discrepancy between the company's public
persona and how it actually operated. He felt constant pressure from
above to tell a story that wasn't true. As he grew more cynical, he
became more reserved and cautious. He found himself putting more
and more distance between his corporate identity and his personal
life, becoming a collector of antique cars and restoring them on
weekends. He repeatedly clashed with his boss and realized that, for
sheer callousness, he could never match either his boss or other
senior managers. Secure yet unhappy, he could say he was staying
primarily for the salary and benefits. In a conversation with a management consultant hired to increase team building in his department, Tom acknowledged how skeptical he had become of any real
improvement in the way the company operated. He said he was now
working for "fuck-you money." One of these days, he said, he would
have made enough money to go into his boss's office and say, "Fuck
you, I'm out of here."

Tom began having trouble sleeping at night. Downsizing in his
department increased his numerous responsibilities and decreased
his empathy for others. When a local newspaper ran an expose that
his company, along with other high-profile apparel makers, was sub-
contracting with sewing shops exploiting Asian women in win-
dowless rooms at below-minimum wage, he exploded to a friend:
"Don't they know that if we don't stay competitive, the work just
goes overseas and these women won't have any work? Don't they
understand this is a ruthless industry?"

Tom's job was to protect the company's image. In a strange
way, his job was made easier by no longer really believing in his
company. The more disillusioned he became, the easier it was to

compartmentalize, to immerse himself in work on weekdays and then tinker with his cars during the weekend. He took medication for his disturbed sleeping, and he meditated more fervently. He found himself calling consultants for any number of proposed change projects, but he never followed up. He had to admit to himself that he was profoundly lonely, but he blamed his boss and the downsizing for the demoralization of his staff. He could no longer even recognize what he really believed. He came to imagine this is what it meant to be a lost soul.

The Hebrew hypothesis of soul suggests that the spiritual and the material are inseparable. Tom cannot balance the ledger by meditating more fiercely in proportion to working more compulsively. He cannot change the deteriorating relationship with his workplace by restoring antique cars. He cannot excuse the exploitation of workers by rationalizing that he also feels abused. The signs of psychic disturbance—troubled sleep, rationalizing, sense of loneliness, identifying with whatever was convenient—all point to a soul in crisis, a mind and body unable to be penetrated by spirit or mobilized by an instinct for what matters. Tom, the whole person, the living soul, finds himself troubled and ill at ease. We might even say that he has lost not so much his soul as his appetite and vision of the soul's responsibility to hold together the spiritual and material.

Tom's predicament, his loss of appetite to struggle with contradiction, his absence of being able to see into the darker recesses of his own and his company's motivations, mirrors a dilemma of modern times. We are all confronted with our conflicting needs to fashion a balance between a personal life that is internally fulfilling and a work life that is stimulating and to some measure externally meaningful. The Hebrew soul hypothesis suggests that being whole implies not simply parallel journeys between these two aspirations but a relationship between the inner and outer worlds. The living soul, the whole human being, is where the inner and the outer world meet.

The Soul in Gnostic Thought

If the soul, as a metaphor for the whole human being, can function as a bridge to an unconscious underworld, then it may also provide a path to a cosmic divinity. The theme of the soul as a transcendent source—a way of practicing eternity—is illustrated by traditions as diverse as Taoism in the East and Christianity in the West. The transcendent suggests the mystery of rebirth, whether of a physical reincarnation, or the renewal of crops after a winter frost, or a reimagining of what it means to be fully human. The transcendent qualities of the soul hint at the awe of nature that has inspired people throughout human history. In the transcendent, we glimpse the eternal, the pattern that is unknowable yet repeats itself again and again through the tapestry of our lives.

The transcendent qualities of the soul were a central motif of Gnostic thought of the first and second centuries of the Christian era. Gnostic writing, branded as heresy by the institutional Christian church, most likely blended Greek, Hebrew, and early Christian views as well as Egyptian and other non-Western religious traditions. Gnostic influence is echoed in the writings of William Blake and W. B. Yeats as well as in the philosophical writings of Rudolf Steiner and the psychology of Carl Jung.

Gnostic legend portrayed the creation of souls as an outcome of an overarching unity that ceased to exist. The story that is told is of a time before time, when there existed only light. The wholeness of the light was shattered, hurtling fragments of the divine unity throughout the universe. The light in flight through the heavens gathered density, lodging in the souls of individuals, tiny sparks hidden within the physical body.

Gnosis, concerned with the struggle for an awareness of these sparks within, hypothesized that in each of us is a particle of the transcendent unity. The particle in each of us is minute, yet it contains the infinite, the "world" as Blake said, "in a grain of sand." The Gnostic legend of how souls were created provides a metaphorical link to the heavens, a way of knowing the world beyond the limiting organs of perception. June Singer, a psychologist and interpreter of the relevance of Gnosis today, wrote:

> The intent of the ancient writers as well as of our own contemporary search for meaning springs from the same source—namely, the desire to liberate the sparks of divinity that have been embedded in the natural world from its beginning. These glimmer—sometimes in the wisdom of old crones, sometimes in the precocious questions of an innocent child. The sparks wander through the centuries, surfacing as Faust in the poetic imagination of Goethe, shining in the symphonies of the child Mozart. . . . It may be that a spark is present in every person, yet many do not recognize it in themselves [Singer, 1992, p. xix–xx].

The contemporary search for meaning, the question of our individual and collective destiny, was echoed centuries ago by the Gnostic teacher Valentinus, who asked: "Who am I? What have I become? Whereunto have I been thrown? Whereto do I speed? Wherefrom am I redeemed? What is birth, what rebirth?" These are the soul's questions. They are questions of origin and destiny, redemption and revelation, choice and fate. They are questions that alert us to our responsibilities in life, our place among others, and our connection to divinity.

The Gnostic soul links a cosmic divinity with the human being, who through direct experience—through trial and ordeal—must discover and recover the knowledge hidden within. The soul hypothesis of Gnosis is fundamentally opposed to institutional codes of conduct or group definitions of morality. Morality acts as a false guide because it cuts too clear a path through the wilderness that everyone must journey. We must each make our own path through wrestling with our fate, through engagement with our creative impulses, and through expressing our own heart.

To approach the soul of Gnosis, we must be prepared to lose some part of our normal ways of ordering and organizing our world. We must be ready to be awakened at a moment's notice, as from a daydream concerning the details of our life. When we talk of losing ourselves in a walk along the ocean, in creative pursuit, or in work that means something, then we glimpse the soul as described by the Gnostics. The soul hypothesis of Gnosis reminds us that our lives are not our own, at least not in the way we normally talk about our lives. Diane Ackerman, author of A *Natural History of the Senses*, described the sensation of losing the normal boundaries of day-to-day reality during her intense periods of writing, as a realization that her life was not her own, "as if my soul has been kidnapped. I can only explain it as a form of love" (Madrigal, 1994, Review p. 7).

Lessons from the Gnostic Idea of the Soul

Laurel, a client of mine, was the chief of anesthesiology in a midsized hospital. She resented how a subordinate, a key manager, dressed in short skirts and flowery blouses. She mentioned repeatedly how this manager never wore a white coat and how this directly affected her credibility with other physicians and technicians. Laurel admired aspects of her manager's performance but did so grudgingly, pointing out many ways the manager did not support her. I asked if there were clear expectations about both dress and performance, but Laurel changed the subject to recount an incident in which her manager contradicted her in front of a physician colleague.

Sensing I was barking up the wrong tree, I remarked that she seemed to have very strong expectations of herself and was conflicted about what it was appropriate to ask of a subordinate. She agreed, saying she wanted to be partners with this women and was uncomfortable with a hierarchical relationship. She also began talking about her own experience, twenty-five years earlier in medical school, of wanting to prove herself in an environment that was largely male and very competitive. "What was it like being a woman in such an environment?" I asked. She reflected for a moment and told me a story about one of her very first classes. The male professor had said, somewhat offhandedly, that physicians wore white coats to hide their genitals. He said it was important that physicians not be seen as having gender.

Laurel told me this story matter-of-factly, noting that at first she had been taken aback but over time had come to see his comment as sensible and appropriate. We talked briefly about how this experience might be influencing her views of the manager's dress, but we drew no grand conclusions from the memory. I did suggest, however, that our expectations of what others should do and how they should be were often buried in assumptions that we rarely took the time to examine.

To my surprise, Laurel returned after an extended vacation and announced that she now felt much less resentment toward her manager: "I wanted her to be an extension of myself, thinking like I thought, making decisions the way I would." She explained how she realized that her desire to be partners with this woman had been only on her (Laurel's) terms. Laurel would have an opportunity to apply her new insight when the two of them next met; it would be "the first time I've met with this woman with the assumption that we might have different approaches and need to discuss them openly," she said.

Laurel told me that during her vacation she had spent time hiking and exploring in Peru, climbing along the high ridges of the Andes. She described losing herself in thought, being back in medical school, remembering and feeling again what that was like. She thought about how much she had internalized a concept of partnering and teamwork as meaning that one does what the institution expects. She recalled how in her first classes she felt uneasy and isolated but overcame those feelings by satisfying her instructor's expectations. What mattered to her now was not to repeat this process with her subordinate: "I actually like the fact that we are different." She smiled, "It actually frees me from worrying about what I'm doing wrong with her." She implied an awareness that she herself could be different, not only the uneasy student who must conform but also an individual who held many competing values.

The soul is spurred by thought that awakens memories and feelings, prompting new assessments of what is significant. Losing herself in the Andes, Laurel discovered a new awareness of herself. She described no mystical experience or life-changing insight, but she sensed something that allowed her to reimagine her concept of partnering with others. The soul hypothesis of Gnosis suggests that we earn wholeness a piece at a time, discovering directly from our own experience how to navigate the mundane and extraordinary events of our lives.

The connection to our own experience as a source of insight propels us forward to new discoveries. The sensation is not so much learning something new as being reminded of our own humanity. The stirring of soul whispers of our dignity and the dignity of others. It can be found in the most unlikely places and situations.

In the inner city of Richmond, California, a contractor working for a local development company found himself increasingly robbed of his compassion as he spent time in neighborhoods with crack houses and "hubba heads," men and women who were addicted, tormented, and dangerous. He bought a pistol and kept a double-barreled shotgun in his truck. He learned to react quickly and violently to threats; he felt nothing but disgust and hatred for the burnt-out "humanity" of the neighborhoods. Returning to his truck one day, he found a man bent over the door. Without the slightest hesitation, he grabbed the man and rammed his head into the truck. As the man's head hit the window with a thud, the contractor's only worry was that the glass would break:

> I violently turned him toward me, prepared to exact an instant conviction with a sentence of pain. I don't

remember what he said, but his face was permanently burned into my memory. He stood there bundled in several layers of stinking clothing and a dirty, torn ski hat. His weathered face looked terrified. His sunken eyes were the saddest I'd ever seen. He had both hands raised in submission, and one of them held a Bic razor. My anger turned to shame when I realized he had been using my mirror to shave himself, in one small grasp at regaining an element of his humanity [Kendall, 1993, p. 12].

In an instant that began with burning rage and a reflexive desire for retribution, a spark of the divine humanity buried within each of us was revealed. In the sunken and sad eyes of this man, the contractor saw a mirror of his own profound detachment and alienation. The contractor could see with other eyes; like Andy imagining a glimpse of a second face in a mirror, or Laurel finding sanctuary for another part of herself, he found a compassion that had become exiled. The Gnostic hypothesis lives on today in our capacity to find a hidden soul through tests and trials, to see an "other" and find reflected some part of our own divine humanity and grace. The contractor and my clients discovered an "other" in themselves, and the revelation propelled them forward to new discoveries and new modes of action.

The Many Voices of the Soul

The soul remains a vital metaphor, particularly during periods of change, because it speaks to timeless longings for meaning and purpose. We often feel that rationality and science have abandoned us to answer on our own the most fundamental questions of human existence. Some turn to traditional religions, others to new-age philosophies. We can all turn to the soul as a way to ground ourselves in something "outside of" and larger than ourselves. Beneath the contemporary language of enhancing workplace productivity (accountability, empowerment, teamwork) lie deeper questions about where we are going, how we will survive, what really matters, what we will surrender. These are the soul's questions. We cannot access the values implied by these business terms if we forsake the deeper underlying questions they imply.

The thread that is woven through the ancient ideas of the soul is that there are many selves whose interactions and struggles shape our thought and our consciousness in general. The journey to Hades is a story of the multiplicity of souls that inhabit an underworld, offering the individual soul advice, prophecy, and counsel—if one learns how to listen. In the Hebrew hypothesis of a living soul, each human being is both flesh and spirit. Our physical nature is fused with our spiritual nature, the breath of life that is blown into us from celestial forces. And the Gnostic vision of a unity of light shattered into fragments that lodge in each individual also suggests many forces that are at once unknowable yet revealed to us through our life experience.

The soul hypothesis of this book is about achieving a greater comfort with the awareness of the many selves within us: flesh and spirit, heaven and underworld, earth and sky. The tension of these apparent opposites strives to link us with the meaning of being a whole human being. I think we miss the value of these stories if we take them too literally, trying to pin down, for example, how a psyche that flitters away like a butterfly in death can also be a living soul that has no existence after the body dies. Each ancient tradition finds its own way, through stories and images, to express the multiplicity of forces inherent in being fully human. Taken together, these ancient soul hypotheses express the importance of appreciating how soul can mean one's essence and vitality as well as a bridge to underworlds and a path to cosmic spheres.

The Dance of Souls in Organizations

The themes that link Andy, Tom, Laurel, and the contractor center on how each of us struggles with different parts of ourselves, wrestling with assumptions and internal personalities hidden from conscious awareness. Tom, who takes "fuck-you money" during the workday and seeks transcendence on weekends, cannot reconcile his divided loyalties. Laurel, who wants partnership but is frustrated with her subordinate, wrestles with her own assumptions about being a genderless physician yet a women who can respect the choices of others. Andy, who prided himself on developing others and remaining undisturbed by ambiguity, finds new regard for his fears and limitations. And the contractor, who rediscovered compassion in the act of seeking retribution, finds that he allowed the hopelessness of his environment to shape his own internal worldview. These are stories of the multiplicity of the soul, brought down to earth by the realities of interaction with other souls and with our social realities.

To approach the soul in organizations, we must be able to hold in our minds the dance of souls interacting within larger and larger circles of participation. The multiplicity that lies within one individual makes even a relatively simple interpersonal interaction complex. If we try to imagine group interaction, the complexity to understand what is happening multiplies arithmetically. The implication, however, is not that we should give up trying to comprehend; rather, we must appreciate that the tensions in each individual soul can also be felt as forces in the larger and larger circles of interacting souls. Each individual wrestles with essential questions of meaning and purpose, power and assertiveness, competence and inclusion—as do groups, organizations, and societies. We might consider the soul as a microcosm that resembles the macrocosm, as in ancient stories where the individual soul resembles the cosmos. The question is how to look at the whole.

Looking at the whole requires an ability to stand back far enough to see the outline of patterns that weave together complexity and multiplicity. In organizations, this is difficult because the farther back we stand the greater the loss of detail. We associate loss of detail with loss of control, with information that is no

longer meaningful. We try to reduce complexity, ignore multiplicity. We look at the whole only to reduce it to its component parts:
technology, information systems, human resources, market influences, and so on. Thus the idea that each individual soul is also an
imprint of the tensions in larger and larger social spheres is disconcerting at first. Yet understanding in depth what one person is experiencing can provide vital clues to what others are going through.
Andy's story, for example, opens a window on how others in his
organization might be experiencing the tension between the rhetoric of caring and the behavior of superiors. His individual story is
a fragment of what might exist as a pattern in his organization and
in other organizations as well. In fact, Andy himself was embroiled
with a subordinate who found Andy's performance review of him
painfully distant and punitive. When we stand back far enough, we
begin to see that patterns of tension take on meaningful form at levels as basic as the individual, yet extending to greater and greater
networks of interaction.

Standing back means gaining enough distance to see patterns in
the sweep of human history as well as in the psychological makeup
of the individual. The importance of the soul, anchored by archetypal themes but constantly being reimagined, is that it is a
reminder that our search to picture the human soul is always tentative. We are not searching for fixed patterns or the ability to
reduce the turbulence of the soul to an unchanging formula. Rather,
we are searching for caution and a note of realism in the challenge
to create organizational and social settings for the whole human
being. The loss of soul in organizations, an experience common to
many of us, must be seen against the backdrop of history and the
choices made along the way. Yet the opportunity remains that the
more we can account for the multiplicity of selves that lie in one
body, the greater our chance of imagining settings that might do
this for everyone.

. . . .

2

Shadows of the Soul

Acknowledging the Dark Side
of Our Best Intentions

*. . . [W]hoever looks into the mirror of the water will
see first of all his own face. Whoever goes to himself
risks a confrontation with himself. The mirror does
not flatter, it faithfully shows whatever looks into it;
namely, the face we never show to the world because
we cover it with the persona, the mask of the actor.
But the mirror lies behind the mask and shows the
true face.*
Carl Jung, The Archetypes and the Collective Unconscious

*How can anyone see straight when he does not even
see himself and that darkness which he himself carries
unconsciously into all his dealings?*
Carl Jung, Psychology and Religion

We are aware that we have a shadow or dark side, parts of ourselves that we are uncomfortable with, indications that something is askew, a chaos within ourselves and our world. The daily papers and news inundate us with evidence that the dark side exists. The portrayal of nations waging war, massacring their own people or those of a different tribe or nation, are visual reminders of the savagery and darkness that lie as a potential of the human soul. Heroes and celebrities, personalities we have become familiar with and feel that we know are routinely shown to be something different from our expectations. Woody Allen, Michael Jackson, and O. J. Simpson are but a few in the cavalcade of stars that have fallen back to earth. Michael Milken and Ivan Boesky are examples from the business world of a dark side to enterprise. Closer to home, we often know personally a family member, neighbor, or friend struggling with the darker elements of mind and body: depression, rage, illness, and death.

It's not that we're unaware of a dark side; it's that we fear it. This chapter inverts the assumption, both understandable and at times necessary, that we must ignore or repress the dark side of the soul. Instead, the dark side must be accounted for in ourselves and others. This means reclaiming responsibility for parts of ourselves and others that we ignore, fear, deem unnecessary, or simply lack the imagination to perceive.

In organizations, both leaders and members have something to gain from attending to the shadow. In Chapter One, Andy, Tom, and Laurel all faced shadow aspects of their own and their organizations' values and attitudes. To varying degrees and with differing results, they confronted tensions between cooperation and submission, responsibility to others and self-interest, compassion and indifference. The contractor from Richmond who saw an enemy in the faces of the community he worked in found in one man's eyes a mirror of his own soul. To see oneself reflected in the eyes of a perceived other is what it means to account for the shadow.

Stories about wrestling with our shadow, like the legends of the origins of soul, are ancient. The darker forces at work in the world are portrayed in stories as diverse as Adam and Eve being tempted by the serpent in Eden, and Buddhist legends of Mara, the great Tempter, trying to stop the Buddha from continuing his spiritual journey. The shadow is portrayed in various guises: as Lucifer, the fallen angel of Christian and Islamic traditions; as the serpent Satan, who embodies darkness; and as an evil spirit, Ahriman, who confronts the good and wise Ormazd in the Zoroastrian (ancient Persian) tradition. Each culture finds a way to make sense of the many forces at work in consciousness and in nature.

In the Western tradition, a duality emerged between the forces of good and evil. It taught that each individual must choose between the powers of darkness, destruction, and temptation and the forces of good. We can sense this tension today in popular culture as well as in management theory. The success of a children's film like *The Lion King* evokes once again the call to battle evil and proclaim the ultimate victory of the good. A cover story in *Newsweek* featured political figures (Bill Bennett, Peggy Noonan, and Hillary Clinton) as angels under the title "The Politics of Virtue: The Crusade Against America's Moral Decline." The article emphasized the need to inculcate such qualities as fortitude, temperance, and prudence during a period of perceived chaos and moral decline. Virtue promises the knowledge of how to choose between good and evil.

In management theory, the emphasis on vision and values, on principle-centered leadership, and on heroic portraits of successful leaders is a cry, especially during morally ambiguous times, for the good to be asserted once again. *BusinessWeek* devoted a cover to the CEO of Levi Strauss and featured the company's values-oriented management philosophy. In management theory, the simplicity of Douglas McGregor's Theory X and Y neatly cleaved the bad, dominating, dictatorial X manager from the enlightened, good Y manager who believed in his workers' capacity for self-motivation, achievement, and personal growth.

In current organizational practice, I hear senior managers talk about their obsession with an idealized vision, such as service or quality, as the only way to change their organizational culture. Recognizing a dark or inferior aspect within the workings of the organization itself would be viewed as a distraction from the leadership mantra of *empowerment, accountability, ownership, and customer focus.* "Of course there are problems with *them*" (the employees), say senior managers; why else would they have to repeat the mantras of productivity? The irony, obviously, is that the workers feel the same way in reverse: why are *they*, the senior managers, so unrealistic, unsupportive, and hell-bent on demanding that employees be accountable for the chaos *they* (the managers) created? Both sides see the shadow in the other.

If we are to create organizational settings that are driven by values which recognize the dignity of employees and that are also socially responsible, then recognition of the shadow is a necessary reality check at both personal and organizational levels. The history of our business organizations is littered with good intentions gone astray; the result is decreasing credibility in both leaders and the institutions they lead. The credibility problem is not solved by recognizing shadow, but recognition gives leaders and organizational members an opportunity to acknowledge and assess responsibility for unaddressed facets of their own personalities and their organization's direction. If our defenses are engaged in addressing those troubling facets, we should not be surprised or too judgmental. One learns to stare into the pool of self-reflection only with practice and with the gradual development of courage.

The Soul's Journey: Ambiguity and Integration

Is it necessary to portray so starkly good and evil, right and wrong, idealized vision and unrelenting reality? Are there stories that might speak to the relationship of good and evil, order and chaos, light and dark in ways that reimagine the polarization between shadow on the one hand and virtue on the other?

Elie Wiesel, writer, witness, and survivor of the holocaust in Germany, tells a story about the battle of good and evil as he heard it from his grandfather. A long time ago, the soul of a great and pious man was to be sent down to earth. Satan petitioned the celestial court, arguing that such a man would be so righteous and his teaching so persuasive that the choice between good and evil would become a moot point. "I will be beaten in advance. I demand justice," Satan argued. The celestial court agreed with his argument. The first soul would still be sent to earth to inhabit a great Rebbe (teacher). But to reassure Satan, another soul would be sent to earth with all the outward manifestations of piousness and righteousness, mirroring almost exactly the virtues of the first soul. What only Satan and the court would know is that this second soul's allegiance would be to Satan.

"How is one to know? How does one recognize purity?" Wiesel asked his grandfather. And the grandfather told the young Wiesel, "But one is never sure; nor should one be" (Wiesel, 1972, p. 164).

In this tale, the clash of good and evil, the ambiguity of knowing right from wrong when neither can be clearly seen, suggests the daunting responsibility of moral choice. We can never be sure—nor should we be. The ambiguity hints at the individual responsibility to examine one's own heart and one's own motivations. How else can one know how to act when there are no outward clues? If we give our whole allegiance to a theory or a teacher or an institution, we give away our power to trust in our intuition, our right to struggle with inward complexity, and our ability to recognize when something that may in fact have been appropriate once no longer is. The senior manager who too fully embraces new management ideologies may be missing crucial information about the reality of her organization, as opposed to the vision. The employee who clings too tightly to behaviors that were once accepted and rewarded as *good* may be limiting his capacity to change in beneficial ways.

The ambiguity of knowing good from evil shifts toward the challenge to perceive how good contains evil and evil good. If we re-imagine Wiesel's tale of the two souls in more human terms, then it is no longer about the wrangling over good and evil in the heavens but the divided loyalties within ourselves. In each of us there is an allegiance to a light and a dark potential: the capacity for courage, personal insight, and compassion as well as the ability to act with timidity, distorted perception, and malice. The metaphysical question about the origins of evil becomes a very practical one about how we mediate the opposites within ourselves. How much easier it is to see our actions as reactions to evil rather than owning the divided voices within ourselves. But if we understand our soul's journey differently—as a need to mediate the opposites within ourselves and among others—then appreciating shadow dynamics becomes an essential tool for honoring the multiplicity of the soul.

The dynamics of light and shadow fascinate those who become aware of them. Thinkers like Carl Jung both experienced and studied shadow dynamics as a way of expanding our sense of personal responsibility and awareness of collective behavior. As individuals, we continuously face shadow dynamics in the workplace and in society. As we see in the cases that follow, shadow dynamics are manifested at different levels and in different ways, reminding us that what we don't see in the upper world of rational behavior also has consequence.

Containing Opposites in Ourselves and in Organizations

Rob Asch was a man with a mission. He had just been appointed regional manager of a large electronics company specializing in customized products for manufacturing plants. The company, still dominant in its field, was at a major crossroads. The senior leadership at corporate headquarters had made clear that their cost advantage had evaporated and their continued success would rest with the development of innovative products and superior customer service. Asch had been selected because of his energy, his ability to delegate, and his "people skills." He was viewed as one of a new breed of managers capable of managing the strategic priorities of the organization while still retaining the loyalty and dedication of his subordinates.

Arriving at his office for our initial conversation about his new role, I noticed how friendly he was with the staff, inquiring about their families, shaking hands, patting people on the arm or back. His interactions seemed genuine and the staff responded with warmth and smiles.

During our talk, I asked him what he believed his core values to be and also what he believed drove him to achieve and be successful. I was struck by how much he relished these questions. He started by saying that he thought a great deal about core values, but much less about what drove him. I suggested he begin with his core values. He answered immediately: respect for the individual, and by extension his own immediate and extended family. He told me that he knew what it was like to have lower status in society, and he hoped always to respect individuals for who they were rather than what economic or ethnic background they came from. Coming from a depressed economic area, he wanted to be a role model and give back to the community the gifts he had received in his own personal odyssey.

When he thought about what drove him, he acknowledged that it was harder to see. He imagined it was very important that he be seen as competent and be well respected as a person. The economic hardships he faced growing up taught him to fear vulnerability and any associations with not being able to get a job done. He said he was driven by success, both for himself and for his family and community.

Rob acknowledged, however, that he could be both conflict-averse and bullheaded. Belying the appearance of the collaborative leader, he was uncomfortable with negative emotional display (anger, panic, weakness) and strongly attached to what he believed was right. He noted that as a child, in his own family disagreement was not valued. As an adult he learned to be agreeable in the presence of others, but he could be dogged, and at times dogmatic, in pursuing his own agenda. He felt I might support him in becoming more comfortable with direct confrontation while also using me as an "intellectual sparring" partner outside the corporate structure.

I was immediately impressed with Rob's openness and awareness of his own psychological nature. He seemed to understand intuitively the relationship of his own personal tendencies and their potential consequences in how he took up his organizational role.

Without using the word *shadow*, Rob indicated that he was prepared to examine his own darker nature in order to pursue the emerging vision he held for the company.

In the sessions that followed, the tension between how Rob wanted things to be and how they really were was constantly tested. He insisted that the problem with his organization was the deadly slow pace at which decisions got made and implemented. He was committed to hiring new senior managers who would, like himself, think strategically and then delegate downward. He wanted an organization that moved swiftly from strategic priorities and broad goals to implementation and action. And he believed that subordinates, understanding that the organization's future was at risk, would respond swiftly to directives from above. He had no intent to micromanage those below him, did not even wish to participate in operational decisions, and assumed that in return for respect, subordinates would set aside turf battles and personal agendas. As he spoke, he sat bolt upright in his chair. His presentation was at once sincere and icily logical.

I listened carefully to his words and observed his body language. He had asked to spar with me intellectually, but he had so tightly packaged his presentation that I could not see where he wanted help or even discussion. I told him he seemed to believe that subordinates would gladly follow his direction even though it might mean dramatically altering the way they currently worked. He seemed to assume they would work harder and with greater focus even as the organization was laying people off and asking others to take on additional responsibilities. I recalled from earlier talks that there was as much fear as enthusiasm for the organization's ambiguous and potentially dangerous future. I also observed that he had neatly cleaved strategic thinking and abstract goals from the operational realities that frontline people had to deal with. I wondered out loud if what he was describing was a new kind of obedience that had more to do with tyranny than with comforting notions of empowerment.

"Tyranny . . . what are you talking about?" Rob nearly stuttered in a controlled but clear flash of anger. His face flushed: "Are you suggesting I'm being tyrannical?" I paused, wondering if I had gone too far in my response.

I told him that I understood he believed himself to be first and foremost an advocate of individuals, and that he would never intend to be personally tyrannical. There are times, I said, when we find ourselves in a conflict of values, in this instance between our regard for individual respect and organizational imperatives to move forward quickly and with minimal distractions. I suggested that at times like these we can too easily rationalize that conflict does not exist; that is when tyranny can take hold. We had already talked of subordinates, acting on Rob's direction, who bullied people lower in the system by simply saying that such and such was what Rob wanted.

Wasn't it possible, I wondered, that his own issues with being conflict-averse but at the same time dogmatic were akin to an organizational culture that portrayed itself as collaborative but remained paralyzed by taboos against discussing how power and decisions were truly negotiated? I added that I did not believe Rob would be the cause of organizational paralysis; that had existed long before he even came to the organization. What I was concerned with was *his* question about how to change those dynamics.

Rob became deeply reflective, and the focus of our conversation shifted. We began to talk about how systems can degenerate from the mission and values portrayed by leaders. We told stories from our own experience about what really happens to people when right and wrong, good and bad, order and freedom are ambiguous and hard to distinguish. I mentioned that a business periodical had recently called the *evil* of psychological numbing among employees a by-product—a shadow—that so often followed the *good* intentions of corporate reorganization. I speculated that *psyche* in the word *psychological* is about the power of the soul to contain the opposites in some creative fashion. When the psyche is numbed, I suggested, individuals learn how to cope, not how to learn.

Rob laughed; his body relaxed. He said he didn't know there was a branch of organizational consulting called management meta-physics. I told him I didn't either, but maybe that was what we needed—if we could keep it grounded in the realities of his role and his organization.

Seeing through the visible world of rational behavior and nar-row intentionality requires an awareness of the other within our-selves. The many faces of the soul are stirred to life by a recognition of opposing forces, conflicts in duty, and deep reflection, as Carl Jung found in his personal grappling with shadow.

Carl Jung and the Exploration of Shadow

In 1957, at age eighty-two, the Swiss physician Carl Jung began to write his autobiography, setting down the forces and influences on his intellectual and spiritual development. He believed that in each of us there is a struggle of opposites: on one hand, a conscious inten-tion to be good, to live up to our ethical aspirations; on the other hand, an unconscious aspect that has within it suppressed motives and even demonic potential. He called this unconscious aspect *the shadow,* the developmental homework of the soul.

For Jung, how we each deal with our shadow constitutes a test of our capacity for self-knowledge, our ability to emotionally com-prehend parts of the self that parallel (and at a deeper level inter-twine with) conscious intention. The recognition of shadow is akin to discovering a stranger living in one's own home. To acknowledge and then resolve the contradictions implied by the shadow requires of the individual considerable reflection and moral effort.

In his autobiography, *Memories, Dreams, Reflections,* Jung recorded his first intuition, as a young man, of an "other" presence in his psyche:

> . . . I had a dream which both frightened and encouraged me. It was night in some unknown place, and I was mak-

ing slow and painful headway against a mighty wind. Dense fog was flying along everywhere. I had my hands cupped around a tiny light which threatened to go out at any moment. Everything depended on my keeping this little light alive. Suddenly I had the feeling that something was coming up behind me. I looked back, and saw a gigantic black figure following me. But at the same moment I was conscious, in spite of my terror, that I must keep my little light going through night and wind, regardless of all dangers. When I awoke I realized at once that the figure was . . . my own shadow on the swirling mists, brought into being by the little light I was carrying. I knew, too, that this little light was my consciousness, the only light I have. . . . Though infinitely small and fragile in comparison with the powers of darkness, it is still a light, my only light [Jung, 1961, pp. 87–88].

Jung understood his dream as visually capturing the struggles he then faced. He had to drive forward into the storm of his future responsibilities and fate—into study, moneymaking, entanglements as well as confusions, errors, submissions, and defeats. But just as certainly, he was dogged by his past, by what he was trying to run away from. He called the figure who bore the light "No. 1," the figure he consciously identified with; he called the figure following him "No. 2," a "specter, a spirit who could hold his own against the world of darkness" (Jung, 1961, p. 89).

These two internal natures within Jung formed a whole that was divided within itself: the one utterly committed to shielding the light, driving forward at any cost, never looking back; and the other a ghostly illumination given shape by the candle of consciousness, a haunting presence not clearly defined but definitely present. The light of consciousness and the specter of consciousness: one fears being overwhelmed, the other fears never being known. What Jung realized was that he didn't have to acquiesce to what haunted him.

The shadow appeared in many disguises. In a second example, in a dream he felt disgust and remorse for having allied himself with an "unknown brown skinned man, a savage." Together, they hunt down and kill the German heroic figure of myth, Siegfried. The year was 1913, and the Western world was on the brink of war. In panic over the dream's content, Jung pondered his own heroic aspirations: "Siegfried, I thought, represents what the Germans want to achieve, heroically to impose their will, have their own way. 'Where there is a will there is a way!' I had wanted to do the same. But now that was no longer possible. . . . After the deed I felt an overpowering compassion, as though I myself had been shot: a sign of my secret identity with Siegfried, as well as the grief a man feels when he is forced to sacrifice his ideal and his conscious attitudes" (Jung, 1961, p. 180).

Here the shadow takes the form of an alien figure, an ally of sorts, partnering with him to do what his conscious attitude could not have done on its own. The revulsion in the dream and the panic on waking offer evidence of the conscious attitude that is being threatened. Here again is the driven Jung of the storm, having to reassess his own heroic mission. To do so, he needs the help of a "savage" who knows the ways of the inner realm. He needs to take seriously the part of himself that wants to hunt down the Siegfried in *himself* so that he does not simply impose his will on others. In shedding the heroic ideal, he creates the opportunity to make new choices about his life.

What is common in both these manifestations of the shadow is its irreverence. In the first dream, the shadow is a presence that doggedly follows the conscious aspect of the person. In the second dream, where the savage must kill the false heroic ideal, the shadow appears as an ally in the form of the "brown skinned man." In each case, the experience of shadow wounds or mocks an idealized aspect of one's conscious identity. Jung, the responsible physician bent on preserving the candle of consciousness, is hounded by a dark figure that holds his past and its disowned meaning and disavowed feeling. Siegfried, the hero of high culture, is destroyed by the savage. Each idealized figure falls short of its heroic persona. The shadow acts irreverently by testing the conscious viewpoint, finding its flaws, and mocking its idealized qualities.

The psychological paradox presented by the shadow is that the more we try to escape our fears, the tighter are we bound to them. The irony is that examining the other side of our conscious outlook is most relevant and most healing when we find ourselves frightened, boxed in by what conscious knowledge cannot explain. There is wisdom to be gotten from the shadow—when the conscious attitude can tolerate it. This is why Jung called the shadow "gold."

To become aware of the shadow is to seek not only self-knowledge but also a portal to the larger world in which we live. Without explicitly looking for the shadow, Rob Asch found a door to his organizational role, illuminating a deeper sense of responsibility for his organizational mission. He could then reflect on his idealized values of collaboration and empowerment and see the shadow of tyranny behind the ideals. His capacity to be irreverent, to laugh in the face of the contradictions I proposed, allowed him to take these contradictions seriously and so remain open to new learning.

What we find in our personal shadow relates intimately with what is also suppressed in the larger collective culture from which we, as individuals, derive our roots. Tyranny and the distortion of reality are not simply personality traits but shadow aspects of group life and social organization. What is difficult for the individual to explore is even more threatening at an organizational level.

Shadow and the Soul in Disarray: An Organizational Case

Liz Kantor was an activist's activist. She understood community organizing: how to get the right people into a room, how to raise money, how to direct the media toward supporting the social programs she developed. Over twenty years, she had helped establish a battered women's shelter, a rape counseling center, and a hospice program for women with AIDS. She understood how to direct the diffuse energies of people toward getting things done. In the space of a few hours, she could walk into a room with twenty-five people who barely knew each other and leave with committees dedicated to fundraising, facilities planning, and program development.

Her pride and joy was the women's hostel, The Haven, which she founded for women who were homeless, drug addicted, or victims of violence. She remained a member of the twenty-five-woman board responsible for fundraising, policy, and finances. The board operated as a collective, as did the staff of twelve women responsible for counseling, organizing programs, and generally providing the varied services needed for their diverse clientele.

Liz was tolerant of the collective process for decision making, but it contradicted her hands-on, get-things-done style. She quietly fumed as a purchasing decision on the cost and colors of towels dragged on for forty-five minutes. She believed, however, that consensus was necessary to model an alternative to hierarchical organizations that concentrated power in a few hands. Yet she secretly tallied in her mind the board members she viewed as cooperative and those who were "bad."

The real concerns began for Liz when four of the five women of color on the board formed a minority caucus to "explore policy procedures that would fight racism." Liz saw the action as a direct threat to her vision of the board as an extended family working together in the communal kitchen to nourish the less fortunate. She did not approve of this splintered-off subgroup, with its own self-serving agenda.

Growing tensions within the board ignited when the issue of working with particularly violent and self-destructive women was addressed. Three staff, two of them women of color, acknowledged that they did not feel they had the skills to handle the severity of these women's problems. They wondered if more harm than good was the outcome of keeping these women within The Haven. The rest of the staff and the majority of the board did not agree. The Haven was a place for the dispossessed; once boundaries were created for one group of women, then other constraints would surely follow. Board members argued that since no physical harm had actually occurred, it was inappropriate to act on the fear that it would.

The staff who brought up their concerns felt dismissed. They viewed this as one further example of their concerns and needs going unheard. They viewed the attitude that was expressed in the board meeting as "if you can't handle it, fuck off." One staff member stated publicly that the collective decision-making philosophy of The Haven was hypocritical: the primarily white staff and board members, who had been around the longest, held the real power and would not give it up. The staff who brought up these concerns characterized the issue as between themselves and white staff who were privileged workaholics.

The situation polarized along issues of race, sexual preference, ideology, and personality. When the minority caucus threatened to expose the board as racist, another subgroup of board members prepared to call the primarily heterosexual caucus members homophobic. When one caucus member accused another board member of being involved solely to soothe her guilt for being part of a racist society, another board member complained about being victimized by "people" who mistakenly perceived her as a member of an international corporate elite. Nothing could be further from the truth, both sides argued about the other's perceptions.

Liz Kantor stayed out of the fray as much as she could. But when she brought to the board's agenda a proposal to open a resource center for past and current clients of The Haven, all hell broke loose. She had expected joy and a respite from the bitter acrimony. Instead, a new member of the board, also involved with the minority caucus, requested an updated needs assessment and suggested that Liz be more consultative with other board members.

Liz exploded. Raising her voice, she declared that this was a window of opportunity and that obstructionists had no place working in organizations that were committed to the community. She was sick, sick and tired of the naïveté and stubbornness of people so wrapped up in their ideology that they could not get anything done.

In the interim between board meetings, the minority caucus met to compose a letter of rebuttal and a request that issues of power and privilege be openly acknowledged on the board. Kalia, the minority caucus member selected to read the letter, broke down crying, testifying how she personally felt silenced and ignored. Many of the board members thanked her for "sharing her pain." Liz Kantor did not. She wanted to know how Kalia could feel this way. Breaking rules of client confidentiality, Liz asked how Kalia could say this after being helped as a former client of The Haven. Kalia bristled, shouting that her gratitude did not hold her prisoner from telling the truth. The facilitator tried to restore order, but Liz continued to shout back at other board members. The minority caucus left the room to discuss what had just occurred. A board member who came over to give Liz a hug was later accused of association with racism.

A compromise to the feud was never found. Liz agreed to apologize for breaking rules of confidentiality, but she would not apologize for her combative spirit or her right to confront others. A coalition of community and board members was assigned to draft structural and procedural changes that would allow more minority representation. One of their recommendations was that Liz Kantor resign her membership on the board.

Liz's letter of resignation came prior to the board's debate on the recommendation for her dismissal. She had no interest in fighting anymore. She felt humiliated, scapegoated, and very tired. However, when her letter of resignation came before the board, there was one final problem. The board could not agree on the wording for accepting the resignation. A subcommittee was formed to review Liz's resignation letter—to determine if it was a racist document.

Steering Through Shadow in Organizations

For those of us with personal experience of organizational issues as portrayed in story of The Haven, our stomachs clench. We have an immediate wish that good people with good intentions should not have to suffer so. We also feel anger and sadness that the tragedy of The Haven could have been avoided if only the individuals could have demonstrated better interpersonal skills, or found a common vision, or recognized that the tensions in their organization are mirrored in so many others. We wish to save people from themselves, or at least rescue the organization from the disarray that hinders their efforts. What tragic spell so envelopes efforts to do what is right and just? What mythic structure helps us understand what has happened here? What feelings must be evoked to draw out empathy and lead us to heal the wounds so deeply festering in our organizations?

What often hinders those of us who wish to choose good are just those qualities that we find repellent in ourselves. We find them as exaggerated qualities in others; at The Haven, the enemy was found at every turn. Liz could not deal constructively with her feelings about the caucus because the members' assertiveness represented a selfishness—having their own agenda—that was so opposed to her own perceived sense of altruism and commitment to others. The caucus members, in turn, so identified with the larger social problems of race and power that they could not imagine themselves doing wrong or victimizing anyone else. The shadow is most virulent in individuals and organizations when unresolved aspects of our own personality are channeled toward blame and the repressed negative qualities within ourselves are projected onto others.

The Haven, founded by the light of Liz Kantor's vision, was an idealized inversion of what was believed wrong with society. If society was male-dominated, obsessed with power and self-interest, as well as hierarchical and segmented by class, race, and gender, then The Haven would be a corrective experiment run by women. It was to be a place for the dispossessed, an extended family operating with collective values that shunned power, inequality, and hierarchy. Liz never believed she held power, let alone institutionally sanctioned authority, but rather only the capacity to influence others for a common good. The Haven was to be a community for those who needed care as well as for those whose role was to be caretakers.

With time, however, it became thick with its own shadow, mired in the unrelenting realities of group process: who feels included, which subgroups maintain influence, how conflict is addressed, why certain needs are given priority and others not. In shadow, as Jung noted in his alchemical studies, there is literally very little light to help us find our way. We feel that nothing is happening; we are stuck and blind in darkness. Yet we also feel our lives falling apart and we do not have the means to pull the parts back together. The multiplicity of the soul is thrown into disarray.

The same process is true in organizations. When individuals in organizations are confronted with realities repellent to their ideals, they split off the rejected parts and project them onto others. While Liz secretly tallied the board members whom she viewed as unrealistic, caucus members whispered dark truths about other members of the board. The organization becomes the container for taboos that cannot be discussed outwardly. Secrets must be shared only with one's allies. Scapegoating polarizes people from each other, relieving the anxiety related to the painful ambiguity of human relationship. People within the organization talk and meet and meet about the talk, but everything has become dark and foreboding. Nothing seems to be happening, and only the sacrifice of a leader or the removal of a subgroup relieves the paralysis in the short term.

At The Haven, the shadow of power, hierarchy, and inequality darkened the relationships among members. Power was seen as dominance leading to the victimization of others, and thus the aspects of power that furthered the organization's goals were rejected. Power could not be valued as an element necessary and healthy for action, so it became twisted. Only those who could declare themselves victims and abused by power could, ironically, have any power within the organization. Negative power, the ability to negate the actions of others, became the currency of interaction. Kalia had power when she declared herself silenced and ignored. The minority caucus held power as long as they focused attention on instances of insensitivity to race and powerlessness. Majority board members negotiated in the same way, declaring themselves victimized by being associated with the inequalities of the larger corporate society or held hostage to the demands of a subgroup. Everyone identified first and foremost with her powerlessness rather than how she actually held power; power became a despised and rejected element within the organization.

The elements of hierarchy and inequality suffered the same fate. Hierarchy was rejected as the source of illegitimate and abusive power rather than as essential to coordinating organizational life. Inequality was associated with the evils of the larger society. Yet boards have legal responsibility for the health and welfare of the organization. Long-term members of an organization have unequal histories compared with those of newer members; founders of organizations have status associated with their initial vision and action. Hierarchy and inequality must exist somewhere in the structure of an organization; they are part of our realities. When we cannot imagine the part they play in organizational life, they become twisted and toxic.

Hierarchy is organizationally sustaining when accountability and responsibility for the organization's actions are at stake. The acknowledgment of inequality is necessary within organizations in order not to create a pretense that all members are the same. Recognizing the multiplicity of one's own soul is intertwined with recognizing the diversity of others. However, if all the conflicting parts of the self are equal at the same moment, one cannot act. If all members of an organization are equal in the same way and at the same time, the organization cannot act. The concept of shadow reminds us that within ourselves there are complementary and at times oppositional forces, but never are they all equal at once. We act from the tension of unequal forces.

The staff who felt ignored when they raised concerns about violent behavior in The Haven were not victims of hierarchy and inequality. They were participants in a system whose membership was uncomfortable with the limitations of their idealized organization. Some wanted The Haven to be a place for *all* women in need. Others wanted an organization that created sanctuary for themselves. The discussion of what to do about violent women darkened and became destructive because the tension of opposites—safety and risk, membership boundaries and inclusiveness, staff development needs and staff competencies—could not be discussed and acted on constructively.

To include soul in our view of organizational behavior necessitates a recognition of its shadows. It also suggests being alert to the mythic patterns that repeat themselves time and again in the drama of organizational life. When Odysseus returned from the underworld, he set out with his ship's crew to navigate a narrow pass between two sheer cliffs guarded by the monsters Scylla, a many-headed creature living in a dark cave, and Charybdis, a powerful, ship-destroying, whirlpool-generating force at the bottom of the other cliff. Circe, the goddess who guided Odysseus in his journey, told him to row like mad and to resist the temptation to stop and fight.

Liz Kantor and her crew also found themselves negotiating a narrow pass guarded by seemingly dangerous forces. They feared the rigidity of hierarchy, which would cause the organization to lose its heart and its spirit. And if collective decision making were mired in blame and shadow projection, then the organization would be sucked down into chaos and disruption. We must row like mad and be willing to risk some losses in order to pass through the sheer cliffs of such opposing forces. We must learn to address shadow dynamics before they become so toxic that we become stuck in our own shadow. Like Odysseus, Liz was fierce and proud, and she had difficulty heeding Circe's warning not to get personally engaged in the battle with these opposites. Once her anger was triggered by Kalia's accusations and she could not back down, she was vulnerable to the whirlpool of the organization's dynamics. The Haven was not the idealized sanctuary that Liz Kantor had sought. Instead, The Haven's idealized values blinded its members to the encroaching, virulent shadow.

The Shadow of the Collective

The collective shadow may be viewed as the disowned parts of individual members of a group, race, or nation projected onto others. The motto for such a group is "Whatever my group does is good; most everything other groups do is bad." When in the grip of a collective shadow, we can tolerate only an idealized image of ourselves; we scapegoat someone or some group to reflect the parts that have been disowned. War psychology has made this principle abundantly clear; every aspect of despised humanity is projected onto the enemy. The story of The Haven, though of a different scale, follows the same course, with the various subgroups becoming the projection screen for the disowned parts of the individual members.

We often see the collective shadow as foreign and unimaginable because we have not recognized the shadow within all of us. How can acts of violence, for example, be understood if I cannot imagine violence in myself? How can acts of senseless and hideous brutality be grasped if I *know* that I could never behave in such a way? For those of us who view ourselves as innocent of the soul's extremities, the reminder of dark forces only furthers our defenses, the sense that evil lies in an enemy outside ourselves but getting closer. Denying shadow, however, is fruitless; the consequence, so often, is the psychological need to scapegoat, to see the long shadow of evil looming only in others.

Jung wrote that what is true of humanity in general is also true of each individual, that our souls are linked in innumerable ways.

If humanity suffers from violence, from willful domination of others, from senseless and brutal acts, then each individual suffers from these things as well. The challenge is to recognize these forces as symptoms of a disturbance in ourselves as well as the world around us. "In this way," Jung wrote, "man becomes for himself the difficult problem he really is" (Jung, 1954, p. 77). Jung suggested the person who recognizes his or her shadow knows the question is no longer "How can I get rid of the shadow?" but instead "How does one live with the shadow without enduring a succession of disasters?" The difficulty of that individual quest is only amplified at the collective level.

In England, two ten-year-old boys abducted and murdered a two-year-old child who had wandered momentarily from his mother in a shopping mall. The public, usually numbed by constant communication of murders, violence, and social decay, was outraged. A crowd of angry citizens rushed the police vans escorting the two boys to their arraignment. The family of a twelve-year-old boy who had been questioned in the incident but later released had to go into hiding as disorderly crowds shouted abuse outside his home. The two major political parties attempted to outdo each other with new programs for public safety, one declaring an "all out war" on crime, the other calling for new measures to lock up young offenders.

I listened to a news report as social workers, psychologists, and politicians each had their say on the matter. Most striking was a minister of the government, who insisted in a raised voice that the one thing that mattered most is that those who did not commit the crime had *no culpability*. The prime minister of England asserted, "I feel strongly that society needs to condemn a little more and understand a little less."

The duality evoked by this comment is startling to contemplate. It associates understanding of the act with excessive tolerance of its viciousness and brutality. Condemnation is the tried but untrue "fix" for deviance. There is no exit from this formulation. We cannot condemn the act and still contemplate its social context. We cannot "understand" and still experience the outrage or examine the capacity of evil to function in the human animal, regardless of age. We are perplexed by the limited choices of either more prisons or more social workers. Most distressingly, we cannot find access to forces within society that would allow us to assess our culpability and to link it with action in the world. The prime minister, who represents the authority of the state, offers a solution—to condemn more—that cannot or will not link the light of society's progress, its onward rush into the storm of the future, with the darkness embodied by the two boys. *What is it these two boys, in their horrific act, "carry" for the collective? What is it we do not want to know?*

These two children who committed the horrific act can be viewed as alien to the good, law-abiding citizens of the state. This is why the government minister insists that there is no culpability for anyone else. The children, from this perspective, are simply bad seeds that must be eliminated. The rest of us can then have the comforting but unwarranted certainty of being "not guilty" of the economic and social catastrophes we live with in the real world. We function as if there is no collective shadow that we must share responsibility for. There is only individual evil to be eliminated. The result is the need for more repressive policies, more prisons, and further applications of a moral varnish to the rough planks of human nature. Yet civilization cannot be held together by moral injunction and social repression. Rather, we must comprehend the cruelty within ourselves and the social conditions that give rise to such horror.

Amidst all the rage and recrimination, I was struck by the calm voice in an article written about this event by William Golding, the English novelist whose book *Lord of the Flies* remains one of the most vivid tales of childhood cruelty. He suggests in the article that to contemplate such an act of horror, we must ". . . live in the real world and not little worlds of our own making . . ." (Golding, 1993, p. D-1). He offers a hypothesis: "If it is true, as it seems to be, that there is a simplicity about human goodness, then it is just as true that there is a corresponding complexity about human evil" (Golding, 1993, p. D-1). But even if complexity allows no single certainty or explanation, there are some conditions, he writes, ". . . in which cruelty seems to flourish, which is different from saying that it has clear causes. What are these conditions? Chaos is one, fear is another. In Russia after the First World War, there were, I believe, gangs of children who had lost their parents. Dispossessed, without anywhere to live or anything to live on, they roamed the country attacking and killing out of sheer cruelty. There was, at that time, social chaos in many countries, and left to themselves, these children found a kind of elemental cohesion in their viciousness" (Golding, 1993, p. D-6).

Golding then makes a connection to current conditions in England, in which offspring of an underclass also face the experience of being dispossessed, are also brought together by fear, and also find that being "afraid together" permits an almost bottomless immersion in violence. The social conditions that twist human action are real and observable, as is the cruelty in each of us. Both are true; one does not displace the other.

The failure to work with shadow dynamics at the collective level is ultimately about the inability to make the connection between apparent opposites. In this case the opposites are represented by the singular responsibility of an individual for his or her own actions and the collective responsibility of caring for others as part of one's membership in a group or a society. If the representatives of the state cannot find that link in their own consciousness, they are hard pressed to help others from polarizing the situation further. The vigilante group that attempted to take the boys away from their police escort and the angry crowd that tormented the family of the boy who was questioned and released are extensions of this type of consciousness, which copes with shadow dynamics by polarizing the opposites more severely.

An entirely different approach can be seen in actions taken by tribal elders of the Tlingit Indians in Alaska. In this well-publicized case, two Indian youths who brutally beat a pizza delivery man for pocket money were banished to two separate islands. The grandfather of one of the assailants sat on the council that sentenced the boys, and the victim of the beating was also present at the tribal hearings. Some journalistic accounts emphasized that compensation to the victim, in the form of a new home built by the tribe, was central to the final resolution. The Indian youths, still facing potential imprisonment on their return, were to be aided in their banishment on the islands by four elders who would give them a crash course in subsistence survival.

I do not mean to compare the murder of a child by ten-year-old boys with the assault on a youth by teenagers. The finality and brutality of the first case far outweighs the violence, even though vicious, of the second. The point is the stark contrast in approach between the two cultures. By their actions, the Tlingit accept responsibility for the behavior of their members. Part of their responsibility is to punish, part to compensate the victim, and part to offer their children—even children whose actions are repellent—some further information for survival. It is as if they are saying through their leaders, "We are all culpable. . . . Where do we start to heal the divisions among us?"

Confronting the Shadow in Ourselves

Today we face a new moment in history. We are at the edge of our understanding of human behavior in a modern, technologically driven society. To a great degree, we face this challenge as individuals without comprehending the power and contradictions of the shadow, believing instead that the inculcation of individual virtues will save us. What lies outside the false duality of virtue versus immorality, condemnation versus understanding, or personal responsibility versus social programs is the question of just how the individual is bound up in the collective. The pathologies of the living soul, of the whole human being in crisis, will not let us ignore this question.

When the institutions that hold communities together—religions, law enforcement, education, health care, workplaces, family—are in disarray, then people begin searching for new models for how to organize themselves. The danger of our times is that we will read the warnings seen in youths out of control and in society falling to pieces as signals for harsher and more repressive policies, or as a superficial call for virtues and values that are viewed as singularly good: romanticized portraits of the nuclear family, instances of self-sacrifice, examples of rugged individualism. Shadow dynamics suggest that the outcome of such initiatives will not result in a more civilized society but instead will lead to attacks on convenient targets: deadbeat dads, violent youths, repeat offenders. These messengers—those who carry the shadow—become thereby not the symptoms of our social condition but scapegoats for our anxiety and sense of soullessness. In such a misguided environment, no one can safely say, without being accused of being an apologist for horror, "We are all culpable. Where do we start?"

If the shadow, whether individual, organizational, or collective, were only evil, we would have cause to ward it off, to keep it constantly at bay. Yet *shadow,* as I have used it, contains wisdom and a warning. When we recognize the shadow as a natural process, following us as Mara followed Buddha and Jung's dream specter followed him as he held the candle of consciousness, then we can begin to respect the multiple selves that lie within. The shadow offers us access to the unresolved issues of our past, the dispossessed feelings, attitudes, and emotions that can offer new vitality and a more comprehensive humanity, if recognized. We learn that we can be both this and that, tyrannical and empowering, just and unjust, altruistic and controlling, compassionate and cruel. The experience of one-dimensionality can give way to a creative polarity that provides the tension necessary for new learning and new approaches to living a more differentiated and psychologically richer life. The confrontation with shadow is the first tentative step we make toward reclaiming wholeness.

Collection and Recognition of the Whole

Organizations reflect and refract the light of the larger society. What happens in society—loss of core values, scapegoating, panic for solutions—happens also in organizations. The challenge to create settings that take account of the whole human being begins with the confrontation of shadow dynamics.

I am reminded of a client, the CEO of a software company, who was concerned that his administrative staff was constantly complaining to him about the degree of stress in the organization. Could I suggest a program for stress management, he wondered? I offered to talk with him about what might prove useful by understanding more clearly his role and his perceptions.

In exploring the question further, he acknowledged that he was furious with his staff and believed that stress was a function of individual capacity to cope: *I did it, why can't they?* He felt like lashing out at individuals who appeared morose and not part of the team.

In the sessions that followed, he reflected more deeply on how the staff's concerns threatened his belief that he was a caring and competent manager. And he agreed to examine how stress was manifest in his life, describing how he often did not sleep the night before a new week began, and how he periodically felt guilty about not being more present with his son. By degrees, he became more interested in understanding the role he might be playing in others' stress, and how he might contribute to organizational strategies in support of his staff generally.

I found it remarkable that he was courageous enough to link his anger at the staff with his doubts about his own self-image. He feared his own capacity to cope. He was able to see, through his own reflections, that stress had multiple sources aside from individuals' capacity to cope. He was able, therefore, to begin to address the experience of stress in his organization beyond what it meant about him; considering more fully now the implications of his staff's relationships to their work, their families, and each other. One of the liberating aspects of addressing shadow dynamics is that it softens our own harsh judgments of others.

We also resisted making stress a "management program." The "morose" individuals were not singled out for condemnation; nor were they subject to the group's pity or misdirected care. Rather, we made explicit an assumption that we all cope with life and that together we might learn more about how we cope as individuals as well as how groups cope with the demands of the workplace.

These conversations led to a focused conversation with his staff. He was able to tell them that he took personally the constant concerns they voiced about everyone's stress level. He was also willing to acknowledge that his responses had gotten in the way of their working together to find approaches that might offer people support. In response to his honesty, his staff acknowledged that they too felt that their subordinates' dissatisfaction reflected on their own performance as managers. They also owned up to the responsibility they shared, admitting it was easier to point out the problem to him than to do something about it themselves.

Together the CEO, his staff, and I agreed to explore the behaviors and conditions that fostered stress in their system. What were these behaviors? Individuals acknowledged that when faced with unfamiliar situations, they often became tentative and felt overwhelmed. As a group, they spoke of how the urgency of multiple deadlines contributed to less careful scrutiny of the choices available and avoidance of hard decisions.

Everyone came to see that behaviors were double edged: useful and problematic. Humor could be used to provide perspective, or it could be laced with hostility that communicated powerlessness. Becoming more organized and working harder was necessary, but it could become obsessive and lead to rigidity and too-concrete thinking. What we began to see was that behaviors contained within them light and shadow qualities that could lead off in different directions. Relying on oneself could amount to both productive independence and a dangerous withdrawal from the group. Ignoring issues that made people angry or frightened could be both appropriate in the short term and dangerous if never addressed. The group broke out laughing when one member quoted Leadbelly's summary of the blues: "In the first verse, you use the knife to cut a slice of bread; in the second, you use it to shave. In the third, you use it to cut your lying lover's throat." The *context* of the behaviors, not the behaviors themselves, had to be assessed.

The discussion of personal and group coping then turned to how departments could work together on behalf of clients and employees. Members began to creatively address how, separately and together, they could channel existing resources toward supporting each other. The human resource director suggested expanding employee assistance programs, previously directed at individuals in crisis, toward fostering interpersonal skills among intact work groups. The head of marketing expressed excitement about talking with his managers about how they coped and how they might better support others. The administrator of operations support recognized how her most recent efforts in developing a service strategy could be a vehicle for remedying confusion and distorted expectations between her departments and others.

The effect of these discussions was to create a new connectedness among these people that had little to do with what is traditionally thought of as team building. They had brought to light the devouring and enveloping forces that they constantly faced. By addressing the Scylla and Charybdis of their collective journey, they began to see more vividly the necessity of their need to row like hell—together.

We all felt the emotion behind the tears of one of the members at the end of the day. She told us this was the first time she had felt

a connection to the group that was not born out of guilt or compliance. She spoke of having feared she would be scapegoated because
she had recently become so overwhelmed. She thought that others
coped so well and that her problems must be evidence of her deficiencies, demonstrating her lack of managerial competence. She
had felt completely alone.

The CEO looked over at her and told her that he too felt in the
dark. He secretly believed that he was the one who would be
blamed, that he lacked the necessary leadership skills. Now, he saw
that although the urgency and deadlines would not stop, his own
way of coping with them could change. He had been generating so
many initiatives that he couldn't see how much they were undermined by lack of integration.

His words allowed other members of the group to acknowledge
that they too, no matter how it appeared otherwise, had fears and
good reason to try out new behaviors. It was as if each member were
saying, "I thought I was the only one who felt this way." I also
noticed that paradoxically the commonality of their experience
allowed each member to differentiate himself or herself in some way.
Senior people were able to openly offer support to newer members,
and individuals with specific knowledge and skills gained recognition for their unique contributions.

The experience for me, being in the room with them, was of
individuals collecting parts of themselves and saying, "This too is
me: both the self-reliant and the withdrawn figure, the organized
person and the obsessive personality, the cheery group member and
the isolated stranger."

The struggle with shadow, as Jung suggested, initiates entry,
through a tight passageway, into a house of self-collection. As I wit-
nessed it here, the dwelling is a place where people can live with
more of themselves. It is not a place of final reconciliation or of static harmony. Rather, it is a place within oneself and among others.

This grappling with shadow dynamics contrasts with intentions,
often benevolent, that end up wounding the whole person. We

create organizational settings that seek to mold personalities as if only the upper world of rational behavior mattered. In the next chapter, we see how organizational structures arose historically to manage the soul's troubling behaviors, to quell a soul too chaotic to manage.

3

. . . .

The Domination of Souls
How Organizations Become Our Keepers

Under the absolute government of a single man, despo-
tism, to reach the soul, clumsily struck at the body, and
the soul, escaping from such blows, rose gloriously
above it; but in democratic republics that is not at all
how tyranny behaves; it leaves the body alone and goes
straight for the soul. The master no longer says:
"Think like me or you die." He does say: "You are free
not to think as I do . . . but from this day you are a
stranger among us. . . . You will remain among men,
but you will lose your rights to count as one. . . .
           Alexis de Tocqueville, Democracy in America

No one can mature in a culture or organization without internalizing aspects of it. We are by nature dependent on family,
community, social institutions, and our workplaces for our survival
and to a large measure our sense of identity. To become aware of
what it is that culture blurs—namely, the distinction between our
utter uniqueness and the demands to fit in—is an essential task of
soul seeking. We must continually confront the questions of meaning: "Who am I?" "What have I become?" "Where am I headed?"
To answer these questions, we must confront our own history and
socialization. We must also confront the power of ideas to shape
both us and the organizations we are part of. The question of how
we become more fully what we are takes on meaning and texture
when we look inward and outward.

This chapter explores how organizations become our keepers, by watching over us, directing us, and attempting to control our actions. It also explores how we are shaped to become our own keepers. In what ways do we internalize the requirements of our organizations in order to watch over ourselves, direct our own behavior, and control our own actions? The dilemma for organizations is how to acknowledge the multidimensionality of a person, without simply molding people to group aims. The dilemma for us as individuals is how to retain more of ourselves in the face of shifting organizational demands that erode our own confidence and hinder access to our own experience.

The weight of these questions came home to me in a recent consultation with a senior manager who was wrestling with budget cuts. Janet Peters was ready to resign in response to the constantly changing and contradictory messages she perceived within the organization. "The question," she told me, "is no longer who's in charge of what, but who's in charge of what *today*? I seem to have lost my emotional intelligence, the common sense, perspective, and judgment I thought were my strengths." With a sigh, she told me that in the past there had been financial constraints, "but we knew we could say when enough was enough. In this new world, since the reorganization, I don't know if that is any longer true."

I asked her to tell me more about this "new world." Janet described an emphasis on analysis and action that devalued common sense and respect for human limitation. I asked her if there was evidence for that description; did anyone actually say one should not use common sense? "Of course not," she said, "but it's implicit in the constant reminders that we must focus on rapid deployment of initiatives and that we must demonstrate a capacity to act. It's the subtle message that now that we've been empowered, we better demonstrate results immediately." Janet was not resisting imperatives for action, but she was troubled by what she saw as the results. The power of these ideas had led to individuals' subordinating themselves to the new organizational structure in ways that decreased the intelligent design of systems and got in the way of bettering the company's products. People actually became less able to respond to genuine customer needs.

What seemed to animate Janet was her memory that, old world or new, she has faced these dilemmas before. She has experienced ambiguity and the contradictions inherent in managing cutbacks while still requiring that staff improve their performance. She rose in her organization because of, not in spite of, her constant questioning of the organization's direction. "What I think has gotten in my way," Janet told me, "is that I've tried to adapt to this new world without questioning it. I've seen this rush to solutions as normal and the plowing-over of people as being beyond my role to question. My peers say they're doing just fine and that makes me feel inadequate. When I'm tired and frustrated, I wonder what's wrong with me. But guess what? My peers aren't any clearer or getting anywhere faster. When I look past their words, I can see that they're also just barely holding things together."

There is no greater challenge to the soul than the forces of authority and the group that seek its surrender. The immense power of the group to demand conformity and inhibit access to our own experience is rooted in the power of ideas and the organizational structure that shapes and organizes these ideas. For Janet, the ideas implicit in the new world she referred to suggested subordination and compliance. Of course, she could have her own ideas, but as Tocqueville warned (in the epigraph that opens this chapter), she risks becoming a stranger among them.

This does not suggest that groups are evil or that conforming to group norms is by itself a problem. We become more aware of ourselves by recognizing that we internalize aspects of the groups we belong to. And we become more aware of ourselves by recognizing our power to transcend the limitations of what we think the group demands of us. The needs of the workplace and those of the individual are not necessarily contradictory, but neither are they necessarily compatible.

Power and Knowledge

Janet's struggle to find herself amidst seemingly new expectations reminds me of my own experience in graduate school. A philosophy professor, teaching a course in organizational theory, introduced us to the writings of Michel Foucault by way of an experiment conducted at our expense. To us, Foucault was an unknown philosopher whose writings were dense, often impenetrable. We placed our recently browsed chapter of his on the desks in front of us and looked expectantly at our instructor.

"What are Foucault's nine disciplines of power," the instructor asked, "and how do they relate to his central thesis?" We looked at each other with anxiety and discomfort. We began burrowing into the chapter in front of us, heads inches from the paper, as if we could hide from the instructor's gaze. One student started to speak, then stuttered and stopped. We looked up and then down helplessly, defeated in our ignorance. I still remember my feelings of that moment: angry, anxious, tentative, without a voice to express what was happening inside me.

Then the instructor's voice softened. "What is happening in this moment is something of what Foucault is describing. He is arguing that power and knowledge are intertwined. Who is viewed as holding power may dictate the scope of what is considered knowledge, what questions may be asked in discussion, and what the format for those discussions will be." The response of those under the gaze of authority, he went on to explain, becomes subject to review, interpretation, study. "Your hesitation becomes the data from which I gain further knowledge, the means by which I make judgments about you in order to develop further methods to teach you about my knowledge, to discipline, reward, and punish you. To measure your compliance against a norm. And when you are able to answer my questions, so that they are also your questions, then I have internalized in you regard for my power and my knowledge."

My instructor's words fell on me like hail in a storm. My class-mates and I sat in silence, looking bewildered. We had been the subjects of my professor's little experiment in group dynamics. We had rapidly lost the power of our own voices when confronted with his assumed knowledge. Literally, students stuttered, lost their thought, became silent. His question, designed to intimidate, had left us docile and potentially more willing to learn his answers than to seek our own.

Yet my instructor's words were liberating. Didn't we at various times in our professional training bristle, complain, and then go along with the knowledge imparted to us? Didn't we feel, at times, that we were losing our own voice and adopting the voices of others? And then didn't we also take our new knowledge and impose it on others, often feeling superior and proud of our achievements? The experience of this interaction was thrilling and transformative, the sense of being high up on a balcony, look-ing down on a scene where actors are learning their roles. But the actors do not know they are actors, and they do not know they are learning a role.

The professor's experiment, conducted at our expense but well worth the price, opened a door in my mind to thinking about power and the willingness to subordinate ourselves to the perceived norms of a situation. The bonus was that it introduced me to the writings of Foucault, who, though well known in academic circles, is relatively unknown in the field of organizational behavior and management theory. To Foucault, knowledge did not emerge in iso-lation but rather was associated with the apparatus of power: insti-tutions, programs, technology. Knowledge was always part of a web of social relations that included dynamics of power, group inclu-sion, and the threat of exclusion. Foucault asked, as my professor had: "Whose knowledge is given authority?" "Who must be observed?" "Who must be taught that their plight is justified and should be accepted?" He applied these questions to moments in history when the confinement of individuals within institutions became a metaphor for the domination of souls.

Suppressing What Does Not Fit

In the historical management of leprosy, mental illness, and social maladjustment, Foucault found analogues of exclusion, domination, and good intentions gone astray. "Who will be society's leper?" "Who will be viewed as maladjusted and subject to cruelty and rehabilitation?" "Who will be regarded as on the periphery of society?" "Who will be confined and judged?" Faced with such questions, one is obliged to ask, "How is it that we come to think of ourselves as normal and rational, and others as deviant?"

In the preface to his book *Madness and Civilization*, Foucault sets the tone by quoting from Pascal: "Men are so necessarily mad, that not to be mad would amount to another form of madness" (Foucault, 1965, p. ix). Pascal's words remind us of the extremes of our own soul, and of the consequences of false ideals, such as narrow notions of reason and conformity, that can be imposed on us. The idealization of reason and social conformity has a shadow: one of domination and false adaptation.

The confinement and domination of an "other" who is different from us is in part protection from our own fear of madness, our own inkling that there are forces within ourselves that need to be controlled and kept at the periphery of awareness. Organizational structure, when coupled with a fear of disorder, sets in motion shadow dynamics that blur our legitimate need for some common behaviors, on the one hand, with punishment for difference on the other hand. The more benevolent our intentions seem, the greater the potential for the encroachment of shadow because we no longer see what lies behind those intentions.

Lepers in medieval times, like the mad who would take up a similar social function later, were seen as wicked and dangerous. The leper was a symbol of the social outcast. The danger of becoming the leper was and still is the danger of being dispossessed: one is no longer included in the social body—one no longer fits in. The leper represents an "other," repository of our fears and reassurance, however tentative, that the rest of us still remain in the light of God's grace.

In the corporate sphere, the lepers are those who are different: minorities, gay men and women, or those no longer of value in the reorganized workplace. As I was consulting to a large financial institution in the early 1980s, a vice president described to me the low morale in the office because many bank officers were waiting for reassignment or termination during a corporate shake-up. "They are our lepers," he said. They hover at the periphery, waiting for corporate action on their behalf, a warning to others of a potentially similar fate.

Exclusion is only one facet of the treatment of those who don't fit. A second strategy is confinement, management, and discipline. The first group in Europe to be confined on a large scale were those with the least power: the poor. In 1656, by edict of the French king, the poor were rounded up and housed in various hospitals, many of which were similar in structure to those used for lepers. The edict was specifically intended to prevent an old sin from being born anew in a changing economic landscape. Idleness and begging were viewed not as symptoms but as the source of communal disorders.

The king's action represented both a form of charity and a warning to those who might refuse to work. The confining of the poor was to provide a cure for unemployment, a remedy for the increasing dislocation of individuals lost amidst changing economic circumstances. However, the institutions that housed the poor also acted as quasi prisons, including the use of stakes, irons, and the dungeon. Domination of the poor was an economic necessity and a social policy mediated by enforcement.

The French hospitals, where the poor were housed, soon made labor an essential aspect of confinement. Labor was regarded as a moral and social imperative, a redemption from idleness and a way to contribute to society. This confinement "solution" to poverty and unemployment, however, became a new social problem. The forced labor of the individuals confined to the hospital created further unemployment for those who were not. As Foucault saw the state's response, poverty had to be recognized as an essential aspect of a prospering nation, which meant the poor had to be maintained outside of the care of the state.

The institutions that for a time confined an undifferentiated mass of beggars, women, madmen, wayward children, and criminals were now expected to differentiate its various populations. The mad and the criminal were to be identified and rehabilitated. At the end of the eighteenth century in France, the poor were freed and those deemed mad were released from dungeons and chains. But this was neither a matter of simple philanthropy nor the progress of medical science. A new form of authority was emerging, one that sought techniques to control the social outcast in a more subtle fashion. The body can be held by chains or kept confined in a dungeon, but the mind is still free to roam, to wail, to curse the tormentor. Now the person must be tamed; the soul itself must be institutionalized.

The Castle of Conscience

Foucault chose for his analysis of these new techniques the work of a man conventionally viewed as the founder of modern psychiatry. Philippe Pinel was physician to the Bicêtre and to the Salpêtrière, two of the leading hospitals in France for the mentally ill in the late 1700s. Until the late eighteenth century, both hospitals functioned as de facto prisons for the destitute beggars, lunatics, prostitutes, and children deemed unruly. Pinel, in taking over the management of these institutions, was one of the leading proponents of a new technique for reining in madness, what Pinel himself called "the rules to follow in the moral treatment of mental disease" (Zilboorg and

Henry, 1941, p. 341). Pinel is known today as the man who released the mad from their chains, responsible for the introduction of humanitarian institutional practices.

Pinel was an archetypal humanist, a scientist in no doubt of his rationality, a man who proposed to lift the mad from the dungeon of their ignorance. Surveying his own motivations for the challenge of treating madness, Pinel discovered only his best intentions, dictated by science and "by a truly sincere love of mankind, or rather by the honest desire to contribute to the general welfare. I shall leave it to the enlightened reader to decide whether I have achieved this aim" (Zilboorg and Henry, 1941, p. 341).

Foucault took Pinel up on his challenge. In him Foucault saw a symbol of monstrous rationality, at times benevolent, sometimes harsh, and always a controlling and judging figure of authority. Pinel articulated a new form of authority that sought to impose moral standards on individuals while having them accept responsibility for their actions in relation to institutional demands. Foucault argued that Pinel and his peers released the mad from their dungeons and chains only to hold them confined in another, moral world, a "castle of conscience."

The castle of conscience was a place of subtle tyranny where outward conformity, fear of isolation, and the imperative of labor ruled. In this world, inmates must always regard their keepers as working on their behalf, and show gratitude for what freedom they have and contrition for bad behavior. Foucault's asylum is a rendition of a nightmare, a "cuckoo's nest" where the Nurse Ratcheds rule and there are no McMurphys to come swinging through the door. It is the asylum as horror chamber, ruled by sovereign reason and misguided philanthropy.

Pinel himself proposed that this new form of therapeutic confinement accomplished "the happy effect of intimidation, without severity; of oppression, without violence; and of triumph, without outrage" (Robinson, 1977, p. 66). His technique emphasized the subtlety needed by those in positions of authority to impose their demands. In *Treatise on Insanity*, which he wrote during a time of revolution in France, he described the meaning of his intervention:

> A Russian peasant, or a slave of Jamaica, ought evidently to be managed by other maxims, than those which would exclusively apply to the case of a well bred irritable Frenchman, unused to coercion and impatient of tyranny . . . [therefore] to render the effects of fear solid and durable, its influence ought to be associated with that of a profound regard. For that purpose, plots must be either avoided or so well managed as not to be discovered; and coercion must always appear to be the result of necessity, reluctantly resorted to and commensurate with the violence or petulance which it is intended to correct [Robinson, 1977, pp. 67–68].

Pinel advocated the threat of confinement, the straitjacket, and the keepers' use of superior numbers to control the inmates. He saw in all these activities not coercion but a treatment strategy that forswore random violence and was always in the patient's best interest.

In one case, of a man freed from twelve years in chains, Pinel instructed the keepers to maintain silence in their relations with him. "This prohibition," Pinel wrote, "which was rigorously observed, produced upon this self-intoxicated creature an effect much more perceptible than irons and the dungeon; he felt humiliated in an abandon and isolation so new to him amid his freedom" (Foucault, 1965, p. 260). Pinel understood that the subtle but very real threat of isolation and humiliation in the midst of seeming liberty was a tactic more "perceptible" by the inmate than the symbols of overt coercion, the irons and the dungeon. Individuals were now expected to take responsibility for themselves in an environment organized by their managers. "Fear no longer reigned on the other side of the prison gates," Foucault wrote about asylum conditions; "it now raged under the seals of conscience" (1965, p. 247).

In his techniques, Pinel concentrated on the individual's conscience, that capacity to internalize social standards of behavior and morality. He documented the case of a man who developed this conscience after being threatened with perpetual confinement for his loud outbursts. The man was told that he would remain confined until he agreed to behave. After three days of actual confinement, the man requested to be released. Pinel wrote that after release,

> a single look from the governess was sufficient to bring him to his recollection . . . lest he might draw upon his benefactress the displeasure of the governor, and incur, for himself, the punishment from which he had just escaped. These internal struggles between the influence of his maniacal propensities and the dread of perpetual confinement habituated him to subdue his passions and to regulate his conduct by foresight and reflection. He was not insensible to the obligations which he owed to the worthy managers of the institution, and he was even disposed to treat the governor, whose authority he had so lately derided, with profound esteem and attachment [Robinson, 1977, p. 106].

The gaze of authority was all that was needed to trigger correct behavior: "a single look from the governess was sufficient to bring him to his recollection." The inmate must watch his keepers, but he must also watch over himself. He must become his own governess, working on behalf of the greater authority, judging himself as the external authority figure would judge him. Only then could a "cure" be awakened that is internal and permanent.

Rehabilitation would be achieved through moral cures. But at the core of this strategy lay the figure of authority who saw to its management. The manager would be immovable, cool, and indefatigable.

The patient, we may imagine, would be disordered, unruly, muddled within himself or herself. Pinel saw in the governor, who administers the asylum, an impressive figure of humanitarian care, his courage unshrinking, his voice that of thunder. In the chambers of La Bicêtre, a symbolic confrontation took place between the figure of chaos and the figure of rationality and conviction. In this confrontation, the figure of authority could not understand what he faces; he knows only that he must dominate what has become so separate from his own personality.

Internalizing the Demands of Authority

In the years that Pinel was freeing the mad of their chains, freedom was also sweeping away the chains of sovereign authority in Europe. The American colonies had declared independence from England. The spilled blood of the royal family in France had consecrated the end of the rule of the nobility. Over the next 125 years, the Russian tsar would fall, the heir to the Austro-Hungarian empire would commit suicide, his successor would be assassinated, and the kaiser of Germany would meet defeat. Freedom was creating new anxieties about individuals' behavior in the absence of a sovereign ruler.

Kings, after all, watched over their subjects and brought order. Subjects offered obedience, and for their dependence they received protection. In the collective psyche, the question was how to retain order now that everyone was free. Freedom demanded new mechanisms of control, new methods for ensuring compliance. Freedom was adding a new urgency to the definition of what should be viewed as normal.

In this changing world, where sovereign authority would no longer dictate order, Jeremy Bentham, an innovator and moral philosopher, became obsessed with an idea and a plan. Bentham, too, had the best of intentions. He had just published a paper entitled *Panopticon Or The Inspection House: A Plan of Management* (1791), in which he hoped to bring order and humane treatment to the horrific conditions imposed on the swelling population of criminals in England. Like Pinel, he grasped instinctively that power would not, as in the preceding centuries, reside in the control of land and its resources. It would be contingent on the control of human bodies, their minds, and their functionality. He set out to develop an architecture for rehabilitation, a means to ensure correct behavior. Freedom must be leavened with order.

Bentham conceived an enlightened prison, whose "shadow" was the capacity to regulate the smallest details of everyday life. The architectural plan for the panopticon was modeled on a factory that his brother Samuel, an engineer, had built in Crecheff, Russia. It was a plan that would balance freedom with control, a structure that could ensure proper conduct. In a preface to his writings on the panopticon, Bentham listed its benefits: "Morals reformed, health preserved—industry invigorated—instruction diffused—public burthens lightened" (Bentham, 1843, p. 39).

Bentham believed, long before the word became popular in our own time, that his creation was empowering. The panopticon would allow the inmate, the pauper, the schoolchild, and the worker an opportunity to adapt their behavior to the conditions around them, to mirror physically and mentally the behavior necessary to fit into the social body.

The word *panopticon* comes from the Greek *panoptes*, meaning *all seeing*. "We know the principle on which it was based," wrote Foucault about the physical structure of the panopticon:

> A perimeter building in the form of a ring. At the center of this, a tower, pierced by large windows opening onto the inner face of the ring. The outer building is divided into cells, each of which traverse the whole thickness of the building. These cells have two windows, one opening onto the inside, facing the windows of the central tower, the other, outer ones allowing daylight to pass through the whole cell. All that is then needed is to

put an overseer in the tower and place in each of the cells a lunatic, a patient, a convict, a worker or a school-boy. The back lighting enables one to pick out from the central tower the little captive silhouettes in the ring of cells. In short, the principle of the dungeon is reversed; daylight and the overseer's gaze capture the inmate more effectively than darkness, which afforded after all a sort of protection [Foucault, 1980, p. 147].

What can be made visible is believed essential to control. The panopticon can be seen as a metaphor and a model for a new form of disciplinary environment, one that embodied the exclusionary nature of the leper community and the classification system of the asylum. The panopticon proposed to confine individuals in order to make them tame.

The panopticon, as in the leper community, had the capacity to identify and confine selected populations. Schoolchildren, workers, convicts, and patients could all be secluded and observed at a distance. As with the mental asylum, the panopticon had the capacity to oversee every aspect of the individual's behavior and movements. The structure of the panopticon insisted on order and was inherently linked to hierarchy, classification, surveillance, and the separation of individuals from each other.

Bentham developed the panopticon during a time of changing economic conditions, when the newly industrializing areas needed a large labor pool. The enclosure of so many individuals under one roof brought fears of idleness, rebellion, and sabotage. The panopticon, wrote Bentham, would be "a mill for grinding rogues honest and idle men industrious" (Bell, 1961, p. 228). He saw the panopticon as a tool to shape conscience by enforcing the "perpetual gaze."

Bentham viewed the surveillance aspects of the panopticon as essential in aiding the individual to achieve correct behaviors and to establish good work habits. "The fundamental advantage of the Panopticon," Bentham wrote, "is so evident that one is in danger of obscuring it in the desire to prove it. To be incessantly under the eyes of the inspector is to lose in effect the power to do evil and almost the thought of wanting to do it" (Miller, 1993, p. 220). Visibility ensures surveillance, and visibility and surveillance are assumed to ensure a wholesome conscience.

In the panopticon, surveillance is maintained at a distance and is one-directional. Special shades were to be constructed in such a way that the inmate could not see inside the central tower. Whether the overseer had his back turned or was asleep or was not even present did not matter. The inmate within the cell believed he was being watched and judged.

The panopticon supported hierarchy by proposing to diminish acts of disobedience before they happened. It lessened the demand that authority be a relationship, albeit among unequals, and fostered an invisible network of methods for monitoring and detecting exceptions to the normal. Bentham anticipated a time when surveillance would be taken for granted, when the individual would anticipate being watched and would therefore police himself or herself. Right conduct would come not only from fear of reprisal but also from the anticipation of guilt if one betrayed the internalized social eye. The chains are removed, but freedom is now bound by the decorum established by the collective will over what is the correct way to think and behave.

The Gaze of Authority in the Modern Organization

The panopticon as metaphor has not escaped writers and consultants on organizational behavior. Daniel Bell, in his essay *Work and Its Discontents: The Cult of Efficiency in America*, noted that the passion for order demonstrated by the panopticon created a "new calculus of time" that disrupted the agrarian and craft nature of work. Work would no longer be dictated by the rhythm of seasons or the art of the craftsman. Instead, work would be internally organized by a clocklike, regular, "metric" beat. Bell wrote: "The modern factory is fundamentally a place of order in which stimulus and response, the rhythms of work, derive from a mechanically imposed sense of time and pace. No wonder, then, that Aldous Huxley can assert: "Today every efficient office, every up-to-date factory is a panoptical prison in which the workers suffer . . . from the consciousness of being inside a machine" (Bell, 1961, p. 229).

Nearly three decades later, Shoshana Zuboff, in her book *In the Age of the Smart Machine* (1988), raised similar questions about how modern technology, involving information and automated systems, creates new and more perplexing dilemmas concerning control. Visibility, she pointed out, is no longer only vertical, as it was in the panopticon. It rests on horizontal scrutiny as well, the collective group watching over themselves and each other. Zuboff (1988, p. 351) wrote: "The model is less one of Big Brother than of a workplace in which each member is explicitly empowered as his or her fellow worker's keeper. Instead of a single omniscient overseer, this panopticon relies upon shared custodianship of data that reflects mutually enacted behavior. This new collectivism is an important antidote to the unilateral use of panopticonic power, but it is not a trouble-free ideal. Horizontal transparency breeds new human dilemmas as well. . . ."

The office with no doors that allows constant visibility, the microprocessor built into the operating equipment to monitor individual productivity, the information systems that monitor compliance with centralized standards are all contemporary extensions of the panopticon. They are not necessarily evil, but they are a new means to harness the power of the group to watch over us and implicitly demand compliance. The effect, though unintentional, can be chilling if the individual senses that their use is unilateral and arbitrary. "Often the level of frustration disables the work," wrote an employee in a workplace environment survey I conducted; "the sense of being inspected and having your words and actions parsed for possible lapses makes me feel more defensive than attentive or productive. This translates into a sense of not having one's judgment trusted." Surveillance evokes a generalized loss of status and personal control.

In contemporary organizations, conformity is gained by way of appraisal systems and a tight corporate culture. Everyone feels watched and judged, even if the manager is less overtly controlling. The organization can depend more on self-regulating units guided by specific boundaries governing what each small unit can influence. Conformity becomes a defense against the anxiety of not knowing who is behind the shades of power, who determines what information is relevant, and what consequences are in store for non-compliance.

What is essential about the panopticon as a metaphor of domination is that it is premised on the structure itself, a machine programmed by its architects for order. All individuals have their established places, with their accountabilities and responsibilities identified. Everyone is interchangeable; no one individual can influence the basic nature of the structure. The underlying rules that govern the system—where power is actually located—are invisible. Domination is not simply a function of one thing, whether surveillance, architecture, or punishment; it is an elemental force that feels pervasive. Everyone feels watched and judged.

The panopticon symbolized a new attitude toward domination, more machinelike than personal. Bentham's proposal offered a solution to the naked power of the autocratic sovereign by stripping power from all individuals. "This is indeed the diabolical aspect of the idea," Foucault wrote:

> and all the operations of it. One doesn't have here a power which is wholly in the hands of one person who can exercise it alone and totally over the others. It's a machine in which everyone is caught, those who exercise power just as much as those over whom it is exercised. This seems to me to be the characteristic of the societies installed in the nineteenth century. Power is no

longer substantially identified with an individual who possesses or exercises it by right of birth; it becomes a machinery that no one owns [Foucault, 1980, p. 156].

The panopticon is a metaphor of a machine with human parts, a system without feeling or creative spirit. The human pieces are subordinate to the will of the machine, adapted gears in a "tremendous clockwork," to use a phrase from Nietzsche. Freedom is replaced by a craving to be happy, to be relieved of the painful choices and struggles to shape how one fits into the larger social body.

The panopticon represents an approach that attempted to change people from the inside out by making it necessary for individuals to tame their own wild and mercurial nature. As their personal identity is stripped away, individuals feel less attentive to their internal world, less able to contemplate the larger system they are in, and finally less able to tolerate the dissonance between the two. It is a disciplinary system that proposes to make individuals conform for their own good. "Call them soldiers," Bentham wrote, "call them machines: so they were but happy ones, I should not care" (Miller, 1993, p. 221). Happiness comes at the expense of a soul too chaotic to manage.

Taken together, Pinel's asylum and Bentham's panopticon offer us overlapping images of what it means to be in an enlightened prison. Everything must be submitted for inspection. We are constantly subject to the power of the prevailing notion of normality, whether it be under the eye of someone in the hierarchy or of our peers, or simply imbedded in the architecture of the system itself. Being under the watchful eye feels like a pressure "applied to the forehead," a colleague told me once. We can't always see it, but we can feel it.

Confronting the Machine

Does the logic of the panopticon and the asylum—precise classifications of individuals based on personality and functionality, surveillance, and treatment of what is perceived as deviant—still infuse the organizational logic of today? Foucault made no attempt to balance out the diversity and contradictions in actual institutions. He did not have the usual academic compulsion to hedge, equilibrate, narrow the questions asked to safe proportions. He acknowledged setting out to write historical fiction, to provoke in the reader a response, to act corrosively upon normal assumptions about power, authority, and institutional life. In this sense he was a consultant to society, acting no differently from the best organizational consultants, who ask of their clients to examine their assumptions, who frustrate their clients' easy solutions, who offer their clients not a new ideology but a method for arriving at their own conclusions.

Foucault joins with writers throughout history who have warned us of any system that promises to meet our needs without considering the costs. Sergei Aksakov, a Russian writer of the early nineteenth century, summarized this viewpoint by warning of the costs of seemingly benevolent social aims:

> However widely and liberally the state may develop, were it even to reach the extreme form of democracy, it will none the less remain a principle of constraint, of external pressure—a given binding form, an institution. The more the state evolves the more forcefully it turns into a substitute for the inward world of man . . . the more closely man is confined by society, even if society should seem to satisfy all his needs. If the liberal state were to reach the extreme form of democracy, and every man to become an officer of the state, a policeman over himself, the state would have finally destroyed the living soul in man [Woodcock, 1962, pp. 401–402].

The idealized image of a perfect society or a perfect workplace is illusory. The living soul, as the phrase is used here, encompasses the full dimension of being human. Humanity has within it pain as well as joy, the unchanging nature of the tragic as well as striving for prosperity and happiness. When we deny one for the other, we can no longer embrace the fully human dimension of experience. The consequence of denial is that part of the self is disenfranchised and goes underground, fermenting fantasies of rebellion, violence, and revenge. The body can be made docile, the mind numbed; but the spirit of the person is free to burn and rage. We are possessed by the very shadows we seek to distance. Irrationality returns in more vivid forms, and disorder does not stay banished for long. Our good intentions, especially our good intentions, can become distorted in ways that subordinate the person and crush the vitality of the soul. What is our freedom if it is purchased at the exclusion of other classes of people, isolated from the rhythms of nature and community, maintained by becoming an officer over ourselves? How do we confront this unintended domination?

One lesson we might learn from these tales is that there are inadvertent outcomes of our best intentions. Pinel and Bentham were reformers who genuinely sought better conditions for those they hoped to help. They believed that by establishing the rules by which others would live, they could cordon off the inner world of emotions, thoughts, and fantasies that sometimes interferes with outward social compliance. What they could not foresee was their shadow, and how destructive their actions would be. They could not foresee how alone individuals would become when removed from participation in the whole. The panopticon, you will recall, was a social machine that no one owned.

Besides realizing unintended outcomes, we must be willing to see beyond our own individual dilemma and identify the larger purposes from which we shape our own organizational role. An example from my consulting work may help illustrate this dynamic in groups.

Recently, I worked with a patient care division of a hospital in which we had addressed a number of organizational issues. In one situation, we were discussing one of the group's main intentions, to create strategic alliances with the financial division of the hospital.

I pointed out that this was not a new aim; they had tried in the past. And they knew perfectly well that this was a critical alliance. Yet the outcome of their effort was invariably the same: distrust and mutual loss of credibility. They not only felt judged by the data from the financial division but also disturbed by oversight from the "bean counters." Repeatedly, during our sessions, I listened to stories of budget information on their operations being put forward that they disputed or felt was irrelevant to their tasks in delivering patient care.

I suggested that they could not find any genuine common ground with the financial division because they were so preoccupied with their anger and sense of humiliation from previous interactions. They were hiding the truth beneath their stated intention, I said; they really had no wish to cooperate. The group was initially silent. Out of this empty space came words from the director of emergency services. He said he had never thought about it this way. He did, in fact, see the finance people as antagonists he continually placated, offering them expense projections that were not realistic, revising his figures later when necessary. "What if they are right?" he said. "What if they do have information that I could use or that might guide me in making different decisions on staffing? I have seen my role as protecting my staffing from them. What if that is not the whole picture? This is scary."

The emergency services director had a real dilemma. If he acted on the information that he was over budget, he might have to cut his staff or services in ways that could further compromise the morale of his department and the safety of his patients. If he ignored the information or continued to placate the finance people, he might jeopardize the fiscal viability of the whole hospital and risk his job. He realized that he must confront more deeply the assumptions of his organizational system, the implications of how the health care machinery operates. He knew, for example, that the majority of his patients did not present serious emergencies but were individuals unable to gain access to medical care in other kinds of clinics. The staffing pattern he maintained was a response to other parts of the health care machine that were not functioning effectively. The underlying purpose of his hospital was to care for people, not to offer a Band-Aid that masked the dysfunctionality of the health care system.

The effect of his insight was liberating, although frightening. He was freed from his own view of the financial division as people unworthy of respect. They had become shadowy figures high up in a tower, peering through the shades of their fiscal knowledge. Now, he realized, they could prove to be a valuable resource in managing during a cycle of cost cutting. He also acknowledged having more personal energy. He escaped the feeling of being suspended between despair—nothing could be done—and fanaticism—marching alone against the impersonal forces of the hospital. He, and by extension individuals in other parts of the system, recovered some additional aspect of a common humanity and a common task. What had happened?

The unintended outcome of bureaucratization within the hospital had left people, like the manager of the emergency department, in tiny cells from which they could not view the whole system, while they in turn felt constantly under inspection. The data from the finance department was perceived as punitive, part of the machinery of the system that gave feedback without engaging in a dialogue. But by confronting these restrictions, and by confronting his own internal feelings of anger, humiliation, and rebellion against the restrictions, he could begin to think in new ways about his dilemma. Unlike the panopticon, a machine that no one owns, he could acknowledge that everyone must own the whole system and that alliances were not simply a function of human relations but an aspect of his core responsibilities. From this psychological stance, he could then proceed to act in strategic ways.

The Soul Emergent

The lesson in all this is a message that lies at the heart of all spiritual teachings: You cannot be someone else. You cannot gain freedom by conforming. You cannot adapt yourself to circumstances and then feel you are a victim or a bystander. I recall a story from my own childhood about a certain Rabbi Zusya, who said, "In the coming world, they will not ask me: 'Why were you not Moses or Akiba or Abraham?' They will ask me 'Why were you not Zusya?'" This question lingers today as it has for centuries, for it is a question about the resiliency of the soul, the utter uniqueness of each individual.

In each of us lies this question about being more fully who we are as opposed to becoming someone else's ideal. We are pulled in so many directions that the inevitable cry from within is "I can't find me." But who is the *I* and who is the *me?* The lessons of the soul teach us to regard the question with reverence. In organizations, we are constantly distracted from this essential question because the pull to live up to someone else's expectation is so profound. The workplace of today embodies a sometimes innocent, sometimes harsh assault on us as individuals—we who need connection to our own experience and our own destiny.

We are on the path to becoming real when our inner work joins with a creative outpouring that is relevant to the world we live in. We are on the way when we attend to our experience, when we recognize both the awe of a larger force operating in the world and also the darkness implicit within human consciousness. This "path with heart" is central to all spiritual teachings.

The soul is endangered by a metaphoric prison in which the inmates and keepers become more machine than human. When we attempt to create an enlightened prison, as did Bentham, we may become shut off from our own experience. For Bentham, as for us, there is an aspect to our consciousness that equates happiness with comfort and order—a painless existence. In contrast, the living soul can be a source of disorder, where competing passions lie, where we journey into alternative realms, sometimes wondrous and sometimes maddening. Nietzsche suggested something of these multiple perspectives of the soul when he wrote in poetic form: "My soul, its tongue insatiable, has licked at every good and evil thing, dived down into every depth" (Thiele, 1990, p. 59).

We elevate reason beyond our own experience and consensual reality above being real, at the expense of what lies creative within us. I am reminded of what Ingmar Bergman said about his art: "I have always had the ability to attach my demons to my chariot." These *demons*, problematic at one level, are the wellsprings of his creativity, the basis, Bergman says, of "a language that literally is spoken from soul to soul in expressions that, almost sensuously, escape the restrictive control of the intellect" (Weiner, 1994, p. 4). Bergman's demons are dual-natured, at once troubling and enlightening. But he could think of them as part of his experience, imagery from the multiplicity of his soul. And experience can give us perspective on ourselves and our organizations.

This capacity to hold the tension of our two natures is what lies on the other side of sovereign reason and group conformity. There is danger, but as Bergman knew, there is at least a chance that our souls can power the chariot of our lives. To approach such an alternative view of the soul, however, we must be realistic about the social threads of our culture, closer to Bentham than to Bergman. We are still just at the beginning of our story as to how organizations challenge the soul.

Part Two

. . . .

Chasing the Dream of Order

4

When Machines Won the Day

Streamlining the Soul to Fit the Industrial Age

> *The village blacksmith shop was abandoned, the road-*
> *side shoe shop was deserted, the tailor left his bench,*
> *and all together these mechanics [workers] turned*
> *away from their country homes and wended their way*
> *to the cities wherein the large factories had been*
> *erected. The gates were unlocked in the morning to*
> *allow them to enter, and after their daily task was*
> *done the gates were closed after them in the evening.*
> *Silently and thoughtfully, these men went to their*
> *homes. They no longer carried the keys of the work-*
> *shop, for workshop, tools and key belonged not to*
> *them, but to their master.*
>
> Terrance Powderly, Grand Master Workman,
> United States, Knights of Labor, 1889
> (Bowles and Gintis, 1976, pp. 56–57)

The themes of Part One—soul that is stirred to life by recognition of multiplicity, the struggle to be aware of shadow dynamics, and the consequences of suppressing what is unruly in the individual and the group—take on new shadings when we apply them to the workplace. The seductive power of the ideas beneath the work of a Bentham or a Pinel is that we can have control, streamline the jagged edges of our humanity so that reason rules, subordinate instinct to the collective good, and make work a requirement of society, irrespective of the wilderness within. We can appreciate this dream of order, but we must also face the distortions and pathologies that arise from the shadow of these ideas.

Part Two explores a related web of ideas that challenge soul in the workplace: ideas about management, efficiency, mechanization, control, and the subordination of individual experience to group demands for productivity. For in these ideas we begin to grasp the ways in which we have come to discount soul and deny the full measure of what lies within the individual. In organizations, we talk about empowerment and individual respect. But so often these are just words to distance ourselves from the individual's inner world of experience.

That inner world of experience can be understood as a skill, the learned capacity to recognize and honor the active soul in relationship to the world. When we honor experience, we are rewarded with imagination, deep emotion, and creativity. When I say that experience is a skill and can be learned, however, I do not mean it is simply taught. To the contrary, more often we teach people to *ignore* their experience, leaving them little incentive to hone what skill they already have. Though we rarely tell them directly to ignore their experience, we do so in subtle ways, masking our request in the cloak of reason or saying we love them, or when our beliefs don't allow us to tolerate another's experience.

The honing of our capacity for experience requires something of the skills of an archaeologist, the capacity to rummage around within ourselves and pose questions about what we discover. The experience of our recent or distant past gives us clues as to how we imagine ourselves in relation to others. When we can plumb the depths of our experience, we invariably find the connections between past events, current behavior, and future choices. We have a greater capacity to find meaning.

Perhaps our biggest impediment to learning is allowing belief systems to override our capacity for discovery. We all know individuals who seem incapable of learning from experience, no matter how obvious the lesson seems. In organizations, we face belief systems all the time that impede learning. Belief systems about such things as order and control substitute for our experience; they constrain the curiosity, imagination, and feelings relevant to relationship with our world.

As Margaret Wheatley has pointed out in *Leadership and the New Science*, we have come to confuse control with order and a mechanistic predictability with the patterns and flow of dynamic living systems. "This is no surprise," she writes, "given that for most of its written history, management has been defined in terms of its control functions. Lenin spoke for many managers when he said: 'Freedom is good, but control is better'" (Wheatley, 1992, p. 22–23).

Our quest for control has been highly destructive to us as living beings. But to appreciate just how destructive, we need to appreciate the social and historical context for its emergence in modern organizations. We need to appreciate the contradictions—the innocence and calculation, the genius and arrogance—that have made of control a language of efficiency and a belief system associated with ever-increasing production and social order. For in this story is a hint of how the living soul has been cordoned off and people subjected to the fragmentation of work.

Prelude to a Tale

In a consulting project with a medical center on team development and strategic planning, I worked with a management team of both physician and nonphysician administrators. Steve, the medical center's assistant physician in chief, was also a surgeon. He decided to have me meet his colleagues in the surgery department as part of my introduction to the medical center. We walked into one of the surgeon's offices, and Steve introduced me as the medical center's new management consultant. "Oh," said the surgeon with a reserved manner, "you're one of those efficiency guys who's going to get us all working faster." He said it good-naturedly but with the air of a man who had no further use for me. He might have even thought it a little comic to have an "efficiency guy" working with surgeons; but if so, he did not share that with me.

When we left his office, I suggested to Steve that we needed a different approach. In the next office we visited, he introduced me as "my colleague, Dr. Alan Briskin. I'm showing him the medical center." I was greeted warmly and asked how I liked the medical center. For a moment the physician imagined I was also a surgeon, and we shared the camaraderie. I then clarified my role as a consultant to the leadership of the medical center. The response remained warm, even curious, and after a brief conversation I left.

Why did this word *efficiency*, coming from the first surgeon, have such a bad ring to it? Why the immediate association with working faster? Was it my imagination, or had a rift been created instantly when I was identified with management? There are clues, many of which grow out of a time at the end of the eighteenth century when efficiency had yet to gain a foothold on the popular imagination.

Serving the Machine: Process and Production

In 1790, Oliver Evans received a patent for mechanizing the process of milling. Grain could now be brought by boat or wagon, dumped onto a scale for weighing, and, by means of a bucket conveyor (functioning as a vertical elevator), brought to an upper floor. From here, the grain would roll down a wide leather strap, descending by its own weight and a system of pulleys. At each step along the way, milling could be performed while virtually eliminating human hands from the process. The automatic mill could process 300 bushels of grain an hour, a vast improvement over mills fed by hand.

Neighboring millers scoffed at the invention, which they saw as a set of rattle traps that defied common sense. Evans would lament that "the human mind seems incapable of believing anything that it cannot conceive and understand" (Giedion, [1948] 1969, p. 82). How could a machine supersede human hands? The prospect seemed impossible long before it would be called monstrous.

The derision of the millers was transformed shortly into anger and fear. As the economic advantage of the mechanized mill became more evident, the other millers were unwilling to pay royalties on Evans' patent. Turning to Congress in protest, they called on Thomas Jefferson as an expert witness on their behalf. Jefferson's testimony attacked the invention as not worthy of a patent. "The elevator," he declared, "is nothing more than the old Persian Wheel of Egypt, and the conveyor is the same thing as the screw of Archimedes" (Giedion, [1948] 1969, p. 84).

Jefferson was correct. There was nothing essentially new about the invention that distinguished it from ancient Egyptian and Chinese methods for elevating water, or the designs of Renaissance theorists whose use of levers, gears, and pulley systems allowed them to raise heavy loads or transmit force. What was different was not the sophistication of the engineering principles that gave the machine its life but the context for its use.

Invention, back into ancient times, was always tied to the wondrous. Sophisticated engineering principles were used to build monuments to religious celebration or memorial, amphitheaters for performance, sites for athletic competition. We still wonder at how the pyramids were constructed. These feats of the miraculous all required techniques for lifting and moving objects. They were awe-inspiring creations.

What Evans accomplished, however, was of a different order. Siegfried Giedion, the master historian of mechanization, placed Evans's discovery in its historical context: "For Oliver Evans, hoisting and transportation have another meaning. They are but links within the continuous production process: from raw material to finished goods, the human hand shall be replaced by the machine. At a stroke, and without forerunner in this field, Oliver Evans achieved what was to become the pivot of later mechanization" (Giedion, [1948] 1969, p. 85).

Evans's mechanized mill stood as a prototype of a new logic in industry. His system of mechanized movement was to be a forerunner of the belt conveyor used in the late nineteenth century; it foreshadowed Henry Ford's assembly line in 1914. Evans's invention accomplished two things, at once practical and revolutionary. For one, he was moving solid materials (grain) along a conveyor system where before only water was moved. And secondly, the mechanized process changed the nature of how individuals would touch what they made with their hands. Human labor could now be replaced with machinery, leaving to individuals the tasks of feeding raw material into the machine and removing finished product.

At the dawn of the nineteenth century, Evans's mechanized milling machine suggested the emerging value of tying work processes to ever-increasing production. Individuals could now serve the machine: watching it, tending to its upkeep, tallying its daily production. And production, the mass production of goods, was to be the language of the next two centuries.

The unassailable logic of Evans's invention was like a snowball rolling down a slope, constantly gaining momentum and bulk. It is a logic of increasing division of labor and a widening net of mechanized assembly. In early nineteenth-century England, for instance, biscuits for naval crews were produced by a human assembly line of five-man teams working in choreography with a machine for kneading the dough and ovens for baking the biscuits. Each man had a discrete task: one molded; one stamped; a third separated; a fourth threw the breads onto a long, wooden shovel; and the fifth arranged them in the oven. But in thirty years' time, the bakers were replaced by a mechanized assembly line needing only two men: one to transfer the dough from the kneader and another to remove the finished loaves (Giedion, [1948] 1969, pp. 88–90).

The notion that organic materials, such as grain, can be disassembled by machinery and turned into a new product (flour) is reiterated in the combination of flour and water to produce biscuits. This logic of continuous production, of assembly and disassembly, becomes the leitmotif of industry in the nineteenth century and its springboard into the twentieth. What can be analyzed and broken down into its parts can also be reconstructed from disparate elements. The origins of the early-twentieth-century assembly line, for example, can be found in the disassembly line at meatpacking houses in mid-nineteenth-century Cincinnati. Here, hogs were disassembled by giving each workman a specific duty: "one cleaned out the ears; one put off the bristles and hairs, while others scraped the animal more carefully" (Giedion, [1948] 1969, p. 90). By 1870, the mechanization of this process had been taken a step further. Hogs were hung from an overhead rail, exactly twenty-four inches apart, and moved continuously past a series of workers who each performed a single operation: one laborer split the animal open, another took out its entrails, and a third removed its heart.

The vision implicit in mechanization is control; control the variables of the process and you ensure the desired final product. Efficiency, as a concept, draws its basic meaning from this vision, where both *things* and *human labor* are broken down into their pieces. How one stands or stoops or swings one's arm can be studied, and this information becomes useful for an engineer of human beings. And when you engineer the body's actions, you cannot help but touch the soul.

Serving the Boss: Engineering Human Souls

In the United States, the dramatic changes in how individuals worked and lived in the second half of the nineteenth century were driven by four key processes: the move from farm to factory, the dramatic increase in wage labor, the explosive growth of cities, and the massive increase in immigration (Rosenzweig, Brier, and Brown, 1993, p. 39). Each of these influences already existed in the first half of the nineteenth century, but they accelerated rapidly from roughly the mid-nineteenth century to the first decades of the twentieth century. Each of these social processes cemented the relationship between working and working for someone else.

Increasingly, individuals were moving from farms and subsistence lifestyles to industrial villages, with their heightened distinctions between wealth and poverty. Prior to 1850, approximately six out of ten families lived on farms and were employed in agricultural work. By the beginning of the twentieth century, fewer than three in ten families lived on farms or worked in agricultural pursuits. The reverse was true for industrial labor. By 1900, the manufacturing workforce grew to six million, four times its size in 1860. Small-scale farms disappeared in large numbers from the American landscape as mills and factories took their place. In the same time period, cities such as Chicago grew tenfold, and immigrants from Europe and Asia came to the cities in the millions.

The disappearance of the farm and the rise of the mill paralleled an increase in the number of people who were employed as wage earners and therefore were managed. In the late 1700s, 80 percent of nonslave adult males were independent property owners or self-employed, as farmers, merchants, traders, craftsmen, artisans, businessmen, lawyers, and doctors. By 1860, half the working population was still self-employed. In 1900, two of every three Americans depended on wages. In the decades prior to these changes, the belief that one could set out on one's own by first being industrious and economically frugal had some validity. In the economic and social turbulence of the latter nineteenth century, this was riskier business. For many, the fact of working for someone else for the rest of one's life was a condition that could not be ignored.

The scope and influence of industry was also changing. Accelerated by new inventions to increase production, steel output grew tenfold between 1877 and 1892; the output of copper rose by seven times, crude oil four times. Railroads rose up across the nation, representing not simply a new method of transportation but also a fundamental part of the redefinition of markets. With transcontinental rail networks, small producers who dominated local markets now found themselves competing with highly capitalized and market-ravenous competitors. In an extraordinarily unstable economic climate, overproduction and fierce competition went hand in hand with business cycles of boom and bust. Economic depression was the rule for at least half the period between 1873 and 1900. Few wage earners could count on full-time employment year-round.

With these changes came a heightened attention to standardization of time, machines, and people. Diversity of all kinds was being invalidated. A federal commission on Indian affairs in 1868 recommended that tribal tongues be substituted with English: "their barbarous dialect should be blotted out. . . ." Wrote the commission of its logic, "Through sameness of language is produced sameness of sentiment, and thought . . . in process of time the differences producing trouble would have been gradually obliterated" (Schwartz, 1994, p. 3). Sameness of language was perceived as producing sameness of experience—how one felt and thought. Trouble was associated with differences.

Trouble was also seen in organizing daily life around the natural rhythms of sun and weather and crop cycles. In the 1850s, most people still told time by looking at the position of the sun. Time was kept haphazardly from locality to locality, not because it could not be accounted for to the hundredth of a second but because it mattered little to most people. What difference did it make if the time in New York was a few minutes different from time as kept in Philadelphia? With the completion of the railroad network in the 1870s, it mattered a lot.

Those who wanted coordinated and predictable rail service so as to engineer transportation of goods and people from one area to the next knew that they first needed a system that organized time. William Allen, working on behalf of the railroads as secretary of the General Time Convention, lobbied businesses and politicians to support a shift to interchangeable standards of time. To do this, however, meant "stopping" time and reorganizing it so that different localities and regions could be coordinated with each other. In biblical myth this had in a sense occurred, as when Joshua requested God's intervention to stop time during the siege of Jericho, but this latter-day intervention required a force of a very different nature, one organized enough to stop time in multiple localities.

On Sunday, November 18, 1883, time was stopped and standardized. On this day, called the "day of two noons," people were
required to reset their clocks by anywhere from two to thirty minutes in order that four new standard time zones, stretching from
Maine to California, could be established. People gathered near
public clocks and jewelry stores to see this feat accomplished with
their own eyes. The *Indianapolis Sentinel* inquired, with tongue in
cheek, whether a man slipping on a banana peel on November 18
would have an extra sixteen minutes (the time correction in Indianapolis) to fall. An article in the *New York Times* of November 19
reported crowds of curious people in front of watch-repair estab-
lishments waiting for the designated moment when time would be
stopped. They were disappointed that the sun did not stop its arc in
the sky, nor did any cosmic force assert itself. "There was a universal expression of disgust," the article related, "when it was discovered that all that was necessary to effect the change was to stop the
clock for four minutes and then start it again" (Rosenzweig, Brier,
and Brown, 1993, n.p.). The curious perceived no great transformation, fears were not substantiated, and nothing changed. Or so
it seemed.

Time Is Money: Power in the Workplace

The implications of the standardization of time dawned slowly on
the American people. Two years after the railroads imposed standard time zones on the nation, time clocks appeared in American
factories. Timeliness took on a new meaning, a precision not for-
merly associated with work. The boss not only owned your time,
but now he measured it in precise units and equated it with profit.
A midwestern newspaper acknowledged this trend by noting: "The
sun is no longer boss of the job. People . . . must eat, sleep, and work
as well as travel by railroad time" (Rosenzweig, Brier, and Brown,
1993, p. 74). Reason demanded that workers subordinate their own
experience of natural rhythms to the logic of efficiency.

The transition to a new calculus of time, however, was still incomplete. The attainment of efficiency and standardization still remained largely outside the boundary of what owners could control. In its origins during the first half of the nineteenth century, the industrial workplace could not determine every aspect of a worker's movements or styles of workmanship. An owner or foreman could only have limited influence, particularly on skilled workers versed in traditional methods of craftsmanship. In these still-developing workplaces, work was organized largely by cajoling workers to get their work done based on vague production standards. It was not uncommon, for instance, that a foreman would periodically negotiate with work crews over pay and output. Industrialists complained bitterly that even unskilled labor took breaks to rest or to discuss the way work was going to be accomplished. This created a charged atmosphere between labor and capital, each side pawing the ground, eyeing the other to gauge the adversary's weakness and strength.

The latter part of the nineteenth century was convulsed with often violent conflict along an increasingly polarized labor-management axis. Foremen, called "minute thieves," tried to find ways to cut back on lunch periods or to keep work going after formal closing times. Managers attempted to create more formal work rules, explicitly associating the laborer's time with the factory's profit. Washing up, noted the work rules in a New Hampshire factory, "must be done outside of working hours, and not at our expense" (p. 74). Unions emerged from this ambiguity over who controlled the workplace to force the hand of ownership, increasingly viewed as the enemy of working people. Owners fought back, using both the carrot and the fist.

The early marriage of mechanization and efficiency often had an underlying premise: to end any ambiguity over who controlled the workplace. When Cyrus McCormick of the McCormick Harvesting Machine Company was stymied by a strike led by his most skilled workers, he vowed never again to be undone by his labor force. He declared, "I do not think we will be troubled by the same thing again if we take proper steps to weed out the bad element among the men." To fulfill his vow, he purchased $500,000 of molding machinery that replaced his most highly skilled laborers (p. 75).

John D. Rockefeller followed the same path when, at enormous cost, he brought in barrelmaking technology that ended the power of the coopers, traditional craftsman of the art of barrelmaking. He was able simultaneously to break their power and lower their wages. In steelmaking, Andrew Carnegie experimented with the same idea, combining technological innovation with brutal management practices. Using elevated trains to carry coal overhead throughout the mill, which replicated Evans's earlier feat of moving solid material along a conveyor system, he was able to eliminate hundreds of shovelers from his payroll. In the mid-1890s, employees at Carnegie's Homestead, Pennsylvania, plant worked twelve-hour shifts as often as seven days a week. They had little choice.

These changes did not come peacefully. At Homestead, for example, workers waged a bloody and ultimately unsuccessful battle with Henry Frick, Carnegie's chief of operations. In the clash over where power lies in the workplace, the Homestead story is one of the sadder accounts of words and deeds diverging. The lesson of Homestead was that when workers could not be won over by the hand of "reason," they would be subjected to the fist. The outcome highlighted a polarization between management and labor that would lead to new beliefs about the necessity of efficiency to determine work intensity, and later to psychological strategies for motivating workers.

The Tale of Homestead: War in the Workplace

Andrew Carnegie was one of a handful of industrial titans who attempted to articulate a benevolent rationale for the growing accumulation of power and capital in the hands of the few. He stressed that competition was good for human nature and that philanthropy and progress, not mere wealth, were the true aims of industrialists. At age thirty-three, he mused in his journal that early retirement from business was necessary because wealth alone was too narrow a goal: "To continue much longer overwhelmed by business cares and with most of my thoughts wholly upon the way to make more money in the shortest time, must degrade me beyond hope of permanent recovery" (Baida, 1990, p. 124).

Carnegie did not retire as early as he had planned, but his wrestling with the purpose of capital accumulation culminated in his writing an article entitled "Wealth," later reprinted as *The Gospel of Wealth*. In this monograph on the positive nature of capitalism, he related a vision of stewardship in which inequality was necessary in order for the most talented to be born from the cleansing fires of competition. The virtues he promoted were those of individualism, the sacredness of property, and the "laws" of competition and accumulation. He held that the race of successful businessmen who survived competition would be the men best suited to serve society, through philanthropy and civic service. The money they accumulated could be considered a fund that they held in trust for the benefit of society. In such a society, individuals would be encouraged to achieve their highest goals through the disciplines of work, education, and right conduct. Carnegie even argued, in other writings, for the right of workers to organize in order to advocate for their individual well-being. As an owner, he declared, he would negotiate in good faith to see that a fair outcome was achieved.

Homestead was one of the most advanced mills in the world. Skilled workers had won wage increases significantly higher than workers at competing mills nearby, and they had joined with unskilled laborers at Homestead to see that their wages also benefited. There was a great sense of community; nearly every family in the town of Homestead had someone working in the mill. Unionism was a shared value, seen as protection from an overdependency on the mill's owner and management.

A fragile balance had been struck between capital and labor that would not hold. Henry Frick, Carnegie's manager in charge, was growing frustrated over his inability to dictate wages, linked as they were with production levels that were increasing with new technology. His aim was to reduce costs in relation to overall output. He set out to break the union by mandating a pay cut, announcing he would deal with the men only on an individual basis, and refusing to negotiate with the existing union, the Amalgamated Association. Carnegie's approval of Frick's plan was ambiguous; he left the matter behind as he sailed to Scotland on vacation.

Knowing the union would not accept his actions, Frick built a three-mile fence, twelve feet high, around the steelworks and topped it with barbed wire, adding peep holes for rifles. He laid off all the workers and hired the Pinkerton detective agency to protect the strikebreakers he anticipated hiring. On the night of July 5, 1892, three hundred Pinkerton guards boarded barges and approached Carnegie's steelworks by water. The strikers had been forewarned; virtually the entire town—ten thousand strikers and sympathizers—waited for the Pinkertons to land. The sheriff was unable to raise a posse since there was hardly anyone left who was not already supporting the workers.

The crowd warned the Pinkertons not to step off the barge. A striker blocked the gangplank and was pushed by a Pinkerton guard. Shots rang out. In the ensuing battle, nine strikers and seven Pinkerton guards were killed. The Pinkertons surrendered to the strikers.

For the next several days, the strikers controlled the area until the governor brought in the militia, armed with Gatling machine guns, to protect Frick's strikebreakers. The new workers were brought in, often in locked trains, not knowing their destination or that a strike was in progress.

Frick won. The union had to submit to a greater power. The union leaders were blacklisted, and the rest of the men returned to lower pay and eventually longer hours. There would be no union at

Homestead until well into the twentieth century. Frick wrote to Carnegie, "We had to teach our employees a lesson, and we have taught them one that they will never forget" (von Hoffman, 1992, p. 45).

Carnegie's benevolent rhetoric concealed a blunt instrument. Henry Frick was the tough and (when necessary) meanspirited shadow to Carnegie's philanthropic actions and philosophical musings. He was an expression of business as war and victory as the only goal worth striving for. He represented realpolitik as well as the efficiency of brute power to shackle dissent and demand the bended knee. Nor by any means was he an isolated case. In 1878, the Brotherhood of Locomotive Firemen published an anonymous account of a railroad official's "statute books" that purportedly (and satirically) demonstrated the intentions of owners. The mandates were written in the form of ten religious commandments, the third commandment being: "Thou shalt not bow down to any other master, and not belong to trades' unions, or lecture on the principles of the working party, or do anything contrary to my wish or command, for, if you do, I will call on the military" (Rosenzweig, Brier, and Brown, 1993, n.p.).

In symbolic language, Frick was the reptilian tail sneaking out from Carnegie's waistcoat. He was a dark reminder of a hidden business virtue: getting the job done at any cost and cutting costs just as mercilessly. In business lore, he was a nearly indestructible figure, not to be underestimated. In the midst of the Homestead strike, Alexander Berkman, an anarchist and colleague of Emma Goldman, represented himself as a business agent and was allowed an appointment with Frick. Pulling out a gun, the story goes, Berkman shot at Frick repeatedly, and then pulled out a knife and stabbed him—to no avail. Some stories have it that Frick stayed in his office and was taken away by stretcher only after he finished his day's work. Charles Schwab, a contemporary and another hard, sometimes dictatorial steel man of the time, said of Frick, "He was a curious and puzzling man. No man on earth could get close to him or fathom him. He seemed more like a machine, without emotion or impulses. Absolutely cold-blooded" (von Hoffman, 1992, p. 47).

"Those Who Sell Us Their Labor"

Frick was a product and an expression of one aspect of the power struggle taking form at the turn of the century. To be successful in the new world of efficiency, some part of the self had to be like a machine, without emotion, hence an enigma to others as well as to oneself. The skill of experience, the living soul aware of itself, had to be streamlined in order to maintain control. One could not let the contradictions of life muddle one's perception of right action either in work or for the self. Frick could not let the traditions or needs of the workers muddle his desire to lower his cost structure and retain command over the work itself. The expression for leaders of this era was (as Jung said about Germany twenty years later): "where there is a will, there is a way."

The double nature represented by Carnegie and Frick was repeated again and again in the actions of businesses during the last half of the nineteenth century and the beginning of the twentieth. At the same time that violence between labor and capital was convulsing the workplace, businesses experimented with what William Tolman in 1898 called *industrial betterment* programs, ranging from hygiene and medical care to profit-sharing programs, libraries, and reading rooms for employees. Tolman stated explicitly that the programs emerged from the self-interest of owners to retain a happier and more efficient workforce. They grasped the idea that workers could not be simply driven like machines. They would become less effective, sullen, easily moved to resistance or rebellion. John Patterson of National Cash Register declared of such programs, "It pays."

Tolman (1909) extolled the value of betterment programs in a second book, appropriately titled *Social Engineering*, with a foreword written by none other than Andrew Carnegie. Carnegie, who sold his interests in steel in 1901 for $250 million, had by then retired to dedicate his time to philanthropic interests. "The hearts of those will be touched," Carnegie wrote in recommending Tolman's book, "who have the welfare of their fellows at heart, and the heads of those will be convinced who wish the condition of the laboring people improved" (Tolman, 1909, p. v).

Yet not every industrialist was convinced. Tolman records the dissent of one prominent industrialist who, disappointed with the results of his betterment efforts, flatly stated the view held among many of his peers:

> We went into it [industrial betterment programs] quite extensively. Whether it was that our people were a class of foreigners who did not seem to appreciate the work that we attempted to do, or whether their appreciation was misunderstood by us, I do not know. . . . We have fully made up our mind that it will be a matter strictly of business with us . . . we shall buy our labor as we buy our material, and we are thoroughly convinced in our own minds that those who sell us their labor will give us as little as they possibly can for what they sell us without regard to whether or not we attempt to go more than our half of the way [Tolman, 1909, p. 356].

He argued what often remained unspoken by those who advocated benevolence: they (the workers, the other) will never be satisfied or show gratitude. Do not bend when you can demand. Do not say "trust me" when you can insist. Do not ask for loyalty when you can require subordination. In the idea of a straight-up trade of money for labor, the soul and its unwillingness to be dominated had no place.

But industrialists, differing over whether the wage earner was someone having a nature worth improving or simply a commodity to be used up with other raw materials, could agree on one thing. They shared a common view that the control over how work was performed should be in the hands of ownership and management, and that the goal of industry was to continuously increase production.

The question that emerged was, what can be done within the plant to lower costs and raise productivity? Pay cuts could not go far enough. Technology, in the form of machine tools, was becoming more commonplace, but it too could not satisfy the quantum leap needed for production increases. The answer lay no longer in new inventions but in new ways of organizing within the workplace. How could work performance be systematized so it was not so idiosyncratic? How could workers, whose labor is purchased, be motivated to perform work tasks closer to the outer limits of their potential productivity?

In the last decades of the nineteenth century, alongside violence on the one hand and industrial betterment projects on the other, a growing number of individuals were working on these questions. An engineer named Frederick Taylor was one of them. He was an answer waiting to be discovered.

5

Enlightenment Born of Fear

Frederick Taylor and the Gospel of Efficiency

*He protects himself with the shield of science and the
armour of reason. His enlightenment is born of fear;
in the daytime he believes in an ordered cosmos, and
he tries to maintain this faith against the fear of chaos
that besets him by night.*

Carl Jung, Modern Man in Search of a Soul

Frederick Taylor, whose name is forever linked with efficiency, is a controversial figure in American history. For some he is a villain and the architect of the dehumanized workplace, whose legacy we are learning to counteract. For others, he was a misunderstood missionary whose basic principles are still instructive today. Both sides view the other with reserved scorn. He is known as the father of scientific management, and his theories are believed by many to be the foundation of modern industrial practices. Some historians believe his contribution to present practices has been exaggerated, and others point out that his theories were never fully understood and therefore never fully implemented in the first place. There is no question, however, that Taylor and his theories had a profound impact on the American imagination in the early twentieth century. Within one year from the time his ideas first gained national attention in 1910, 219 articles on scientific management had been written. Harper and Brothers published a collection of his major articles on the subject of efficiency, and the work was translated into nine languages. Taylor societies were formed, and efficiency expositions were held. President Theodore Roosevelt praised Taylor's work, and for years after Taylor's death businessmen made pilgrimages to his home in Philadelphia.

The concept of efficiency, especially as Taylor refined it, extended the machine metaphor to the human body. But it did so in a way that transcended both the arguments of owners to dictate arbitrary rule over the workplace and the advocates of industrial betterment who sought cooperation through humanizing gestures. Taylor was one of the first individuals to systematically study work processes themselves, and in so doing to make work subordinate to knowledge. But the rule of reason has a shadow, the twisted knot of knowledge intertwined with power. Just as Bentham's panopticon sought a harmony won by subjugating soul, so too did Taylor's ideas of scientific management seek harmony at the expense of the richness and complexity of experience. The missionary zeal with which Taylor pursued his engineering of work processes masked the subordination of work itself as meaningful and a necessary extension of the living soul. Today, as we begin to assess the human damage in the wake of our high hopes about reengineering, we have reason to listen to the story of Taylor once again, to recover lessons we thought we had learned.

The Rules of the Game—and Its Limits

Playing with his friends in the fields around Germantown, Pennsylvania, in the early 1860s, the young Frederick Taylor insisted on the strictest observance of the rules, whatever the game. More to the point, he insisted that there were rules and that he could frame what they were. Birge Harrison, a childhood friend of Taylor's who later became an artist, offered this description: "Fred was always a bit of a crank in the opinion of our boyhood band, and we were inclined to rebel sometimes from the strict rules and exact formulas to which he insisted that all our games must be subjected. To the future artist, for example, it did not seem absolutely necessary that the rectangle of our rounders' court should be scientifically accurate, and that the whole of a fine sunny morning should be wasted in measuring it off by feet and inches" (Copley, 1923, vol. 1, p. 56; all subsequent citations in this chapter are of volumes and pages in this work unless otherwise indicated).

But to Taylor it did matter a great deal that the boundaries of the field should be measured just right and that the rules be adhered to with uncompromising consistency. Harrison noted, however, that "once this observance of the law was conceded and agreed to, he was most generous to his opponent, allowing him every possible chance to win and conceding every doubtful point." Frederick Taylor, having established the correct boundaries of the field and the proper parameters of acceptable interactions, was most gracious once the game began. He understood—and this was evident throughout his life's work—that to set the boundaries for others is to control the game and ultimately the behavior of the participants. And he understood also that controlling the rules of the game implied that individuals experience something similar to each other, for were they not then motivated by the same principles?

Taylor's inclination toward invention and organization found its way into all aspects of his life. When he found at age sixteen that a bean bag toss game between boys and girls left too many children idle for moments at a time, he added bean bags to quicken the game's pace. And when, at twelve, he determined that the fearsome dreams terrifying him came only from the position of his sleeping body, he constructed a harness of straps and wooden points that dug into his back to wake him up whenever he turned over.

Taylor felt an enormous responsibility, even a burden, that reason should triumph over all forms of disorder, whether disorder be in the form of idleness or the unknown. He was at his best when he could test the limits of a mechanical process, such as the impact of a mallet on a croquet ball or the efficiency of a hiking stride. He seemed to show little interest in why any of this mattered in a larger sense, but it mattered to him a great deal that every task be done with precision, logic, and order. He applied these virtues to everything mechanical, and he eventually extrapolated them to human organizations as well. He seemed to have a creative and desperate need to know the hidden potential of mechanical and human activity. Yet his behavior was also reflective of an arrogance toward internal experience, a willful disregard for what was not measurable or rationally discernible—forces beyond his control.

Perfecting the Tools

Taylor's experiments with finding the hidden nature (and potential) of a mechanical process began in earnest in the mid-1890s when, at the Midvale Steel Company, he invented a steam hammer that not only worked at three times the speed of similar steam hammers but also didn't wear out as quickly. He did this by studying all the previous designs that he could locate, taking the most resilient parts from each, and incorporating them into his final design. He designed unique features to the hammer only when he could not find an acceptable design for a specific part. His most important discovery was that the resiliency of the machine depended on the elasticity of the parts during motion. The hammer was mounted on an apparatus resembling steel spider's legs that absorbed the power of each blow. In this way, he was able to keep the hammer snapping back into proper alignment. The lesson would not be lost when he later devised processes for human labor: the redesign of work processes was also to account for human fatigue.

Frederick Taylor was concerned with limits, the outer limits of pressure that could be applied to an object and the maximum limits to each object's elasticity. This quest for the outer reaches of utility, for the rules that govern the engineering of tools, was applied equally to the human body and to human organization. How hard could people be driven without breaking down? How elaborate a structure must be created to ensure a consistent alignment of human labor with the work processes that maximized production? With

utmost conviction, Taylor was discovering the most efficient ways
to turn the human body into a mechanism.

In 1898, Taylor accepted an offer from the Bethlehem Steel
Works to institute a piece-rate work system that promised to
increase production and cut costs. Although hired directly by the
president, Robert Linderman, Taylor was primarily encouraged in
this endeavor by Joseph Wharton, a financial backer of the steel
works and a member of its board. Wharton believed in experts and
was willing to bring in a hired consultant to improve the financial
efficiency of the operations.

The choice of Taylor did not go unnoticed. There was general
unease in the town of Bethlehem as news of Taylor's methods raised
fears of layoffs. He was given the name "Speedy" Taylor, and rumors
questioning his character spread throughout town. For many, he was
a hired gun whose presence was disquieting.

Taylor, for his part, had come to expect resistance and took it
upon himself to do things right. He attempted always to be disciplined about the process by which he sought change. He put in
writing all suggestions for reform and reviewed the suggested directives with Linderman. He sought the buy-in of senior leadership by
giving talks on his methods to the officers of the steelworks. He
understood from past experience that if a new set of rules were instituted, he would have to keep senior leadership informed and malleable to his prescriptions. He also grasped very quickly the reality of
the situation: authority rested in no one person at the steelworks.
The functions of the organization were run by various fiefdoms, with
no one in charge of the works as a whole. To proceed, he needed a
clear line of authority.

Robert Linderman gave Taylor the go-ahead. For Taylor, this was
the opportunity he had hoped for and calculated on. He recommended centralizing all operations under a new role, the superintendent of manufacture. Taylor orchestrated the selection of the
individual he wanted to fill this centralizing role and simultaneously
began preaching the necessity of standardization.

The Logic of Efficiency

Taylor argued that, far from discouraging originality and innovation among workers, standards created the baseline from which improvements in efficiency could be judged. No worker, Taylor noted, should have to reinvent what someone else has already learned. Learning as well as authority was to be centralized and transmitted along a clear chain of command. Taylor proposed that he himself was in the best position to learn how to make work processes more efficient. He believed learning was a product of the efficiency studies that he would conduct and that they could then be used as the parameters for determining a piece-rate system of compensation.

Consistent with this logic, Taylor set out to discover the rules governing the most efficient cutting of steel in the machine shop. To do this, he had to determine the outer limits of the cutting tools themselves before he would investigate the maximal use of their human counterparts. To cut steel, one needs a cutting tool made of a harder steel. This was a new science; the mass production of steel was relatively new and the methods for producing a cutting steel were in their infancy.

In 1895, three years before joining Bethlehem, Taylor had methodically figured out that mushet steel (named after Robert Mushet and also called air-hardened or self-hardening steel) not only cut harder types of steel more efficiently (which was known) but also the softer varieties. Taylor also found, contrary to conventional wisdom, that the self-hardened steel tools performed fastest when the tip or nose was lubricated with water and reground frequently to retain its cutting edge. At a time when few engineers were even asking the question as to how to speed up cutting production, Taylor was isolating the variables that would almost double the speed of these tools.

When he came to Bethlehem, Taylor was still experimenting with a variety of self-hardening steels, each somewhat different in its chemical composition. After extensive study, in which he fitted a lathe to do the testing, he chose a specific self-hardening steel made by his former employer at Midvale.

To prove his point about the necessity of standardization and to gain the acceptance of the various superintendents and foremen, Taylor specially made four tools from a single bar of Midvale Steel. He had them ground to his specification, and then he set up a formal exhibition to display his findings. He called together all the managers of the various shops, friends and foes, and before them tested his specially designed tools against various other competitive steels. Something, however, went awry, and Taylor's tools failed miserably. In transcripts from a patent suit some ten years later, Taylor recalled:

> These tools were then run in competition, as it were, in the presence of these men with all of the other brands which had proved themselves in our experiments worthy of consideration, and much to my humiliation the four Midvale tools carefully prepared for this exhibition proved to be the very worst of all those that were tried.
>
> I, of course, was of the opinion that being a newcomer in the Bethlehem Steel Company the blacksmiths who made these tools had overheated or burnt them for the purpose either of playing a joke on me, or, possibly even, of discrediting me in my work [vol. 2, p. 93].

Taylor was to discover, however, that he had not been betrayed, at least not yet. The tools had not been purposely damaged by overheating them. He had chosen a steel whose performance excelled only when heated within a very precise range. And given that blacksmiths judged temperature primarily by color (bright cherry red signifying a temperature of approximately 1,500 degrees Fahrenheit), precision was difficult. Most likely the blacksmiths had been overly protective when heating his special tools. They knew that the utility of this make of steel could be destroyed by taking it to temperatures much above 1,500 degrees; they probably did not know that heating them to just slightly below the critical temperature also rendered them less effective.

A New Zone of Efficiency

The rest of the story is like a dream—or a nightmare. Humiliated in front of the very people he was bent on convincing, Taylor next set out with renewed conviction to learn what had happened. The tools he had named L1, L2, L3, and L4 were now heated by eye, under his orders, to bring them to temperatures ranging from cherry red to a bright yellow heat. A yellow heat would be closer to a temperature above 1,890 degrees, higher than the steel's original forging temperature and surely a recipe for disaster. Taylor wanted to test the limits.

The experiment was pushed even further. Tools L3 and L4 were accidentally heated to a temperature of yellow and beyond, to almost a pure white heat that signified the moment just before melting. And here lay Taylor's Promethean discovery. He found that steel tools of this composition were ruined when heated to a range of 1,500 to 1,750 degrees but start to increase in their cutting efficiency above 1,850. There was an undiscovered zone of efficiency, "the greatest improvement taking place just before the melting point, or at the maximum temperature to which it was possible to bring the steel without destroying it" (vol. 2, p. 103).

The breakthrough came when they tested L3 and found that its cutting speed showed an increase from twenty-eight to fifty feet per minute. Its speed and the heat it produced were so great that the shavings of steel being cut turned blue as they flew off the lathe. The machinists and foremen stopped what they were doing and flocked around the lathe to observe this miracle of resurrection, of performance never before seen. One of the assistants was assigned the task of shooing the men away, encouraging them to go back to their worktables. They were not allowed the thrill of the discovery. Both the risk and the reward were to be Taylor's.

When L4 replaced L3 on the lathe, anticipation was great. Taylor was becoming aware that he had made a huge discovery. He watched in amazement as his superheated tools grew red hot from the friction of their efforts but still remained capable of cutting the cold steel. "I could hardly believe the evidence of my eyes," he remembered afterwards. L4 reached forty-five feet per minute and was still speeding up when suddenly it cracked—"a large piece out of the front of its nose."

Was this a forewarning? Was the mechanism driven too close to its outer limit? Was there a zone of performance that carried within it the seeds of its own destruction? No, said Taylor in his testimony: "This tool was not ruined from the sense of being run at too high a cutting speed" (vol. 2, p. 102). Instead, Taylor surmised, it was flawed in its nature; it had left the smith shop with a slight crack during its forging process. If they were properly engineered, these superheated tools would withstand speeds unknown within production machine shops.

The new tools would be valued for their "red hardness," a property such that they maintained their cutting edge sufficiently to cut steel even after becoming red hot. They were not technically harder than the steel they replaced, but they were more resilient to the pressure and the friction put upon them. Taylor believed this superior race of high-speed steel tools would eventually make other tools of the kind obsolete. There was only one right way to make the best tools, and the highest standard of efficiency must always be the choice. In a machine shop, even one tool of lesser speed could slow up the work of an entire operation.

The Collective Awe of Technology and Efficiency

Frederick Taylor's red-hard, high-speed cutting tools made their entrance on the world stage at the Paris Exposition in 1900. Owners and officials of machine shops in the United States, Germany, and England came, together with their foremen and shop superintendents, to witness this production miracle. Taylor exhibited his experimental lathe, showcasing his high-speed steel in runs of twenty minutes with breaks of no longer than ten minutes. He recalled, "there was a great rush of people from all parts of the building to see the tools cutting with their noses red hot, and turning out blue chips, and the entire exhibit, together with all the space around it, was jammed with people trying to get a view of the tools cutting" (vol. 2, p. 102). Even the traditional makers of steel-cutting tools and blades, the men of Sheffield, England, had to grudgingly acknowledge that their supremacy was now challenged.

Tradition was also being challenged on a larger scale. Taylor's display of his newly patented discovery only heightened the already high-pitched exuberance of technology crossing over to a new psychological, even spiritual frontier. The historian Henry Adams circulated through the Paris exhibit and reported being enraptured by the hall of dynamos—the generators of electricity—that "became a symbol of infinity" and "a moral force." Adams wrote: "The planet itself seemed less impressive, in its old-fashioned, deliberate, annual or daily revolution, than this huge wheel, revolving within arm's length at some vertiginous speed, and barely murmuring—scarcely humming an audible warning to stand a hair's breadth further for respect of power—while it would not wake the baby lying close against its frame. Before the end, one began to pray to it" (Adams, [1918] 1961, p. 380).

For Adams, the dynamo, with all its implications of unfathomable power, dizzying speed, and humble presence, was a monument to a new secular faith founded in science and technology. Mystery and religion must now yield. Where once technology served the creation of monuments to religious awe, now technology and its efficiencies would themselves be worshipped. The supremacy of the machine, mass production, and the corporations that organized human effort now reached toward new heights, asserting themselves in the day-to-day consciousness of modern times. In comparison, nature and experience were seen as inferior and chaotic. Where could soul fit into this new world?

The parade of technological innovation suggested something further. From now on, as we sought solutions to material desire and increased physical comfort, for order and hope, even for moral and spiritual purpose, we looked increasingly with the eyes of the engineer, who, as priest of this new order, saw the human condition and the complexity of work processes as problems whose parts must be broken down and reorganized, as mechanistic systems simply lacking the proper instrument.

The success of high-speed steel also had analogies to how people would be expected to perform alongside the new technology. Steel is a modified form of iron, harder and more elastic. Individuals would now be expected to reach a zone of higher efficiency, beyond mere incremental increases. High-speed steel was made of a composition that failed when forged at only slightly higher than normal temperatures. To become efficient, people had to be brought nearly to their melting point as well. Some might fail—like L4—if they had a crack in their nature. Other individuals, however, would flourish. Flourishing was something akin to red hardness, a resiliency that would allow for working at maximum output without succumbing to excessive wear.

I recall a colleague whose father worked the steel mills in Sheffield after World War II. He described men with their shirts off, glowing red from the reflection of the fires, drinking beer while they worked to cool themselves down. These men were literally red-hardened, cooled down by liquid running past their noses. Many had lost a finger or were mangled in some fashion by the machinery they served. Yet there was pride in my colleague's father's description because these men survived and could hold a family together by working in these "caves of smoke." But really there was no romanticizing these infernos; they were straight from Dante's hell.

Frederick Taylor's fascination with efficiency made him an appropriate administrator for hell. He could not distinguish between the striving for perfection and an addiction to perfection. The hell constituted in the workplace of this century has an obsession with speed, is infused with surveillance, controls all behaviors, and distorts emotions. The shadow of a fantasized perfect workplace is the curtailment of all individual fantasy, where individuals must make themselves over into mechanisms of production.

Seeking the outer limits of a tool's efficiency mirrors a similar obsession with human efficiency. Taylor's conscious virtue, a belief in optimal performance, was turned inside out and became an edict for directing human nature against itself. Taylor was in the grip of this belief system as much as he was a proponent of it. His official biographer, Frank Copley (1923), noted that "the spectacle of a man doing less than his best was to [Taylor] morally shocking. He was concerned for the effect of it on the man's own character. He enthusiastically believed that to do anything less than your best is to add to the sum of the world's unrighteousness" (vol. 1, p. 207). The belief in optimal performance comes to have a religious undertone, a moral mandate associated with perfecting oneself.

Perfecting People: "The First-Class Man"

Taylor's mission of perfection led him straight to conceiving of a "first-class" man. This was a hypothetical being of Taylor's imagination, a being whose self-improvement is synchronized with the industrial workplace. The first-class man does what he is told and is glad to put in a fair day's work. He is to be a man, like Taylor, who manages his life according to reason and systematic regulation. First-class men demonstrate *character*, which Taylor defined in one of his lectures on success as "the ability to control yourself, body and mind; the ability to do those things which your common sense tells you you ought to do; the ability above all to do things which are disagreeable, which you do not like. It takes but little character to do difficult things if you like them. It takes a lot of character to do things which are tiresome, monotonous, and unpleasant" (vol. 1, p. 84).

The internalized traits Taylor admired would create an individual driven by the necessity of labor and the desire to control himself and others. The discipline of doing what is tiresome, monotonous, and unpleasant teaches self-control of the body and its desires, of the imagination and its fantasies, of emotion and its vulnerabilities. The ability to do what is disagreeable provides the experiential basis for controlling others, since a manager must demand from others that they do disagreeable tasks. The individual becomes part of the machine that no one truly owns.

Taylor's vision of a first-class, or "high priced," man was a democratic one; we all could achieve this state if we accepted the authority and care of management. The requirements of a first-class man depended on aptitude and compliance with the task assigned, not on any superior qualities per se of the individual. "I believe," said Taylor, "that the only man who does not come under 'first class,' as I have defined it, is the man who can work and won't work" (vol. 1, p. 180). He described this unwilling individual as "a bird that can sing and won't sing." For Taylor, the necessity of labor and obedience was a mandatory song of life.

The tune that Taylor insisted upon was not his creation. Rather, it was the culmination of voices heard randomly for at least one hundred years, from Bentham and Pinel to Taylor. The utilitarian choir had sung of the benefits of rationality, control, productivity, and the inculcation of virtues specific to the marketplace. Anyone satisfied with less than what was most efficient was simply singing out of key. Taylor recalled being asked by a workman, "Fred, if you were in my place, would you do what you are asking me to do?" His answer was, "No; if I were in your place, I would fight against this as hard as any of you. Only if I were you, I would not make a fool of myself. When the time comes that you see I am succeeding, I would work up to a proper speed" (vol. 1, p. 207).

The first-class man knows "proper speed." It is a function of the time studies Taylor and Emlen Miller performed on behalf of management by observing the most efficient and fastest individual in relation to a specific task. Taylor associated proper speed with the notion of a fair day's work, which represented the idealized relationship between a first-class man and an engineer's sense of proper speed. What hindered this marriage of character and efficiency was idleness, a condition of human behavior that originally meant useless and worthless before it came to mean simply lazy. Taylor feared idleness. Idleness, embodied in what Taylor called "soldiering," was an enemy to the idealized relationship he hoped to foster. Soldiering took two forms. The first was the individual's natural inclination toward idleness, a regrettable but correctable aspect of individual behavior. The second, and more serious, form of soldiering happened in groups. Taylor had seen, during his short time as a worker on the shop floor, numerous examples of workers thwarting the production goals of management. He had watched, for example, machinists fooling ignorant foremen by banging hammers on sheet metal, appearing busy when really just noisy. The notion of a fair day's work, arrived at scientifically, would surround the soldiering of idleness with the objectivity of knowledge and law, forcing it to surrender.

But how does one determine a fair day's work? Taylor turned to mathematics, or at least the metaphor of mathematics, as a tool for rational justification. He had been delighted with a slide rule created by his associate, Carl Barth, to determine the proper speed of cutting metals. Could not mathematics be used to determine a simple formula for productivity?

At Bethlehem, Taylor was trying to determine the most efficient way of moving ninety-two-pound pigs (crude castings) of iron onto rail cars. Was there a formula waiting to be discovered that could determine the proper rate for moving pig iron? Taylor attempted calculations based on foot-pounds of work per day and experimented with measures of manpower as a fraction of horsepower.

None of his formulas, however, proved meaningful. They could not account for fatigue. At a loss for how to proceed, he turned to the mathematically inclined Barth.

Barth demonstrated to Taylor that the answer lay not in the "horsepower of the trotter" but the "pulling power of the cart horse." The question Taylor and Barth asked themselves was how long an animal could be "under load." They developed a formula that calculated how much exertion by lifting, pushing, and pulling must be offset by a percentage of rest. Taylor figured that a man carrying a pig of iron could be under load 43 percent of the day. With this calculation in mind, they determined that close to forty-seven tons of pig iron could be loaded in a day by one man, nearly four times what his current workers were achieving.

An Ox Named Schmidt

The question now was how to put into practice the theorem they had developed. An individual had to be found, from among the seventy-five men who loaded pig iron, who could work according to Taylor's specifications. This individual had to be motivated and willing to accept direction. In his book *The Principles of Scientific Management* ([1911] 1967), Taylor depicted his process for identifying such an individual:

> Our first step was the scientific selection of the workman. In dealing with workmen under this type of management, it is an inflexible rule to talk to and deal with only one man at a time, since each workman has his own special abilities and limitations, and since we are not dealing with men in masses, but are trying to develop each individual man to his highest state of efficiency and prosperity. Our first step was to find the proper workman to begin with. We therefore carefully watched and studied these 75 men for three or four days, at the end of which

time we had picked out four men who appeared to be physically able to handle pig iron at the rate of 47 tons per day. A careful study was then made of each of these men. We looked up their history as far back as practicable and thorough inquiries were made as to the character, habits, and the ambition of each of them. Finally we selected one from among the four as the most likely man to start with. He was a little Pennsylvania Dutchman who had been observed to trot back home for a mile or so after his work in the evening about as fresh as he was when he came trotting down to work in the morning. We found that upon wages of $1.15 a day he had succeeded in buying a small plot of ground, and that he was engaged in putting up the walls of a little house for himself in the morning before starting to work and at night after leaving. He also had the reputation of being exceedingly "close," that is, of placing a very high value on a dollar. As one man whom we talked to about him said, "A penny looks about the size of a cart-wheel to him." This man we will call Schmidt [Taylor, (1911) 1967, pp. 43–44].

Taylor continued his story of Schmidt's transformation by stating that his task was to convince Schmidt to handle forty-seven tons of pig iron and to make him "glad" to do it. Taylor's recollection of this conversation, complete with his version of Schmidt's accent, continues:

> "Schmidt, are you a high-priced man?"
> "Vell, I don't know vat you mean."
> "Oh yes, you do. What I want to know is whether you are a high-priced man or not."
> "Vell, I don't know vat you mean."

"Oh, come now, you answer my questions. What I want to find out is whether you are a high-priced man or one of these cheap fellows here. What I want to find out is whether you want to earn $1.85 a day or whether you are satisfied with $1.15, just the same as all those cheap fellows are getting."

"Did I vant $1.85 a day? Vas dot a high-priced man? Vell, yes, I vas a high-priced man."

"Oh, you're aggravating me. Of course you want $1.85 a day—every one wants it! You know perfectly well that that has very little to do with your being a high-priced man. For goodness' sake answer my questions, and don't waste any more of my time. Now come over here. You see that pile of pig iron?"

"Yes."

"You see that car?"

"Yes."

"Well, if you are a high-priced man, you will load that pig iron on that car to-morrow for $1.85. Now do wake up and answer my question. Tell me whether you are a high-priced man or not."

"Vell—did I got $1.85 for loading dot pig iron on dot car to-morrow?"

"Yes, of course you do, you get $1.85 for loading a pile like that every day right through the year. That is what a high-priced man does, and you know it just as well as I do."

"Well, dot's all right. I could load dot pig iron on the car to-morrow for $1.85, and I get it every day, don't I?"

"Certainly you do—certainly you do."

"Vell, den, I vas a high-priced."

"Now, hold on, hold on. You know just as well as I do that a high-priced man has to do exactly as he's told from morning till night. You have seen this man here before, haven't you?"

"No, I never saw him."

"Well, if you are a high-priced man, you will do exactly as this man tells you to-morrow, from morning till night. When he tells you to pick up a pig and walk, you pick it up and you walk, and when he tells you to sit down and rest, you sit down. You do that straight through the day. And what's more, no back talk. Now a high-priced man does just what he's told to do, and no back talk [Taylor, (1911) 1967, pp. 44–46].

What is significant about Taylor's recounting is how often he repeated to Schmidt that he already knew what a high-priced man was. By accusing Schmidt of holding out on him, Taylor created the psychological conditions for obedience. He linked humiliation—"you're wasting my time"—with the necessity of following orders—"Do exactly as you're told." The worker must internalize the boss's commands in lieu of understanding their origins or rationale. The meaning behind the commands remains shrouded in mystery for Schmidt, all the more because he is told he already knows it and is playing dumb. Schmidt's experience of himself—his knowledge and feelings—are irrelevant to becoming efficient. "Now a high-priced man," Taylor summarized, "does just what he's told to do, and no back talk."

There was back talk, however. Some workers threatened a strike and were initially discharged; some apparently were discouraged from meeting the new quota by other laborers resisting the increase in workload. The local newspaper lambasted Taylor. The president of the company was reluctant to back him. Linderman feared losing three-fourths of his workmen, who lived in South Bethlehem and whose families were renting homes from the company owners as well as shopping in their company stores.

Taylor stood firm. He threatened to leave if Linderman countermanded any of his orders. Behind him, he knew, stood Joseph

Wharton, who did not live in Bethlehem, and who had hired him to bring financial efficiency to the steelworks. For Taylor, efficiency was a higher value than a worker's temporary dissatisfaction or a manager's narrow financial interests.

At Bethlehem, Taylor acknowledged that barely one in eight of the seventy-five men were physically capable of moving forty-seven tons per day. He wanted to make a point, though, that this fact did not dissuade him from believing it was the correct amount of physical labor. He wanted to demonstrate that "first class" did not denote superiority, but rather a relationship between an individual's skills as measured by management and work as defined by management: "He merely happened to be a man of the type of the ox," Taylor said of Schmidt, "no rare specimen of humanity, difficult to find and therefore very highly prized. On the contrary, he was a man so stupid that he was unfitted to do most kinds of laboring work, even" (Taylor, [1911] 1967, p. 62).

In the beginning of the industrial age, the traits that were selected at the lower end of the labor pool often favored strength, dexterity, and speed. Today, we echo these tendencies in our search to reduce the level of skills required on the job to preliterate functions, such as the recognition of an icon on a computer or repetitive assembly. We also demand certain emotional traits of workers such as the ability to be pleasant in often difficult, sometimes intolerable service roles. However, even at senior levels, the skills required are not always what is written on the job description.

I recall a senior manager I worked with who was being encouraged to move to a new position within the central corporate offices. He was highly skilled, excellent at problem solving, and always open to new ideas and innovation. He was, however, unsure of why he was being courted. I suggested he ask these senior officers directly what skills they thought necessary for him to be successful in this new role. He reported back that they talked mostly about loyalty, honesty, and a willingness to work hard and serve the company. He reflected for a moment and said, "I'm bothered by this. I'm honored that they associate these traits with me, but as I left the interview, I kept thinking that what they want is a St. Bernard, not an administrator with ideas of his own."

Upton Sinclair's Voice of Dissent and Taylor's Reply

When Taylor published his account of Schmidt in *The Principles of Scientific Management* ([1911] 1967), there were pockets of outcry. Some didn't like the tone of Taylor's lecture to Schmidt, or that he would refer to someone as stupid and oxlike. Upton Sinclair, the muckraker journalist, who would go on to write of the meatpacking plants in *The Jungle*, wrote a letter to the editor of *The American Magazine*. Sinclair questioned the economic assumptions behind scientific management and asked if scientific management was not simply exploitation by another name. His comments stirred a sparring match with Taylor himself. Sinclair wrote:

> I have been reading with a great deal of interest the first installment of Mr. Frederick W. Taylor's account of "Scientific Management." He tells how workingmen were loading twelve and a half tons of pig iron and he induced them to load forty-seven tons instead. They had formerly been getting $1.15; he paid them $1.85. Thus it appears that he gave about 61 percent increase in wages, and got 362 percent increase in work. I shall not soon forget the picture which he gave us of the poor old laborer who was trying to build his pitiful little home after hours, and who was induced to give 362 percent more work for 61 percent more pay. I wonder how Mr. Taylor and his colleagues arrive at the latter figure. He tells us just how by scientific figuring he learned that the man could lift 47 tons of pig iron, but he does not tell us by what scientific figures he arrived at the conclusion that he should receive $1.85 for the work, instead of, let us say, $2.85.

Can it by any chance be that he figured upon this basis?—The workingmen for the steel plant are at present producing $1,000 worth of value and getting $168.00; therefore, if we can induce them to produce 362 percent more, they would then receive 16.8 percent of the additional increase [Copley, 1923, vol. 2, p. 50].

In his letter, Sinclair challenged the assumptions of industrial efficiency, pointing out that workers will be subjected to constant dislocation and continuing obsolescence and markets will be hostage to cycles of boom and bust. He suggested, a few years before the outbreak of World War I, the connections among efficiency, dependence on new markets, and countries' willingness to wage war: ". . . He tells us we have no need to worry because seven men out of eight are turned out of their jobs by the new system, because there are plenty of jobs for them in other parts of the plant. Is that really so? And is it so everywhere? . . . When they have taught one-fourth of the workingmen to do the work of all the workingmen, is it their plan to organize the remaining three-fourths into armies, and send them out to conquer new foreign markets?" (Copley, 1923, vol. 2, p. 50).

Sinclair offered an analysis that would dog the optimism of his emerging century and remains current amidst the downsizing of our economy today. What are we to do with people when they are replaced by machines, made obsolete, used up as fodder for changing technologies? Will there be enough armies, prisons, and mental asylums to house them all? What will become of the families, children, and communities torn apart by dislocation? What will become of soul? How will nations wage war over markets and resources? His warning was that we place efficiency over humanity at our peril.

Taylor hammered back his answer on the anvil of progress: the prosperity of civilization is advanced with the increase in material goods. Dislocations of workers are temporary, the triumph of material progress inevitable. Consumers will demand that the greed of industrialists be slackened and the employee's demand for higher wages moderated. Increased productivity is the only bulwark against massive unemployment and stagnant markets. Scientific methods to enhance productivity will uplift character, create incentives for new discoveries, and promote an enlightened populace. There is no turning back. The march of progress must go forward. We must be willing to step past archaic management practices that fear new responsibilities and burdens; we must be willing to confront workers disinclined to give up their idiosyncratic habits.

Taylor argued that his methods were far from exploitative. They offered the potential to reduce workers' hours and to increase their pay. He reminded Sinclair that his formulations did not include the cost of the small army of efficiency planners and foremen who must plan and oversee these new methods. The worker makes a limited contribution to how work is made more efficient. The capitalist, on the other hand, must not only risk his capital but he must pay for the costs of improving the work processes that enhance productivity.

Taylor told Sinclair that he was also naïve on what motivates workers. He argued that there is a psychological relationship between the extent of higher wages and what is best for the worker. When men are paid up to 60 percent of their former wages, they work more diligently and become thriftier. However, when paid much more than 60 percent of their former wages, Taylor told Sinclair, they are less inclined to steady work and become "more or less shiftless, extravagant and dissipated. Our experiments showed, in other words, that for their own best interest it does not do for most men to get rich too fast" (Copley, 1923, vol. 2, p. 53). Taylor's economic assumptions about what constitutes fair wages are tightly intertwined with his assumptions about character and what is required to maintain a labor pool. The few work for greater achievements, but the many must be brought along by just the right amount of financial incentive. Thus the good of the individual and the well-being of industrial progress are merged.

Taylor went on to chide Sinclair for reducing his formula of what constitutes value and fairness to simply the owner and laborer. The consumer is the benefactor of greater production, representing a third party distinct from the employer and employee. The more a society hitches its wagon to production, the greater do all three parties benefit: the employer gets better returns on investment; the employee gets higher wages, better working conditions, and fewer hours of labor; and the consumer receives more goods at less cost. These, Taylor argued, are the benefits that accrue when machinery replaces hand labor and human efficiency complements the machine.

Behind Productivity and Efficiency: Taylor's Management Assumptions

Sinclair and Taylor, on behalf of all us, argue the relationship of knowledge and power, efficiency and community. They frame the uncountable permutations of beliefs that attempt to mediate progress and exploitation, manipulation and freedom. Taylor gives voice to the position of a ruling class, a voice perhaps within each of us who have gained material benefits from the industrial order. He states explicitly assumptions that today are rarely referred to in public discussion: the assumptions of individuals who feel entitled by their wealth, education, or position to make the rules for others, to determine what is morally uplifting and what personal and emotional sacrifices are worthy of social and financial reward. Taylor tells us, in his philosophy and his actions, what his underlying assumptions are:

- The poor are ennobled by adversity; they must be managed for their own good.

- Some individuals can be developed for their value; others must be relegated to repetitive tasks.

- Order is maintained by an enlightened elite, dedicated to scientific principles.

- The greed of financiers can be moderated by the competition of markets.

- Each individual must sacrifice himself or herself for the social good, regardless of inequity.

These assumptions represent an internal discipline of thought that has religious as well as economic meaning. According to Copley, Taylor knew that the engineers who followed his methods often bristled at the emphasis he placed on the "mental revolution" that takes place when one adopts efficiency as a credo. "Yet," Copley wrote:

> it actually was the fact that men to follow after him had to undergo a mental revolution singularly like that of a religious conversion. To the undeveloped soul, liberty of self-expression means liberty to follow one's individual ways. That it is hard to give up these ways, no one can deny. It is a giving up of one's self. And life knows no fiercer battle than the struggle of a soul with its self-will. But here arises the paradox that lies at the heart of all religion. To give up one's self is to find one's self. The individual, having sacrificed his individuality, becomes a greater individual. He becomes a participant in other lives besides his own [vol. 2, p. 125].

Through the discipline of efficiency, Taylor sought to sacrifice the individual to the industrial workplace. He offered the repentant soul boundaries set by engineers and rules defined (primarily by white males) as fair and unalterable. Taylor conceived the soul, as he did the body, to be malleable and capable of domestication. He had no sense of the soul's own wellspring of archetypes and gods. He had little inkling of how the body and mind rebel when hemmed in too tightly. For Frederick Winslow Taylor, the greatest good was achieved through an industrial-strength Puritanism, that extreme form of surveillance over one's interior conscience. The dream of Puritanism, embedded in the strategies of efficiency, was the hope that all impurities could be purified in the heat of right thinking, a mind's attempt to rein in the idiosyncrasies of the body and soul.

There is little value in discrediting or discounting Taylor's assumptions. They are embedded in the fabric of our management practices. For each of us born into a century of valuing technology and production over soulfulness and relationship, we carry a little bit of Frederick Taylor within us. We know that he was right in many respects and wrong in some fundamental ways, particularly regarding respect for individual experience and collective solidarity. The failure of efficiency is all around us, but the lessons we have to learn are still elusive.

Organizations that are reengineering today are still grappling with Taylor's legacy. There remains a belief that once reengineered, organizations will run like the clockworks they were meant to be. Among leaders of the workplace, there still exists a dream of order. Implementation of new technology, redesign of work processes, and clearer accountability of employees still holds a seductive allure for those who wish to control the workplace. Taylor's story should be a warning.

The story of Frederick Taylor, however, is not simply a lesson to avoid or a historical fable without consequence. There is opportunity for dialogue in the assumptions that propelled Taylor and the realities we face today. The discussion between Taylor and Sinclair suggests some of the assumptions that still must be questioned. Is material progress inevitable? Is ever-increasing productivity truly the answer to employment? If so, what are the human consequences of market economies' constantly vying for the greatest productivity at the lowest cost?

If the workplace no longer needs people or relegates people to too narrow a function, both subsistence and meaning are frayed and lost. People cannot simply become mechanisms of production without losing connection with their own experience: fragility, wonder, passion, and mystery. These qualities are critical to health, creativity, and compassion for others. We compartmentalize the soul at our own risk.

Postscript: The Dark Night of the Soul

The story of Frederick Taylor has a mythic quality. And like the myths of legend, it is retold differently each time. Management consultant Marvin Weisbord (1987) points out in *Productive Workplaces* that even Taylor did not get his own story right. Taylor probably never made the speech to Schmidt he reported in detail some ten years later for his article on scientific management. He made his offer to the whole work crew. There were seven men who initially volunteered, not one; the rate that was offered was $1.68, not $1.85. Schmidt, whose real name was Henry Noll, was no more an ox than was Taylor, both physically small men. Carl Barth's theorem for "heavy laboring," which was the supposed rationale for the forty-seven-ton workday, was most likely developed after, not before, Schmidt was put to work.

I suggest, however, that Taylor, wrong on the details, gave a psychologically accurate accounting of the events involving Schmidt. His recollections described how it felt to *him* to be pitted against the resistance of laborers on the one hand and the self-interest of the managers on the other. Taylor was, within the organization of his mind, a heroic figure overcoming the multiple obstacles placed between him and future progress.

Even his choice of calling Schmidt an ox can be seen as something other than simple condescension. The ox is a castrated bull, symbolizing patient toil and animal strength. What better symbol could there be of his attempt to yoke the industrial workforce toward productive ends? The apparently imaginary speech he gave to Schmidt was a window on the dialogue taking place inside Taylor, the culmination of his actual battles to retrain a stubborn and resistant workforce. His speech summarized what he had learned from these battles: how one must offer a mix of intimidation and anticipated reward to motivate the ox. In essence, he says to this inferior being: "You want the extra pay, you want to be called first-class and high-priced; then do as I say. You make me sick with your neediness. I will show you how to be somebody, but no back talk."

The intricacies of the story of Taylor and Schmidt have comic and contradictory edges. Schmidt, whose treatment as described by Taylor evoked a popular outcry, became the subject of speculation that he had died of overwork. Following a congressional investigation of scientific management in 1913, Taylor commissioned a physician to report on Schmidt's health. Schmidt was found in Bethlehem, relatively healthy and still working ten-to-twelve-hour days, now handling graphite.

Taylor, on the other hand, fared less well in both his health and employment. At Bethlehem Steel, he was summarily dismissed within a year of his success at the Paris exposition. He had one final and losing battle with Linderman over his authority, this time to standardize the care and storage of tools within the machine shop. Taylor had written to Joseph Wharton for support and was confident of his backing—so confident that he went on vacation to practice his golf game, leaving Linderman an ultimatum, in writing, on his authority. When he returned in late April, Taylor found a note on his desk:

Mr. F. W. Taylor,
South Bethlehem, Pa.

Dear Sir:

>*I beg to advise you that your services will not be required by this Company after May 1st, 1901.*

>>*Yours truly,*
>>*[signed] Robt. P. Linderman,*
>>*President* [Copley, 1923, vol. 2, p. 153]

Rumor had it that Taylor was a pawn sacrificed by Wharton in negotiation with Linderman over the potential sale of Bethlehem to a rival English firm. Linderman, it seemed, wanted from Wharton a commitment to stay out of his dealing with Taylor. Whatever the behind-the-scenes arrangement, Bethlehem was sold in August 1901 to Charles M. Schwab, who soon after dismissed Linderman and much of what remained of Taylor's reforms.

Taylor suffered from chronic indigestion and insomnia. Most likely, he continued to have terrifying nightmares; he was known to spend nights sitting bolt upright in bed, staring into the darkness. Frederick Taylor's dream of order had within it a nightmarish side. He could not ward off the demons that tormented him. "There is evidence," wrote Copley, "that, haunting some part of the nature of this courageous man, was the ghost of a fear, a horror" (Copley, 1923, vol. 1, p. 59).

Copley noted Taylor was never a man of introspection. The time came when he could not endure what his mind could not explain: ". . . what his intellect could not grasp, comprehend, was to him as a shadow" (Copley, 1923, vol. 1, p. 438). He appealed at one point to his physician to help him stop thinking, to ward off the thoughts that oppressed him, but he received little relief. There was no instrument that could sever Taylor from his fears. He died in 1915, at fifty-nine, from a bronchial condition that turned into pneumonia. At 4:30 A.M., shortly before he died, he was heard in his hospital bed, winding his watch.

6

. . . .

Separating Action from Meaning
The Legacy of Efficiency

Then he was told:
Remember what you have seen,
because everything forgotten
returns to the circling winds.
Lines from a Navajo chant *(Cousineau, 1993)*

Frederick Taylor's legacy is with us in all areas of organizational and corporate life. Each time we determine an appropriate degree of centralization and standardization, we make choices about how individuals will be allowed to think on their own. Each new technological breakthrough has implications for how work will be performed and whether human labor will still be needed. Each new attempt at work redesign holds within it assumptions about how people derive meaning from work and how individuals will relate to a larger system. We cannot distance ourselves from the social forces behind efficiency—the history of the power struggle, the rationale for work redesign, the methods for control over employees—because we are still subject to their influence.

Each time we struggle with the question of why employees still do not "think" or seem too preoccupied with their job descriptions or cannot work well with others, we face Taylor's legacy of efficiency in the workplace. Taylor was fond of telling workers, "You're not supposed to think; there are other people paid for thinking around here." He said this to be provocative and often followed his comment by engaging in a heated conversation with workers over this principle. His point was that work had become so complex and the knowledge of how it was best performed so precise that both laborer and manager benefited from allowing a third party, the efficiency engineer, to be the arbitrator of best practices. He could not foresee how seriously his injunction not to think would become woven into the unwritten rules of the workplace. Why should employees think when their tools were taken from them, when their physical behavior at work was determined by someone else, when their time was no longer their own?

Thinking is both an analytic and a creative act. It is part of the skill of experience, meaning it is active, internal, and dynamic in relation to our environment. To think as a living soul is to challenge and be challenged by our surroundings. If our surroundings are rigidly determined or if we have come to believe that thinking is being done for us, then thinking no longer carries the necessary sense of discovery and reward that reinforces it as part of experience. Repetitive tasks cannot destroy thinking, nor can domination alone obliterate it. These are external to the individual. What undermines thinking is passivity, the learned response to our environment that what we discover is unnecessary, will not change a thing, will not matter to those around us. The corrosive legacy of efficiency was that it was too effective; we came to believe that someone else really did have a better understanding of the bigger picture. And the result was a splitting off of work from the soul's search for meaning, its familiarity with limitation, and its capacity to seek wholeness.

The Soul's Search for *Logos*

If we think about the soul as being nourished by going beyond the literal, by getting underneath what is initially apparent, and by linking with others for collective aims, then we can begin to imagine the loss of soul that accompanied the frantic dash toward organizational efficiencies. Efficiency took things apart in order to control the fragments. But breaking things down meant that work lost its internal coherence. The soul's desire, in contrast, is to understand how fragments can be viewed as part of a whole. The soul seeks *logos* (literally *the word* in Greek), which is associated with qualities such as meaning, understanding, voice, language, and expression. From ancient times to the present, logos has been associated with the expression of inward thought that tries to understand the principles of wholeness and universal action. For the ancient Greeks, the recognition of logos gave the cosmos its character and its coherence.

Individuals require both reflective time and dialogue with others to achieve logos. To go beyond the immediate and literal, we need to enter the soul's domain, which includes the metaphoric and imaginal aspects of inward journey. We need time and space to fantasize, to wonder, to see meaning emerge from apparent disorder. Efficiency suggests there is no time for such activity, that someone else has the answer, that answers are found by a linear process. The notion of logos, on the other hand, suggests that without reflective time our worldview becomes fragmented and chaotic.

Logos, deriving from the Greek word *legein*, meaning to speak, is also a reminder that soul is intimately related to developing one's own voice. When logos is denied and replaced with another's *logic* or displaced with a system's *logistics*, the soul has no voice. Logic becomes the thin crust that suppresses meaning rather than fostering its awakening within the individual. Communication plans within organizations, designed to inform employees about the logic of change, become instead inhibitors of logos when only the voice of leadership is heard. Logos implies the need for speech from many constituencies within an organization, and not just at the beginning of the process. Logos requires opportunities to gain a voice so that fantasies of what is really happening under the crust of logic can be explored, questioned, and engaged. Logos is sought through redundancy, through repeated opportunities to voice one's inward thought so that it may be heard, challenged, and allowed a place among the ideas of others. But we are impatient and see redundancy as an inefficiency to be cut short.

Efficiency challenges logos in the workplace. The soul is relegated to a corner where it cannot seek understanding, where wholeness is out of sight, hidden behind the door of the efficiency engineer, the financial officers, and the management consultants. People do not possess the big picture; it is contained in the efficiencies of a bureaucracy and in the automated processes of machinery. Whenever we hear employees say defensively "It's always been done this way," or say with puzzlement "I don't know why, but it never made sense to me," we are hearing the loss of logos in the workplace and in the individual's soul.

Logos is awakened when we leave the literal, allowing individuals to strive for depth, to entertain ideas, to explore the full range of experience found in their own imagination. Thought takes on texture, is associated with images, has resonance with internal values. No creative work, no work of significant value takes place without some space for logos. It is ironic that efficiency destroys logos at its own expense, making the solutions of yesterday the problems of today. Over time, efficiency degenerates and the human dimensions of work that are ignored in the engineering of work processes return in the circling wind. We need new images of how things work; logos suggests understanding that is rooted in wholeness and relatedness.

Logos may also be imagined as the thought of the heart expressed by the tongue. Among the ancient origins of the Greek concept, logos was suggested by Egyptian hieroglyphs that associated divinity and creation with the symbols of the heart to express "thought" and the tongue to express "speech." The ancient Egyptians believed thought lodged in the heart, not the brain; they would unceremoniously toss out the latter in the embalming process before sending the dead on their journey. The symbolism is useful if we speak of the search for logos as heartfelt, pulsating, and alive with new blood. Efficiency is too often coldly analytic, up in the head, without sufficient awareness of how ideas circulate through the body of a person. The search for meaning does not require us to throw out analytic reasoning, but it does suggest embodying logic with heart and passion.

What happens when the words we speak do not arise from both our head and our heart? What happens when we pay attention to the words of others and find the sounds empty of any real meaning? I recall working with an organization whose managers complained to me that their leaders managed by way of catch phrases: *service excellence, managing by walking around, continuous improvement*. In my mind, I thought they were describing to me a kind of sickness, an illness in which leaders believe they are being consistent by institutionalizing a certain sameness of language. I suggested to them, somewhat humorously, that they suffered from the disease of platitudes, which I defined as the chronic displacement of meaning by repetitive phrases. They insisted that was the case; their problem was that leadership offered no real direction. I challenged them to consider that it was not direction they were lacking but *their own words* for describing what they did and why they did it. I see now that I was challenging them to seek logos, to find in their own experience and the experience of others the principles and patterns that gave their world character and coherence.

Logos suggests depth and profound understanding, the downward journey into the realm of the soul. In ancient times, Heraclitus first suggested an intimacy among soul, depth, and logos when he wrote: "You could not find the boundaries of the soul, even by traveling along every path, so deep is its logos." When we let our minds wander into these depths we come upon images, often surprising ones. When we struggle to understand their meaning and express them in language, then we are once again entering into the ancient partnership between soul and logos. Logos is an act of self-expression, but not simply of clever logic or surface feelings.

In organizations, logos is constantly bounded by the immediate rush for solutions. Deeper reflection is suspect, considered potentially wasteful, associated with "paralysis by analysis." The source of solutions is seen in pieces outside oneself: in a new program on excellence, a course on communication, or revised incentives. Logos suggests not the efficiencies of taking things apart, but the internal coherence of putting them back together. Logos, the offspring of wisdom in myth, the source of creation in various religious traditions, suggests the solution is within the people who own the problem, those who will look inward and with some depth.

Work, Jobs, and Meaning

The legacy of efficiency was that work became a job: a set of tasks and a relationship to a boss. Taylor wrote that workers should ask themselves only two questions: "What is the name of the man I am now working for? What does this man want me to do, right now?" Once again he was being provocative. He meant that the disassembly of work processes into tasks had to be administered in clear chains of command. The man you are working for also receives instructions from his supervisor, who receives them from someone else, and so on, the end of the chain being linked to the analysis of work processes developed by efficiency studies. In this way, the whole network of actions is linked together by a coherent plan of action. We know from his own struggle with the president of Bethlehem Steel that he did not simply believe in authoritarian rule. But he could not anticipate the limitations of his mechanical metaphor on how work was accomplished over time; nor could he foresee how literally his instructions would be taken. In the absence of any deeper reasons for why work should be performed, employees simply defaulted to accommodating their boss or fulfilling a discrete set of tasks.

The relationship of work to creating something, seeing the end results of one's efforts in a finished product, or taking pride in one's labor was lost. Work became something immediate, cut off from others, subject to the idiosyncrasies of supervisors who also did not understand the larger purposes of their efforts. Work became doing things, action without relationship to individual experience or collective aims.

When work becomes a job, its intrinsic value vanishes. The theologian Matthew Fox puts it very nicely when he writes that work, in contrast to the external limitations of a job, "comes from inside out; work is the expression of our soul, our inner being. It is unique to the individual; it is creative. Work is an expression of the Spirit at work in the world through us. Work is that which puts us in touch with others, not so much at the level of personal interaction, but at the level of service in the community" (Fox, 1994, p. 5). Fox points us in the direction of work and meaning, the expression of soul as mediator between spirit and service, between individual and community.

A consultant known nationally for his work on corporate culture once told me of an experience where he was sitting with a group of chemical engineers and scientists who were watching a teleconference on their parent company's successful new product line. At the end of the conference, one of the men turned to him in frustration. "You know, I always took pride in the work we did. We developed the means by which pollution was controlled and crops made more resilient. But now we're a subsidiary and our emphasis is elsewhere. Our biggest products are for the household. Am I suppose to have the same pride in carpet fresheners and toilet cleaners? Am I an outcast of this new corporate culture?"

This man's questioning goes to the heart of the challenge we face in associating work with meaning. We each must wrestle with the larger purposes of our work. In a world connected with soul, our collective efforts matter. The spirit in which we do our work is intimately related to the product of our efforts, to the service we provide to the larger community. The risk involved in asking about purpose is revealed by the man's second question: "Am I an outcast of this new corporate culture?" He asks what prophets and visionaries have asked, who pay the price of not being true believers, who cannot go along with the consensual agreements of the group. His questions take us far from Taylor's injunction to ask only what is wanted from the person we work for. His questions take us into the deeper regions of soul.

An example from my own work in health care organizations further illustrates the deeper connections between work and meaning. I was asked by a management team to structure a discussion of values related to administering a medical center during a time of increasing pressures for cost containment. I did so by proposing one question: "What do you care about, not in general, but specifically in relation to what your organization does?" I suggested that their values discussion was not a debate but an opportunity to explore each individual's own assumptions about the meaning of his or her work.

The conversation began with the physician leader stating that what he cared about was staying in business. He noted that the health care business had become predatory. He believed there was general agreement in their marketplace that only five or six health care providers of forty currently operating would still be standing in five years. He wanted theirs to be one of them, and that meant maintaining and building on market share while reducing the costs of delivering care. He valued actions leading in that direction.

His immediate subordinate, also a physician, did not want to stay in business simply to survive. He believed that the future held opportunities for better and more cost-effective care, but it also held challenges to the ethical and moral foundations of medicine. He believed health care, as a business, would be vulnerable to the same kinds of expediency and short-term solutions endemic in other organizations threatened with survival. He wanted to be a "voice" for better ways of practicing medicine.

I found it remarkable that the conversation did not become polarized between cost of care and quality of care, nor between generalizations of business as profane and medicine as sacred. Rather, both physicians acknowledged their dual pressures: to stay in business and to honor their Hippocratic oath. The meaning of their work took on greater dimension as they struggled openly with this tension. How could the medical center reduce hospital admissions without screening out people who need care? How could pharmaceutical costs be lowered without jeopardizing those who need more expensive medications? How could referrals for laboratory tests and imaging (X ray, CAT scans, MRIs) be decreased without denying appropriate measures for patients needing diagnosis? They discussed openly what the chemical engineer in my earlier example feared was unmentionable: what was the purpose of their collective efforts? If it is simply to survive, to promote cost containment in a vacuum, or to promote carpet fresheners because they provide revenue, then something at the core of why we do what we do is lost. Work, as Fox reminds us, is an expression of the soul. During turbulent times, we need more than ever to ask the questions of meaning that underlie our efforts.

The challenge to meaning should not be underestimated. A *Vanity Fair* article on the new entrepreneurs of American industry cites an observation by David Rieff to point out the social context for new enterprises. Discussing the unique nature of a popular culture that minimizes historical perspective and intellectual depth, he writes that its genius "resides precisely in the nihilism of its entrepreneurs and, finally, out of the society from whence they spring. . . . There is a staunch refusal to admit that anything needs to be taken so seriously as to get in the way of its marketing, and a confidence that anything can be marketed, anything made appealing, if it is packaged well enough and given the right advertising spin" (O'Shaughnessy, 1994, p. 235). His words trouble me, not so much because he is right or wrong, but because I think he describes the modern context for the struggle to find meaning. In a time when little is taken seriously, when meaning itself can be packaged and sold, how does one find meaning and coherence? How does one maintain faith? How does one question the value of what comes from our collective efforts? Meaning cannot come from corporate mission statements; it is sought through dialogue and reflection, through the courage to ask troubling questions and a willingness to face the consequences of our collective and individual actions.

High Performance: The Embodied Soul at Risk

To look at efficiency with the perspective of soul means also to question how the physical body is valued and viewed. Our culture has typically divided body and soul, or merely viewed body as a receptacle for the soul. An alternative view would be to imagine the soul as "em-bodied" in us, relating to the world through the senses. The senses by which we taste, touch, smell, see, hear, and intuit are the portals by which the soul knows itself and others. The soul is not "inside" but rather at the boundary between inner experience and outer events. When we forsake the senses, we forsake the soul by driving the idea of soul into the interior of the body. Soul and body are not divisible. "Man has no body distinct from his soul," wrote William Blake in "The Marriage of Heaven and Hell," "for that call'd body is a portion of soul, discern'd by the five senses. . . ."

In Frederick Taylor's world, the body was a machine that had to be kept healthy through proper nutrition, steady exercise, and positive mental outlook. He viewed the body's resiliency as a fundamental factor in how he designed work processes. By determining how long the body could be "under load," he calculated the most efficient work schedule for Schmidt. His followers continued this avenue of study, exploring not only physical motion but also mental activity. One of them, Frank Gilbreth, experimented with "happiness minutes," focused periods of inactivity that he hoped could combat fatigue and substitute for conventional rest periods.

The body as machine deserving of proper maintenance and the soul as worthy of mediating between internal and external reality remain components of a subtle conflict in today's workplace. In Silicon Valley, a human resource employee confided to me a disconcerting interaction she had had with her firm's CEO. She had noted to him an apparent discrepancy between the health and fitness emphasis he championed and the typical schedules of employees working twelve to fifteen hours a day. "What is the problem?" he responded in genuine surprise. "To work those hours, you have to stay healthy, you have to work out in the gym, you have to keep a good mental outlook." He saw no contradiction. She was troubled. She believed that the consideration for employee health masked a deeper disrespect for the limitations of the body. "Yesterday," she told me, "a woman who works here approached me and told me how she was required to be at a 6 P.M. teleconference with an overseas affiliate. The problem was it was 6 P.M. Australian time—2 A.M. in California. How can people be empowered, how can they stay healthy, when they can't even control when they go to sleep?"

The maximizing of human performance is rooted in a fundamental ambivalence about the nature of the human body. When are we honoring the human spirit in its call to attain the heights of achievement—athletic performance, creative pursuits, intellectual discoveries—and when are we submitting our bodies and minds to danger? In the name of transcending physical limitations, have we denied the necessary limitations and ultimate frailty of the body?

Our reverence for athletic performance, for example, is challenged when we hear that the pressures for ever higher achievement lead an athlete to fall into drugs, depression, or desperation. The executive who works maniacally until suddenly brought down with heart palpitations also reminds us of the physical limitations associated with stretching one's limits. The body reminds us of our mortality, our limits, and our potentially fatal quest to go ever faster. That quest jeopardizes not only our bodies but also our embodied souls.

The workplaces of today are highly stressful, in part because we don't distinguish very well between the call for ever-higher performance and the injunction to work people to near their melting point. The downsizing of industry, more and more a financial tool to lower cost structure rather than a response to business cycles, has put an ever-increasing burden on people to either work harder or not work at all. And technology has intensified, not eased, our flight to the heights of performance.

The promise of mechanization was that our burdens would be lightened and our workdays made shorter. As Juliet Schor (1991) has pointed out in *The Overworked American*, this has not been the case:

> Working hours are already longer than they were forty years ago. If present trends continue, by the end of the century Americans will be spending as much time at their jobs as they did back in the nineteen twenties. . . . The experts were unable to predict or even see these trends. I suspect they were blinded by the power of technology—seduced by futurist visions of automated factories effortlessly churning out products. After all, they say, if we can build robots to do humans' work, what sense is there in doing it ourselves? Appealing as this optimism may be, it misses a central point about technology: the context is all important. Machines can just as easily be used to harness human labor as [to] free it [pp. 1, 5].

Not only has the time we work increased but the pace and intensity has increased as well. Technology has created the means by which we can work continuously. Phones in our cars, faxes in our briefcases, multiple locations from which we do our work all add to the feeling of work being something that has us, rather than work being an aspect of our lives. During the writing of this chapter, I received a phone call from a manager who was having thoughts of resigning. She was feeling depleted and used up. She voiced her concern that work had become all-consuming: "There is no time here for us to be people." She was not talking just about herself but about a collective dilemma. She wanted to be reassured she was not alone.

When Taylor's high-performing steel-cutting tool L4 cracked, he could easily dismiss the incident as a flaw in the tool's forging because it was simply a tool. Humans are not so easily dismissed. When we crack, we are not easily repaired. The embodied soul has a way of creating symptoms—illness, disorder, and suffering—when subjected to too much stress. When we ignore these symptoms or "fix" them too superficially, the underlying causes are sure to manifest themselves even more dramatically. The living soul is not a passive entity.

The hope that in the new information age work will be mediated by brains, not physical endurance, misses a crucial element of reality in the workplace. Working to the outer limits of performance in the information age requires a kind of stamina just as potentially destructive as the physical strength and exertion demanded in the industrial era. Humans must now compete with the speed of modems and the information-processing capacities of computers. "BRAINS, SURE," begins an article in *Fortune*. Titled "Stamina: Who Has It, Why You Need It, How You Get It," it goes on: "Brains are useful. But these days it could be your stamina that really counts. Downsizing forces survivors to work ever-longer hours, and the global economy has stretched the executive itinerary to China, Indonesia, and Malaysia. Mind and body end up in faraway places trying to adjust to new times, new climates, and new germs—from routine stomach bugs to an outbreak of pneumonic plague in India" (Smith, 1994, p. 127).

The article cites numerous examples of individuals who have "it" and suggests ways to get it or be doomed. One executive is touted as absorbing "technical and financial data like a four-megabyte memory chip." Another notes that "We measure time in dog years . . . seven years of activity for every calendar year." The pictures of executives portray one woman working out in a gym, and a man lying next to a tennis star is learning stomach crunches from a sports psychologist. Lessons are offered from nutritional science, as are the words of a physiologist who counsels on ways to shave off hours of sleep—down to three a night when necessary. As with Gilbreth's exploration of "happiness minutes," there is also advice on the importance of attitude and "recovery strategies needed to balance the stress." A chart of eight chief executives highlights their sixty- to eighty-hour workweeks, with sleep limited to as few as five hours. The article suggests that *staminacs* are different in subtle ways from workaholics because they work from necessity and choice, not compulsion.

I am struck by the marshaling of human sciences—physiology, psychology, nutrition, sports psychology—all to promote one goal: the extension of the boundary of human performance. One executive quoted in the article feels he's missing something when he sleeps; another practices visualizing the ten issues on his agenda during rest periods, "numbers each, and puts them in an imaginary box while he dozes." The article stresses that these feelings and activities are self-imposed, useful, and oftentimes necessary. I admit finding it exciting to read about the extent to which we can stretch the limits of human activity. Deep in our souls, there is an undeniable fascination with how far we can take possession of our destiny, whether cheating sleep, human endurance, or even death.

I also think, however, that the article demonstrates a flight from the aspects of soul that mediate between spirit and earth, between conscious and unconscious, between control of our physical nature and acknowledgment of our limitations. The executives in the article, often found high above the ground in a plane, are extreme representations of the struggle we all face to encounter our humanity, to live within the reach of our senses, to stay planted with our feet on the ground. The boundaries of performance should not be confused with the boundaries of the soul, for performance is so much narrower a goal, so much more inherently personal and self-absorbed.

As exuberant and practical as this *Fortune* article seeks to be, it is also cautious: it asserts that there is a difference, though subtle, between staminacs and workaholics. There is a potential downside to shaving off hours of sleep. There are penalties for pushing too hard. There is a shadow, a dark side: collapse, exhaustion, and a fall from the heights of achievement. In *Working Ourselves to Death,*

Diane Fassel notes this shadow side: "Everywhere I go it seems people are killing themselves with work, busyness, rushing, caring, and rescuing. . . . John O. Neikirk calls it 'the pain others applaud'. . . . I call it the cleanest of all the addictions. It is socially promoted because it is seemingly socially productive" (Fassel, 1990, p. 2).

It is one thing, however, to note the shadow side and another to recognize the idealized qualities that continually attract us. Pushing the limits of technology and the boundaries of human performance allows us to gauge the degree of control over our lives. The mythic story of Icarus flying too close to the sun before he falls should remind us of the initial delight and mastery that comes with taking wing. Creativity, exuberance, the sense of being a god defying gravity are no small potatoes when compared with the labyrinth he escaped from in the mythic tale. The demands of a vital living soul are problematic if we think of these demands as inherently beyond our capacity to control, a labyrinth of sorts that we can never escape. We fear capture by our own inner complexity.

To grapple with the shadow side of performance, we must somehow learn to embrace the inward complexity of our lives. We need a vision of inward work that extends outward into community, into service that is worth doing, into productive aims that offer an opportunity for meaning and relatedness. It is then we can fly and still regard the labyrinth of our soul as worthwhile—and even view it with a sense of awe. Only when there is less fear of what lies within can we stop proving ourselves against the limitations of our body.

Fit into My Order or Else: Efficiency and Obsolescence

After my father's death, I went to help my mother with the small family business she and my father had run. He had invented and patented a hand tool that placed rhinestones and nailheads into fabric and leather. In our little shop we assembled the tool from various standardized parts, including metal plungers, springs, and caps, all machined to the most stringent tolerances, allowing for inter-changeable assembly.

I set about organizing the various supplies—different-sized rhine-stones, nailheads, adapters—that were sold with the hand tool. The more I set to the task, the more immersed I became in getting it just right. I worked over the weekend so as to be undisturbed by the interruptions of the regular workday. I decided there should be just so many premade packets of product, consistent with our orders. I arranged the boxes of product so that the most commonly sold items were also the most easily accessible. I created a consistent pattern for arranging the various colors and sizes of rhinestone on the shelves, a necessary improvement in order that anyone could imme-diately understand how they were arranged. I finished my work with a great sense of achievement and satisfaction.

When I returned later in midweek, everything had been restored to its original place. My mother explained that she knew where everything was and found it confusing to change her habits. She acknowledged her way was confusing and time-consuming and difficult for others to figure out, but this was her office and where she spent her time. "I'm old-fashioned," she said shrugging her shoulders.

I stood in shocked silence. I had worked it all out, even adjust-ing for her height in the placement of the boxes of product. The feelings that arose from out of my shock were anger and humilia-tion. All I had achieved was being undone. I looked at my mother and thought to myself, "You can be replaced." The absurdity of this thought shook me. "You can be replaced, you have become obso-lete," I was thinking, "just like the machine parts that do not con-form to the tolerance levels we set for our tools."

How easy it is to see in others the overweening desire for con-trol, the vain attempts to dictate predictable outcomes, the futility of insisting on certainty. How much more difficult to stare into the pool of self-reflection and see there one's own desire for control, pre-dictability, and certainty. The interaction with my mother was star-

tling because it revealed to me how subtle and seductive the practice of ordering and arranging *things* can be in the way we look at
people. In the workplace, there is always that temptation to act from
a secret assumption: fit into my order or be damned.

I could hear the echo of Frederick Taylor in my efforts to arrange
and organize: "In a scientifically run modern machine shop, then,
all of these implements have been standardized, and are maintained
in a tool department in perfect order at all times, thus entirely doing
away with the old fashioned judgment of each workman as to what
kind of a tool he liked best, and also doing away with his individual making and care of his tools" (Copley, 1923, vol. 1, pp. 356–
357). For Frederick Taylor as for me, the "old-fashioned" ways were
assumed to be flawed and without merit.

More disconcerting, however, is the view that the person associated with the old ways is also expendable. "You can be replaced,"
I thought as I faced my mother in anger. In this case, the thought
was absurd since no one else, especially I, had any inclination to
take over the business. But that is not the case for businesses in virtually every sector of our economy. We have institutionalized obsolescence in the workplace, without a coherent plan and without the
psychological awareness of its effect on people.

The difficulty with following the logic of efficiency is not the
desire to improve upon how we work, but rather its isolation from
human meaning and relatedness. To be associated with soul, work
must have its dignity. The machinist who cared for his own tools
formed a relationship with those tools that offered him some measure of control over his work life. My mother, who defended her
idiosyncratic methods of stocking product, also achieved some dis-
cretion over how she got her work done. When we interfere with
this process we commit a form of violence that, although at times
necessary, should not be underestimated or trivialized by asserting
only the benefits and advantages of the new.

The rationale of efficiency severed the necessary relationship
between work and identity: what I do and how I do it is part of who

I am. In the era of efficiency, we began to think of work as doing isolated tasks that someone else thought were a good idea. And though all work contains some drudgery, beyond a certain point isolated tasks become a drudgery that is numbing and disorienting. When work becomes simply a job someone else has thought up, we begin to lose ourselves; that is what was at stake in Taylor's tool shop almost a century ago and in my mother's words to me.

The critical question is how work renders meaning and relationship for those who undertake to do it together. Without work that has internal substance as well as external incentive, we lose access to our very sense of being. Without work, we decay inside. The tragedy of individuals who have never known work to be anything but temporary or demeaning is that they begin to disintegrate physically, emotionally, and spiritually. For those who are told they have become obsolete, there is also a sense of decay. Work demands our respect because without it we lose connection both to what is inside us and what is outside in the world. We have reason to honor how we do our work and to regard work as an extension of our souls acting in the world. We may ask ourselves, how can we afford to do this in the workplace? But the answer, in part, is that we cannot afford this decay either in the workplace or in society.

The Renting of Souls

Frederick Taylor viewed labor "both as a commodity and as a soul" (Copley, 1923, vol. 1, p. 159). As a commodity, people were something useful, an asset that afforded the owner a potential advantage. As a soul, workers were allowed certain rights, such as wages and opportunities to choose where they work. The distinction had certain limitations. At the beginning of the twentieth century, labor could increasingly be bought with the proper wages and channeled by limitations of choice. Henry Ford's assembly line was the prototypical example.

The assembly line both extended and replaced Frederick Taylor's ideas on efficiency because it even eliminated the need for reengineering work processes. Once the assembly line was established, human labor was reduced to repetitive actions orchestrated by the speed of the line. Ford had to pay top dollar to get workers to submit to such constraints. In the years before the introduction of the assembly line, building automobiles was a highly skilled craft. Each car was put together in one spot by numerous mechanics working together. Base wages were often supplemented with incentive pay and bonuses. With the introduction of the assembly line, Ford initially abandoned incentive pay for one flat wage: $2.34 per day.

Workers left in droves. So great was the distaste for the new mechanized line that in the months before it became fully operational, Ford had to hire 963 men for every 100 he wanted to add to the line (Braverman, 1974, p. 149). As long as there were alternatives to working in Ford's mechanized plant, workers would have no part of it. Ford's solution was to increase wages to five dollars a day for eight hours.

The move was rooted in solving the problem of how workers could be made to submit voluntarily to unpopular and unappetizing jobs. His five-dollar-a-day wage answered the dual threat of intensifying union activity and the flight of workers from his factory. He got a steady stream of laborers willing to take their chances in exchange for an opportunity for higher wages. In being able to run his mechanized assembly line, he could then exert his competitive advantage over his competitors. "The payment of five dollars a day for an eight-hour day," Ford asserted in his autobiography, "was one of the finest cost-cutting moves we ever made" (Braverman, 1974, p. 150).

Following Ford's lead, businesses adopted a strategy to pay higher relative wages to a shrinking proportion of workers in order to maintain uninterrupted production. When labor was skilled or individuals had employment alternatives, wages went up. When work could be mechanized or surplus labor existed, wages would flatten or be lowered. Economist Juliet Schor called these higher-wage jobs a form of property that owners "rent" to employees. "The five-dollar day," she wrote, "created a 'carrot'—a sophisticated economic incentive. . . . In its simplest terms, the employment rent is the value of a job to the worker" (Schor, 1991, p. 61). She noted that Ford celebrated the docility of his new higher-paid workforce, demanding greater productivity. As a production foreman in the plant recalled, "[They] called us in and said that since the workers were getting twice the wages, [management] wanted twice as much work. On the assembly lines, we just simply turned up the speed of the lines" (p. 65). A deal was struck: employers would rent to employees a higher-paying job and expect in return that employees rent their bodies and souls.

Today, the wheels on that deal are starting to shake. In October 1994, a strike at a General Motors plant in Flint, Michigan, made headlines across the nation. Workers struck not over wages but because downsizing had made them work longer and harder. A single mother of two reported having to put her son into psychological counseling and fearing for her eighteen-year-old daughter, who was unmarried and pregnant. "I keep thinking," she says, "that maybe if I'd been able to spend more time with them this wouldn't have happened. But there's constant pressure to be at work" (Genasci, 1994, p. 28). She knows there are limited financial alternatives to the relatively high wages she earns on the line. She hopes something can be negotiated with General Motors to limit her six-day, fifty-seven-hour-average workweek.

The gap between jobs that pay more and jobs that do not pay enough has intensified the view of labor as a commodity and as a soul. And not just in blue-collar jobs. Over the past ten years, the largest companies in virtually every business sector have collectively eliminated one-quarter of their workforce. The simple mathematics of financial efficiencies that dictated Henry Ford's actions also play a significant role today. The rising costs of benefits make it financially sounder to pay higher salaries or overtime to a few, while at the same time paying lower salaries or no salaries at all to others.

Upton Sinclair's warning to Taylor that workers (and now companies) would face a future of constant dislocation and obsolescence has taken on a prophetic quality. From 1991 to 1993, 4.5 million workers over the age of twenty lost "permanent" jobs that they had held for at least three years. By mid-1994, a majority had found new work. However, only 18 percent of these workers found jobs with significantly higher wages (20 percent increase or more). Approximately one-third found jobs earning less, and another third were still looking for work or had abandoned searching for work altogether. In such an economic environment, jobs with higher salaries carry a premium, and individuals will be reluctant to challenge the demands made on them.

This new economy has created two classes at either end of the economic spectrum and a dwindling middle group that Secretary of Labor Robert Reich calls the "anxious class." Reich warns that statistical models showing average wage earnings going up can be deceptive in an increasingly bifurcated system. To illustrate his point, he likens averaging his height, which is 4'10", with that of basketball star Shaquille O'Neale, who is 7'1". Together, they average six feet. The analogy that we have a six-foot economy made up of two vastly diverse groups is a warning about the lack of common ground that is necessary for community and the recognition of soul in each of us.

I am suggesting that soul mediates between spiritual awareness and material betterment. We cannot pursue prosperity at the cost of the whole person or the whole community. The employment rent on jobs demanding that the individual be entirely consumed or drained of any separate initiative is as damaging as the enforced idleness of a minority who cannot find work. We must transcend the labor-as-commodity, labor-as-soul duality, because it has fostered an unworkable agreement. Employers cannot hold up their end of the bargain without changing the rules whenever necessary. Workers simply cannot pay the "rent" expected of them without violating their connection to family, community, personal health, and spiritual longing. I am reminded of Tocqueville's warning of the excessive love of prosperity. He cautioned that under certain conditions the pursuit of prosperity could do harm to those who seek it: "There is a closer connection than is supposed between the soul's improvement and the betterment of physical conditions. A man can treat the two things as distinct and pay attention to each in turn. But he cannot entirely separate them without in the end losing sight of both" (Tocqueville, [1840] 1969, vol. 2, p. 546).

Efficiency and the Search for Meaning

The final legacy of efficiency is that it left the workplace without core human values about collective purpose and individual meaning. The pursuit of increased material prosperity fragmented the way work was performed and how work was shared. Efficiency gave owners dominance over work processes and made workers dependent on management to dictate the terms of their employment. Today, we mourn the loss of individuals' ability to cultivate their own sense of purpose and direction in work. I cannot imagine going into any modern corporation and *not* hearing from management that staff are overly dependent, do not adequately identify or solve problems on their own, and need constant support to work together cooperatively. One manager told me that she finally came to realize that the call for empowerment in her organization was simply a code for telling workers to stop whining. At the same time, I would be surprised if employees did not communicate a feeling that they lacked direction from management or simply felt resigned to put up with the changes going on around them.

As a rationale for management control, efficiency was (and still is) simply not persuasive as a philosophy to engender the workplace harmony that Taylor sought. Work cannot simply be broken down and then reassembled to management's satisfaction. Something else is needed to supplement the machine metaphor of workplace organization and reliance on wages to satisfy the full spectrum of human need. Mechanistic assumptions ignore the nonrational human dimension of work.

Taylor, of course, also understood that managers could not assert arbitrary power without resistance from workers. But he believed the rational process of engineering the workplace according to "laws" of efficiency would make managers the servants of workers. In exchange for loss of control over the workplace, workers would see the benefits of everyone sharing in greater productivity. No one would really have arbitrary power; both management and workers would share the same value of increasing production by means of scientific study.

Arbitrary power, however, did not go away. The creation of greater wealth through engineering greater productivity was not shared across the board. The rational, mechanistic breakdown of work created a loss of shared purpose among workers. The justification for management to oversee labor was without a human rationale distinct from watching over people and dictating how work was to be performed. The need to humanize the workplace, to give management and workers some greater purpose than efficiency alone, was ironically its final legacy.

The next chapter takes up the challenge created by the need to humanize the workplace. Efficiency, after all, tended to leave the internal world of the worker alone. When we attend to the needs of human connection, however, we are entering the domain of emotion, attitude, subjective experience, and personal fantasy. For organizations, the challenge to the soul is how what is inside us will be harnessed for greater productivity. The recognition of feelings and the need for collaboration binds us closer together but does not guarantee that the search for meaning and connection with others can be satisfied.

7

The Management of Emotion

Elton Mayo and the False Enchantment of Human Relations

And now about the caldron sing,
Like elves and fairies in a ring,
Enchanting all that you put in.
William Shakespeare, Macbeth, *act IV, scene 1*

Imagine this: a group of three human resource employees sitting around a table in a corporate office suite. They are sharing the gossip of group behavior within their organization: a senior executive heard expressing his frustration with all the corporate whining; a manager leaving after breaking down in tears and frustration; a less-than-admired co-worker being promoted, to the dismay of his subordinates. They are unhappy with how the corporate restructuring is going. They were skeptical but hopeful. Now, they are skeptical and putting together their resumes to see what else might be available.

"We wanted to believe in the values promoted by leadership," says one. "We will be a value-driven company," says a second, mimicking a marionette on strings. "Were we naïve?" says the third. "I still believe in the values; those values still matter." The first one to talk grows serious: "I believe in those values, too, but something is

---

Note: I wish to acknowledge Robert Howard's discussion of enchantment in his book *Brave New Workplace*, and F. J. Roethlisberger and W. J. Dickson for their detailed analysis of the Hawthorne experiments in *Management and the Worker*.

going on here that is more than simply good values and bad execution. What is happening here is happening all over. I don't think values are enough, and maybe they even get in the way." "Get in the way of what?" asks the second person, puzzled. "In the way of reality, the reality that we're a business, that we really don't give a shit about people, that we tell people change is good, when it's a mixed blessing. I don't know, the reality of being caught between intention and what really happens."

"Maybe what you're saying," says the third, "is that we all want to believe so much in something, something good, that we can't tolerate both sides of the coin. Emotionally we need the coin to keep coming up heads, so we intellectualize the other side and feel crushed when it actually shows up tails. Nothing that happened here is so surprising, yet I can barely face it. I hate coming to work. I hate feeling that I'm still supposed to be positive." "But you are a positive person," says the second. "You're right. I hate feeling disenchanted. I hate feeling like I can't be myself."

The three get up and depart into a labyrinth of hallways. They share a set of values that have been embraced by their corporate leadership. But the inspiration at the core of these values seems to have flitted away. Where has the animation gone? Why has soul fled, just as everyone was in agreement about what mattered? As does their leadership, the three believe in the value of empowerment, participation, personal development, group cohesion, and collective problem solving. They believe in high-performing teams, self-managing groups, results-oriented thinking, partnership, customer focus, and redesigned process flows. They believe change is inevitable, and that after suffering some disequilibrium a new pattern will emerge. Underlying this belief is a hope that change is good and fruitful. Although no one lives in a perfect world, they believe productivity and profits will rise and those who come through the transition will benefit and be rewarded.

The Challenge of Enchantment

The human resource employees mirror a conversation taking place throughout the corporate world. They embrace a language of corporate change that, like Taylor's view of efficiency, is right in many ways and deceptive in subtle areas of execution. They believe that work can be a forum for personal growth, interpersonal cooperation, and institutional learning. Unlike Taylor, they believe that the design of work should be generated by the workers themselves, in teams, and implemented only after workers understand and buy into the changes. They believe work is part of an intricate social system and cannot be mandated from above or broken down into pieces by efficiency experts. Most important, they value personal qualities such as trust, feedback, expression, and honesty. Their knowledge is grounded in social science, not engineering. They believe change is a human process that requires attention to existing social networks and the development of skills in communication, change management, problem solving, and negotiation.

The expression of their *disenchantment* raises the question of the nature of their *enchantment*. Why does their strong belief in empowerment, partnership, and teamwork mean that they have trouble accounting for the need to speed change, cut costs, and downsize the number of employees in the organization? How do deeply held beliefs in the organization's commitment to value people, be tolerant of mistakes, and support fairness make them unprepared for the haphazard way people are treated, the way mistakes are not forgiven, and the ambiguity of fairness as a guiding principle? Enchantment suggests a magic spell that can be captivating and transcending. But it also suggests being held captive, unable to deal creatively with contradiction.

The organizational ideas and values of these human resource employees have their origins in conversations that began in the early twentieth century. In reaction to the increasing mechanization and bureaucratization of work, a growing alarm was voiced about the capacity of workers to sustain their productivity and their spirit. Sociologist Max Weber warned of a "disenchantment of the world" brought about by new methods of managerial and mechanical control. The time was ripe for ideas that would suggest ways to diminish the loss of human connection, a means to reenchant the workplace.

Elton Mayo and the Inner Organization

Elton Mayo, an Australian educator, came to America to preach a fundamentally different view of industrial labor from Frederick Taylor's and the assembly line model of Henry Ford. Taylor and Ford sought harmony and control through a precise manipulation of the physical surroundings. They believed in adjusting the outer organization as a way to foster human efficiency and character. Mayo sought to modify the inner organization, to adjust the individual's mental outlook and emotional attitude to his or her surroundings. In his ideas, he held the promise of reenchantment that was being sought for the workplace.

Mayo believed deeply in human potential and the need to recognize the influence of social systems on human development. In his writing and speeches, he promoted the idea that human behavior could not be reduced to mechanical metaphors or economic calculations based solely on individual self-interest. His teachings and writings spoke of a horror he felt toward a world that had lost its moorings. He hoped to save industrial progress from itself by promoting a philosophy that embraced social cohesion.

Mayo's name is identified with the human relations movement and the experiments at Western Electric's Hawthorne plant in Chicago. The "discoveries" at Hawthorne are now part of the folklore of management and social science, a story about how organizations turned their attention toward the inner organization of the worker's mind and emotional attitude. Mayo challenged industrialists to make use of the whole person. Henry Ford had once complained that when you wanted to purchase a pair of hands, you also had to hire a whole person. Elton Mayo wanted to demonstrate that there could be an advantage to this "compromise." In so doing, he invested management with a moral mission and a new mandate. The worker was cast as a psychological being, one more likely to submit to authority when his or her needs and motives were properly understood. The role envisioned for management was to oversee the worker's need for significance and belonging.

The Life and Times of Elton Mayo: Social Crisis in the Workplace

In 1900, the year Taylor was exhibiting his high-speed cutting tools, Mayo failed an examination that would have steered him toward medicine in the tradition of his father and grandfather. After failing again, this time in a medical school in London, Mayo worked for a mining company in West Africa and later on the staff of a men's college. He returned to Australia in 1905, where he took up studies that ranged through ethics, philosophy, psychology, and anthropology. Appointed to an academic position at the University of Queensland in 1911, Mayo spent the next ten years building up his career in academia. He came to the United States in 1922, and in 1926 he received an appointment to Harvard.

Mayo's mission was to bring an enlightened application of psychology and the social sciences to bear on the industrial workplace. He came to the United States in 1922 amidst labor unrest that still echoed the turbulence of the Homestead strike of 1892. In those thirty years, economic turbulence and worker discontent had gone hand in hand, creating a fiendish undertow to notions of social progress. Union activity and strikes for better pay and working conditions convulsed industries as diverse as textiles, steel, and agriculture. For Mayo, the solidarity of the workers against management was misdirected. Like Taylor, but with very different tools, he sought to create a workplace that banished conflict and embraced a form of social cohesion grounded in productivity.

Labor unrest and economic inequality in the midst of growing prosperity were not the only ills that troubled society in Mayo's time. Industry had disturbed the traditional ways that people lived and worked so that even those who benefited from an expanding economy suffered from some unnamed loss. The "roaring" 1920s were an age of change; women petitioned for the right to vote and explored new roles (one of Mayo's early papers was on the psychology of flappers); music came in new rhythms in the form of jazz; and mechanical gadgets brought new forms of status and convenience ranging from alarm clocks to radios, refrigerators, and automobiles. For all the new opportunities, Mayo sensed a certain rootlessness in people's lives that left them feeling empty and lost.

In 1922, the year Mayo arrived in America, Sinclair Lewis published his fictional portrait of George Babbitt, a social climber and civic booster who lived in the mythic city of Zenith. On the surface, Babbitt was a successful businessman and solid citizen, but underneath he felt dissatisfied and longed for expression. In a passage that captures the decade's self-doubt in the midst of optimism, Babbitt confides his fear of disillusionment to his only real male friend, who responds:

> Good Lord, George, you don't suppose it's any novelty to me to find that we hustlers, that think we're so all-fired successful, aren't getting much out of it? You look as if you expected me to report you as seditious. . . . Course—competition—brings out the best—survival of the fittest—but . . . But I mean: take all these fellows we know, the kind right here in the club now, that seem to be perfectly content with their home-life and their businesses, and that boost Zenith and the Chamber of Commerce and holler for a million population. I bet if you could cut into their heads you'd find that one-third of 'em are sure-enough satisfied . . . and one-third feel kind of restless but won't admit it; and one-third are miserable

and know it. They hate the whole peppy, boosting, go-
ahead game, and they're bored. . . . Why do you suppose
so many Substantial citizens jumped right into the war?
Think it was all patriotism? (Lewis, 1922, pp. 61, 64–65)

Sinclair's *Babbitt* revealed a disorder at the zenith of America's
dream of prosperity. There was a gap in people's souls that left them
vaguely dissatisfied and restless. Mayo would write some ten years
after *Babbitt* was published that "the problem is not that of the sickness of an acquisitiveness society; it is that of the acquisitiveness of
a sick society" (Mayo, 1933, p. 147). Mayo's word play was meant
to dramatize that the sickness lay in the social domain. The Bab-
bitts of the world were not sick because they craved possessions; it
was deeper than that, rooted in loss of tradition and loss of genuine
collaboration in work and community.

The Individual in the Group:
The Birth of Human Relations

Mayo located the problems of the industrial workplace in the concept of anomie, "of planlessness in living, which is becoming char-
acteristic both of individual lives and communities. This is due, at
least in part, to economic development. . . . Defeat takes the form
of ultimate disillusion—a disgust with the "futility of endless pursuit" (Mayo, 1933, p. 125). Building out from the sociological
insights of Emile Durkheim and the anthropological studies of kinship patterns in tribal groups, Mayo articulated a hypothesis that
rapid development in industry had disrupted the patterns of community life that gave individual actions meaning and connection.
In ways similar to Robert Bellah's more recent assertion (1985) that
we have lost certain "habits of the heart," Mayo asserted that an
emphasis on individualism had undermined the capacity of individuals to move forward as a society. When social order is disrupted
by change, Mayo argued, we see its effects in the individual; but the

illness is in the social body. The affliction that troubled a George Babbitt could not be found by analyzing him or even his relations with his family; instead, it must be looked for in the entire pattern of his life and relations with others.

Mayo brought this insight into industry by arguing that external conditions such as pay incentives or trivial adjustments to working conditions could not alleviate the maladjustment of workers to their work. Instead, the workers' relations with each other and their supervisors must be studied and reformed so that the kinship patterns of their group could be brought back into equilibrium. The individual, Mayo felt, must once again be subordinate to the group. By this, he did not mean domination by an authority figure. Rather, he envisioned a group that responded to individual needs in such a way that the individual, without conscious effort, would want to belong and thereby submit to the goals of the group.

For Elton Mayo as a social scientist to assert his point of view, he needed some empirical evidence of his hypothesis. He needed something akin to the experimental laboratory of the physical scientist to propose his theory to the public. Just as Taylor had needed Schmidt for his theory, Mayo needed a group of people to demonstrate his formula for the happy effects of togetherness. The opportunity came in the form of a study at the Hawthorne Works at the Western Electric Company in Chicago.

The Hawthorne Experiments

The Hawthorne experiments, a story where the details matter, comes to life in its contradictions. The original studies taking place at Hawthorne involved measuring worker output under varying conditions of illumination. In one group the lighting was kept constant, and in another the light in the assembly area was gradually diminished. Contrary to an initial hypothesis that a single variable such as light could influence efficiency, no difference in worker output was observed between the two groups. The productivity of *both* groups increased, up to the point that workers in the area of diminished lighting protested that they could not see what they were doing. Something other than a purely external variable was at work, something that involved the psychological attitude of the employee.

In a follow-up experiment, two women were selected to work together under varied lighting conditions. At one point in the experiment, they were allowed to suggest their preference for increased lighting. In reality, however, the replacement bulb was the same size as the one removed. The women, unaware they were being deceived, commented favorably on the "change." As in the prior experiment, no decline in productivity took place, whether light was increased or dimmed. The researchers at Western Electric became convinced they were onto something important.

This may all seem a bit ludicrous today, but in the early twentieth century the obsession with the outer limits of human productivity and human resiliency needed to maintain such production was a constant concern for industrialists, as we have seen with Frederick Taylor. At the heart of the debate was how best to mitigate the effects of fatigue and monotony on worker output. Industrial work, with its repetitive movements and endless stream of things to be assembled, was taking its toll on human souls in the forms of injury, sickness, and deteriorating morale. The question of human productivity now had to be measured against the capacity of workers to sustain the gains brought about by efficiency studies. A singular question arose with multiple avenues for exploration: what sole or combined interventions would keep the pace of industry moving forward? What optimal lighting was needed? What were the effects of varying rest breaks? How should pay incentives be tied to performance? What effect did mental attitude have on increased production? These questions formed the framework for the investigations at Hawthorne and led to a second phase of research that Mayo was to champion.

Mayo's Solution: Social Cohesion

Mayo believed monotony and fatigue were not a self-evident result of repetitious work. Rather, the relationship of workers with each other and with their supervisor was an unexplored key element in worker satisfaction and productivity. Whereas Taylor tried to bring efficiency to Schmidt's moving of pig iron, Mayo sought to demonstrate the palliative effects of teamwork on the repetitious nature of assembly.

The researchers at Hawthorne sought to design experiments that would measure every possible variable. Six women were chosen to assemble telephone relays in an area shut off from the main shop area by a ten-foot wooden partition. Five women, working independently, put together some thirty-five separate machine parts into an assembly fixture secured with four screws. A sixth woman picked up and distributed the parts to the five sitting at a workbench. Assembly took approximately one minute, and a record of their efforts was hole-punched onto a special tape created specifically to measure their output. For over five years, the holes signifying completed relays were punched onto this tape, ten feet of tape per day, approximately five holes every minute, for at least eight hours a day, five or more days a week.

The researchers measured the temperature and humidity in the secluded area, as well as the women's blood pressures and their vascular reactions to pressure applied to their wrists. Physical exams of the women judged their relative health and any changes that might occur. To test hypotheses involving fatigue and monotony, changes in the external surroundings were to be matched against the internal physiological changes of the women.

In order to control for psychological reactions to the experiments, the researchers sought cooperation and consistency. They offered to talk with the women about the changes being contemplated: the introduction of rest breaks, a midmorning lunch, and variations in the hours and days worked each week. They told the women they were interested in their thoughts and comments regarding the changes. The superintendent of the company's inspection branch informed the women that this was not at all about boosting production rates, but instead an attempt to learn about changes in working conditions that might be desirable for employees. The women would be kept informed of all results. Most important, they wanted the women to work at a comfortable pace, with no forced efforts at increased production. Everyone involved wanted the women to express their feelings so as to objectively evaluate the effect of external conditions on health and performance.

Both company officials and researchers sought to be reassuring. When the women, suspicious of authority, questioned why they needed a second physical examination, the physician and his staff met with them afterward to calm their fears. They all agreed to have ice cream when next they came for examination. An observer stationed in the secluded "test room" sought their continued cooperation. His job was to keep track of production but also to lend some supervisory help. He came to know the women and over time even became the target of some of their teasing.

The experimental tests were organized into thirteen periods, each representing the number of weeks during which different combinations of rest intervals, meal breaks, and hours worked per day were tried. In the first three periods, baseline data were collected. In the next periods, IV through VII, rest periods of five and ten minutes were introduced. The women were working less time, yet their collective output rose. In period VII, a fifteen-minute rest period was introduced with a midmorning lunch. Their collective output rose again. Periods VIII and IX were concerned with varying work hours, lessening the day by half an hour and then by a full hour. Total output declined. The women seemed delighted with the shorter workday, but the lost wages in combination with the decline in production apparently discouraged any further interest in this model.

In period X, the full forty-eight-hour workweek was resumed, but rest breaks similar in length to those of period VII were continued. Total output reached a new peak, although hourly output generally declined from the previous period. Yet the researchers took this as a sign that something wonderful was taking place. Mayo wrote: "It was, perhaps, this 'high' of production which brought to expression certain grave doubts which had been growing in the minds of the company officials responsible for the experiment" (Mayo, 1933, p. 61).

He and his colleagues concluded that up until period X, changes in production seemed to follow, in some fashion, the introduction of different experimental variables. But the logic of the experiment changed with the "high" of period X. The external conditions were the same as in period VII, but total production was significantly higher. And the productivity came despite disappointment among the women that the full forty-eight-hour workweek had resumed. But the fifty feet of tape that measured their weekly rate was clear: total productivity had never been higher.

In period XI, a brief concession to the worker's interest in a shorter workweek was tried by eliminating Saturday mornings. Total output once again declined and was dismissed as not particularly relevant to their research. In all periods besides IX and XI, however, total production increased regardless of fewer actual working hours per week.

The seed for a new discovery that was planted in period X came to full bloom in period XII. With the understanding that the change was temporary, working conditions returned to their original hours: no rest breaks, no midmorning lunches, and a half day of work on Saturday. This was the crucial test. If external factors played a major role, then surely the return to the original work conditions would show a return to the original output. But it didn't happen. In the annals of management lore, this absence of deteriorating performance was the defining moment in birthing a human relations approach to both productivity and morale.

Initially, at the start of period XII, the women approached work tentatively. They expressed their displeasure with the loss of rest periods, midmorning lunch, and shorter hours. They worried that they would be too tired to get through the day, and one operator actually suggested it would be a "miracle" to finish the day. But their productivity shot up 17 percent from the baseline of period III and was 12 percent greater than period VII, which had rest periods. This was the miracle at Hawthorne.

Like Taylor watching L3 and L4 cutting ever faster, the test room observer watched as new behaviors among the women aided them in cutting through the work day. The operators passed candy around to each other, they took extra time to chat with each other after lunch, and they even became boisterous, laughing and joking with each other. The report reviewing the outcomes of the experiment noted an "increase in contentment among the girls since entering the test room group," and "an eagerness on the part of the operators to come to work in the morning" (Mayo, 1933, p. 65).

By the mid-twentieth century, the marvel of the experiment at Hawthorne had grown to become the authoritative outlook on industrial work. In a 1954 textbook on the social psychology of industry, the author cites what "Elton Mayo discovered in his investigations at the Hawthorne plant. The worker is not an isolated machine. . . . If four men can each as individuals shovel 25 tons of material a day, the four working together can shovel 100 tons. It may be that they can—but will they? The emphasis in industrial psychology has shifted from studies of the isolated individual and the physical environment to the consideration of motivation and morale. It is now clear that the most important single factor in determining output is the emotional attitude of the worker towards his work and his workmates" (Brown, 1954, p. 17).

Human Relations and the Soul: Managing Feeling in the Workplace

Mayo and his successors' emphasis on the emotional attitude of the worker tended to mask the contradictory nature of work and the workplace. The goal of creating a workplace free of conflict, arranged to stabilize and promote gains in productivity, was illusory at best and potentially manipulative. The language of human relations became a repository of hope, an enchanted realm of ideas, models, and examples of what might be possible. Rather than truly influencing the actual conditions of the workplace, the rhetoric of "feeling" was concerned with detachment from the total experience of work and the workplace.

Work is contradictory. Sometimes it is engaging, challenging, a source of inner satisfaction. Other times work can be a drudgery— endless tasks without purpose. Sometimes it can be exploitative and cruel, as when we are humiliated, watched over with the intent to control, or simply used up by others and thrown away. Our ability to distinguish the differences within ourselves—how we experience the contradictory nature of work and our work environments—is a critical challenge to facing the world with soul. As Jacob Needleman has said, ". . . the soul is not a fixed entity . . . it is a movement that begins whenever man experiences the psychological pain of contradiction" (Needleman, 1980, p. 175). Soul, then, is not a fixed entity but rather a quality brought into being when we must face the sometimes painful and contradictory nature of our own experience.

Elton Mayo wished to demonstrate to the leaders of industry that they needed to attend to the psychological nature of the worker. He wrote of the studies at Hawthorne in magical terms: "What the company actually did for the group was to reconstruct entirely its whole industrial situation." This is quite a statement about a group of six women in a room assembling telephone relays. His point was that a new atmosphere had been injected into the setting where the women worked, "a milieu in which their own self-determination and their social well-being ranked first and the work was incidental" (Mayo, 1933, pp. 70–71). And herein lay the first of many contradictions. Work is not incidental. The process of how one works with one's hands and mind is not incidental. The quality of one's labors is not incidental. The influences of the products we create in society are not incidental. For a bit of self-determination and a portion of social belonging, Mayo offered a formula that split feelings—how one felt about work, how one felt about supervision, how one felt about wages—from the actual conditions of labor. And workers know this at some level; beneath the overt behaviors of social cohesion can lie deep and more personal resentments toward managers and co-workers.

The power to set rates of productivity, change the nature of how work was performed, and determine what was produced were viewed as beyond the parameters of human relations. By the mid-twentieth century, in the same time period that textbooks on industrial psychology proclaimed the victory of Mayo over Taylor, the actual contracts of the workplace sounded much closer to Taylor's time studies and narrow job classifications. A "fair day's work," read a 1946 agreement between the U.S. Steel Corporation and the Congress of Industrial Organizations, was judged as "that amount of work that can be produced by a qualified employee when working at a normal pace . . . a normal pace is equivalent to a man walking, without load, on smooth, level ground at a rate of three miles per hour" (Boorstin, 1974, p. 368). In the following year, U.S. Steel developed 1,150 jobs within 152 different classifications. General Motors followed the same logic, dividing the hour into six-minute periods, fragmenting the work to fit each time period, and paying the worker on a tenth-of-an-hour basis.

The contradiction that could not be acknowledged was that the heirs of Mayo's discoveries—human relations experts, group dynamics theorists, organizational development specialists—did not replace the logicians of cost and efficiency in the workplace. Rather, they served as a soft appendage to the body of technical experts directing workplace conditions.

Peter Drucker (1954), in his book *The Practice of Management*, suffered no delusion about the division of responsibilities: "Personnel Administration and Human Relations are the things talked about and written about whenever the management of worker and work is being discussed. They are the things the Personnel Department concerns itself with. But they are not the concepts that underlie the actual management of worker and work in American industry. This concept is Scientific Management" (Drucker, 1954, p. 280).

The reforms instituted at the Hawthorne Works were a good example of this attitude. One outcome of the research was the establishment of a counseling program. The counselors, primarily women, were available for workers and supervisors in manufacturing areas to express their grievances. The counselors, who reported to a separate department within the division of industrial relations, were given no authority, expected to keep all conversations confidential, and asked to gain the confidence of workers in order to support their adjustment to the industrial setting. The supervisors, on the other hand, were identified as having authority because they were accountable for discipline and output. "No synergy was created between managers and workers," wrote one analyst of the program years later, "or between toughness and tenderness, feeling and intellect, distance and relationship. . . . On the contrary, workers, tenderness, feelings, relationship . . . femininity would all be in one department: and management, toughness, intellect, distance, . . . and masculinity would be all in the other. The latter would, of course, dominate the former" (Hampden-Turner, 1970, p. 192).

The division of labor between human relations experts, who managed feelings, and technical experts, who managed the external conditions of the workplace, mirrored a schism within the experience of work itself. How one felt personally about work—one's own comfort, status, social position—became disengaged from the relevance and meaning of work. Work became something incidental to one's individual and social achievements. The inflated emphasis on internal relations—how we cooperate, how we attend to each other's feelings—though important, tended to blur the distinctiveness of what work was really about.

The consequence of splitting "feelings" off from the goals of work carried with it a certain infantilization of the workforce. Taylor had "freed" the worker from having to think; the logic of scientific method was proposed as the way to determine how work was best performed. Mayo and his colleagues now offered to relieve the worker of the responsibility of having to feel. Management that took responsibility for fostering harmony often did not recognize that people must look at their own behavior and generate their own hypotheses about what was happening with work and with themselves. Instead, the techniques of getting along predominated over the content of why getting along mattered. William Whyte, Jr., captured this dilemma of "cooperation" in his book *The Organization Man*: "To preach technique before content, the skills of getting along isolated from why and to what end the getting along is for, does not produce maturity. It produces a sort of permanent prematurity, . . . and those who believe that they have mastered human relations can blind themselves to the true bases of co-operation. People don't co-operate just to co-operate; they co-operate for substantive reasons, to achieve certain goals, and unless these are comprehended the little manipulations for morale, team spirit, and such are fruitless" (Whyte, 1956, pp. 396–397).

Ironically, what began as a method of control for managers to motivate and channel their workers' productivity became instead a failed psychological contract. The promise of being cared for was often a hollow offer of false love. Human relations was perched on a contradiction: advocating for personal development and democratic principles on the one hand, and on the other serving in a subordinate role to the increasingly bureaucratic and mechanized workplace.

The consequence of managing feelings and relationship as separate from the actual demands of the workplace can lead to a false understanding of what actually drives decisions in that sphere. The hopes engineered by proclamations of caring are often dashed by the realities of work and the turbulence of economic markets. The relay-assembly experiment at Hawthorne, for example, that engendered so much long-lasting interest for social scientists was abandoned in the midst of economic depression in 1932. Beyond the values of a caring attitude and some measure of participation were the costs associated with work time lost to shorter work hours, longer rest periods, additional lunch periods, visits to health care professionals, and discussions of the results of work and changes in the experimental conditions. In addition, there was a higher ratio of layout operators to the number of assemblers, and less variation in the types of relays that could be assembled. Of course, there was also the cost of a full-time observer whose main responsibility was to support the work of the women and offer them supportive counsel. The actual requirements to run the experiment were far too costly to be integrated into shop operations, despite increases in productivity. Additionally, the success of Hawthorne set up a false either-or perspective: managers are either caring or all business oriented.

In recent times, we have seen a continuing cycle of corporate promises offered and then regrettably withdrawn. I remember in the mid-1980s when Apple Computer first laid off employees, negating its no-layoff policies. The sense of disenchantment was unmistakable, captured by one employee in particular who made the stinging accusation that the company was "acting like a business." He could not believe the external world of the marketplace, filtered through Apple's management, would permeate his enchanted world.

Today, under the forces of downsizing, we might wonder how he had the impression that Apple was immune to market forces. However, the greater lesson might be that we all have a self-protective need to believe in something—an idea, a guru, a benevolent work setting—and organizations have a need to manage these beliefs. One unintended legacy of human relations was that it became viewed as too touchy-feely, but the promise of a method to shape harmony and adjustment within the workplace continues, balanced precariously between hope and false hope, substance and illusion.

The Illusion of Control: *Perceptions* of Meaning in the Workplace

The driving interest in new human relations models of motivation was the belief that good employee morale translated to higher productivity and sustained performance. The logic was simple enough: if workers benefited directly from a more hospitable work atmosphere, then the company would benefit indirectly by their increased efforts. The logic seemed so straightforward that it was stretched further: could the worker's *perception* of benefit be influenced by the organization? If so, how?

The very origins of the Hawthorne experiment foreshadowed this challenge. As you may recall, the relay-assembly experiment was preceded by a perplexing occurrence. In testing the effects of illumination, researchers found that the two women were fooled into thinking that the lightbulbs were being changed to provide greater illumination. Although the same size bulbs were used, the women, who had been allowed to suggest their preference for more light, commented favorably on the "change." They "felt" more involved.

If the perception of being allowed a choice could influence the estimation of light in a room, how far could the principle be taken? What might be the association between the perception of employee involvement and improved morale? Could a central principle of marketing, namely that people *will act from perceptions*, be used to influence the emotional reactions of workers to the workplace? Could the image of work itself be given a touch-up?

Journalist Robert Howard took up these questions in the 1980s when he toured corporate America in order to identify the opportunities and dangers of an increasingly technological workplace. One of the lingering images from his book *Brave New Workplace* was an IBM advertisement popular at the time. In the ad, a Charlie Chaplin look-alike plunks down in front of a personal computer, his face filled with wonder and delight. His chair is tipped back, his hat blown off by a passing breeze; the imagery of the ad suggests a wild, thrilling ride into the future of work. Howard wrote:

> Designed to sell computers, this ad sells a promise as well. Charlie Chaplin was the first popular media figure to express the reality of alienating work on the assembly line. For more than a generation, his film *Modern Times* has provided the images governing how we see industrial work. And yet, here, Chaplin's factory worker finds fulfillment . . . through the wonders of new technology. The computer delivers him from the prison of dirty, boring, alienating work. Within the frame of the ad, the former critic of work becomes a persuasive advocate for technology and for the corporation itself. Through technology and the corporation that provides it, Chaplin seems to be telling us, we too can be, like him, test-driving the IBM Personal Computer. And our work can become a realm of freedom—fluid, infinitely mobile, freighted with enormous possibility [Howard, 1985, p. 3].

The IBM ad captured hope for the future of work, a hope dependent on a workplace that required personal initiative and individual skills of problem solving, communication, and independent management of time. The conveyor belt no longer brought along components to be assembled. Efficiency studies could no longer be satisfied with the "normal pace" of a man walking on level ground. The tremors of the information age mocked a normal pace to work, or a level ground to judge performance. Now speed was of the essence, and the ground could be shaken right out from under a person. Mayo's assertion of the need for self-determination and social well-being took on added significance in a workplace built upon a fault line. The high-rolling 1980s and economic volatility of markets created a need for a "modern" Charlie Chaplin who could immerse himself in the adventure of the workplace. The new worker, hair blowing in the wind, eyes fixed on a computer terminal, became a blueprint for corporate management in creating and then directing activity.

The workplace as a setting for enchantment kicked into high gear with the publication of the management book *In Search of Excellence*. The best-selling nonfiction book of 1983, it offered a blend of philosophy, psychology, and business tips to foster the link between morale and productivity. I remember seeing the book in the offices of clients as diverse as the Federal Bureau of Prisons, Bank of America, and a Catholic college. Senior administrators described themselves as "people managers," who enjoyed "interfacing." As I became more familiar with the lessons people were learning, I began to appreciate how deep was the need to break out of old patterns and foster a new spirit in work. Yet I also realized that the *talk* of empowerment and collaborative work relationships was far more seductive than the *actions* necessary for change to take hold.

Buried within the book's discussion of transformational leadership and revitalizing corporate culture, *In Search of Excellence* offered a formula strikingly reminiscent of the corporate response to human relations. Authors Tom Peters and Robert Waterman, Jr., wrote: "So we observed, time and again, extraordinary energy exerted above and beyond the call of duty when the worker (shop floor worker, sales assistant, desk clerk) is given even a modicum of apparent control over his or her destiny" (Peters and Waterman, 1982, p. xxiii). For a modicum of *apparent* control and a dollop of social recognition, workers could be motivated to go beyond the call of duty. But the line separating more control from apparent control was elusive.

To illustrate the importance of perception, the authors referred to a field of psychological inquiry called "the illusion of control." They described a study that echoed the illumination trials at the Hawthorne Works. Two groups were given problem-solving tasks.

In the background were loud, randomly occurring, distracting noises. One group was instructed just to work on their tasks. The members of the other group were shown a button, an off switch, that apparently could shut out the noise. The group with the button solved five times the number of puzzles as the control group. "Now for the kicker," the authors proclaimed citing the research, ". . . 'none of the subjects in the off switch group ever used the switch. The mere knowledge that one can exert control made the difference'" (p. xxiv). The latent implications of the lighting experiment at Hawthorne, where the lightbulbs only seemed to be changed, are validated in this modern experiment on noise. The distractions of the external environment can be minimized by the perception of control and the offer of participation.

Although few workers would actually be fooled for long if lighting were not actually increased or noise were not really shut off, the deeper implication was of a new function for management. Authentic participation would require taking account of the actual work to be done and the richly varied circumstances of workers in the context of their work roles. The perception of participation, however, could be managed more symbolically through the orchestration of rhetoric, programs that called for participation, and initiatives that suggested inspirational outcomes. In the actual confinement of the workplace, the search for excellence, though often sincere, offered the latter more than the former. The need was not to fool workers but to get them "on board" with as much haste as possible.

The old rules of corporate management, to keep people focused on discrete tasks and offer them some sense of social belonging, now were giving way to a desire to forge meaning for people at work. At the root of Mayo's diagnosis of anomie was an incapacity for people to create meaning for themselves. In the context of shop work that included repetitive assembly, the prescription was social cohesion. But in the new workplace, the desire to motivate people suggested a direct appeal to workers to find meaning associated with corporate performance. "We desperately need meaning in our lives," wrote Peters and Waterman, "and will sacrifice a great deal to institutions that will provide meaning for us" (p. 56). The paradoxical expectation of leaders was to foster dependency on the one hand—fill the worker's void of meaning with corporate purpose—and on the other hand to promote independence and the perception of self-determination.

The soul is in the details of things. The problem with emphasizing perception over action, or illusion over substance, is not simply that it is manipulative, though it can be. The problem is that in the details of living, the false promises and grand abstractions slowly unravel. The soul cries out against deception, against all things manic and hollow. If the corporation could actually satisfy people's needs for security and meaning, then for a time there would be no reason to grapple with the contradictory nature of experience. We could look to the workplace as a sanctuary in which our sacrifices of time and energy were rewarded with love and understanding.

But in the real world, where details matter, the competing demands of workplace and family, the tensions of working for a salary and finding one's passion, and the paradox of working for others and attending to one's own needs reassert themselves. The high-flying spirit of work, as suggested in the IBM ad and the language of management books, is distanced from the more grounded elements of soul found in relationship, failure, and even disenchantment. A dependency on organizations to manage meaning and connection for us deepens rather than alleviates the dilemma of living with authenticity.

The new demands of the workplace posed contradictions for both the organization and the individual. At an organizational level, the causal relationship of employee satisfaction and productivity is suspect. Sometimes there is a link between high morale and greater productivity. Sometimes there is fairly good morale and low productivity. Sometimes there is low morale but high productivity. The danger for organizations is a tendency to avoid conflict in the name of keeping people happy, or conversely throwing away any pretense of caring for people when times get rough.

The result is a kind of deadening of feeling toward work itself. "What reengineering has not accomplished," a manager recently told me, "is any change in how people come to work, any sense of pride in wanting to come to work, the feeling you want to make a contribution." Describing why she thought this was so, she suggested it was due to a kind of game in which "management says it wants everyone's participation but can't figure out what that really means and staff say they'll play along but end up sabotaging every effort to change when it affects them personally."

The management of perception can cut two ways. Just as managers hope to create the perception that they care and invite participation, workers can create the perception that they want to change and welcome the opportunity to participate. Both parties may be sincere, but underlying the good intent is an underworld of feelings: fear of being adversely affected, suspicion of betrayal, and ambiguity about the value of change. The danger to the organization is that the very methods used to get employees to "buy in" can create a superficial acceptance of change. The real reasons, including the employee's recognition that there is no alternative, go unnoticed and remain unspoken.

The danger to the individual is also daunting. The trials necessary to find meaning for oneself cannot be orchestrated by others. The workplace, as a place for creating "rich tapestries of anecdote, myth, and fairy tale" (to use language from Peters and Waterman), does not create meaning for people but a temporary enchantment that inevitably wears off. The more immersed we become in the workplace, the less of ourselves is available for the full continuum of living. When the reflected glory of the organization pales, we are once again left with the questions of soul: where have I been? Who am I? Where am I going?

Each new generation finds a language and an image to describe this dilemma. Just as Chaplin stood for a human cog in an industrial machine, today's employees search for a metaphor of their own. In Douglas Coupland's "fictional" account of life at Microsoft, the character Todd offers this cry of disenchantment: "What we do at Microsoft is just as repetitive and dreary as any other job, and the pay's the same as any other job if you're not in the stock loop, so what's the deal . . . why do we get so *into* it? What's the engine that pulls us through the repetition? Don't you ever feel like a cog, Dan? . . . Wait—the term 'cog' is outdated—*a cross-platform highly transportable binary object?*" (Coupland, 1995, p. 60)

The tension implicit in managing the contradictory nature of work becomes polarized. Work becomes an all-consuming adventure—"Why do we get so *into* it?"—or a sentence of death. Both Chaplin as cog in the industrial machinery and Todd as binary object of the electronic age are transformed into something less than human, something resembling the technology they were meant to control. In contrast, soul reminds us that we remain our own agents, that by attending to the contradictory nature of experience, we are grappling with what it means to be fully human.

My quarrel with the emphasis on perception over experience is that we will slowly come to view reality as an illusion that can be overcome. We will become so skilled at avoiding the psychological pain of opposing forces within ourselves and in the world around us that we will settle each day for a convenient story, an easy rationale, a new inspirational motto. The underworld of soul will be something for writers and filmmakers, a commodity to be sold for entertainment. We will not be forced to give up our soul. We will simply ignore its relevance to nourish our lives.

The Continuing Dilemma: Reengineering the Soul in the Workplace

The current crisis of the workplace has shifted the rhetoric of change away from the machine metaphor of Taylor or even Mayo's social cohesion philosophies of human relations. Today, the language of success in the marketplace emphasizes a blend of "hard" strategies related to changing work processes and "soft" strategies stressing corporate cultures that value learning, commitment to change, and results-oriented thinking. There is even an effort to talk about the workplace as a setting for an individual's spiritual journey. The question remains, however, whether the emphases on learning and spiritual reward, proposed as outcomes of the future workplace, are real or simply convenient.

The call for a new spirit in the workplace carries the same danger that accompanied the adoption of human relations as the language of personnel departments, academics, and inspirational corporate speeches. The danger is that spirit and soul will be talked about but split off from the actual conditions of the workplace. Just as Mayo once suggested the need to adjust our emotional attitude, we now must adjust our mental outlook. "Everyone must change," declares James Champy in *Reengineering Management*; "The change will go deeper than technique. It touches not merely what managers do, but who they are. Not just their sense of task, but their sense of themselves. Not just what they know, but how they think. Not just their way of seeing the world, but their way of living in the world" (Champy, 1995, p. 10).

A whole industry of books, videos, and motivational speakers offers to help us achieve the habits of highly effective people or embrace the spiritual laws of success. Management books offer whole companies a language and a rationale for their change efforts. The message is that attention to people can infuse a company with a spirit of commitment, zest, energy, care, love, and passion. Work is compared to a jazz ensemble, a championship N.B.A. team, a place to be managed from the heart. The promise is of a workplace in which personal meaning and corporate purpose are fused together, a place in which everyone gladly plays their part in concert with a "master script." The workplace is presented as a setting for a spiritual journey.

In contrast, in an article for people struggling with career choices, *Fortune* magazine presents a far different portrait: "Production engineers or telephone marketers who speed inventory turns or sell more software are driving vast increases in productivity and creating layoffs. This has spurred a Darwinian battle for jobs and pay. It's no use grousing about your compensation when thousands of laid-off managers are ready to take your place. Companies have the whip hand. They're scrimping on raises and working people harder than ever. Managers are willing to strive like Trojans" (Tully, 1995, p. 68).

The split between work as spiritual journey and work as a Darwinian struggle for survival does not suggest that one vision must necessarily negate the other. However, it does pose a challenge to hold both these "realities" in tension with each other. The manager who says, "Sure, we're working people hard and asking them to do twice as much with half the staff, but we really care about the people here," just isn't making the connection. But some, as the following story of Floyd Simon illustrates, do understand that the contradictions of the workplace must be attended to.

Floyd Simon is participating in a company-sponsored session called "The Spirit of Work: Vision and Values 2000." In this session, designed to get employee "buy in," a chorus of voices instead raises a protest. "Isn't there an awareness that cutting down on the workforce is screwing the customer?" a man asks, almost shaking as he holds his hands out in front of him. A man standing by an easel writes down *Decrease in workforce affecting customer*. Another employee asks, "How can we be expected to do more when we don't even know if we'll be here in another month?" The man at the easel writes down *Uncertainty affecting staff morale*. A third questions the salaries received by the CEO and his top lieutenants at the same time there has been a hiring freeze and a limit on wage increases. The man at the easel writes down *Issues of equity*. Floyd sits quietly, jotting down notes. He has been with the company for twenty years and has seen the good with the bad.

The seminar leader, the general manager of customer services, nods in agreement. "Yes, I agree with you. We can't just keep cutting costs; we need to grow our revenues. But we also need to make sure we're getting the best use out of our resources. The question of CEO salary is not determined internally; the company's board determines that and it's set relative to comparable companies in our market." The general manager faces the room of anxious employees and reassures them: "We think we have the best people working here right now. But we need to make sure they're in the right places and working in the best way. We want you each to feel like you're an owner of this company. We need you to be empowered."

The afternoon session takes on the air of a revival meeting. The company's vision and values have been laid out, and now employees are being asked for their commitment to the new challenges of the workplace. They are asked to write down answers to three questions: what can you do to serve your customers better? What is your commitment to your team? How can you help improve work processes? The answers are shouted out. One is a commitment to be more receptive to change, another is to recognize that the customer comes first, and a third promises to partner with others to improve quality. Floyd is skeptical.

"I know what they're facing," Floyd says, back in his office, about the challenge facing senior management. "I know that we're in a death spiral if we don't move out in front of our competition. But this talk of empowerment and every employee being an owner is just too much to take. I know what they're doing in that seminar. They're letting people express their grievances and then hitting them up for commitment. But they won't get it that way.

"I kept thinking of that scene in the movie *The Outlaw Josey Wales*," Floyd says. "Clint Eastwood was in it, and so was Chief Dan George. There's this scene where he's listening to Chief Dan George tell him a story about how all the tribes came together to meet with Union army officials in Washington. They explain to an official how their people are dying and their lands are being taken away. They wait expectantly for his answer. And all the man says is, 'Endeavor to persevere.' That's it. And that's the answer here as well: endeavor to persevere. Well, the Indians declared war, but here it will be more subtle. People will be jockeying for position and not getting a whole lot of work done."

Floyd looks down at his desk. "I guess I need to look at things differently, at least as long as I stay here. In that same movie there's another line I remember. 'Don't piss down my back and tell me it's raining.' I need to keep my attention on what work can get done and not be pissing down the backs of my own people. It's quite a challenge. I feel anxious, furious, depressed, and just damn tired."

Floyd Simon is an example of someone with enough of his own experience not to become enchanted by corporate language of empowerment. Yet he still recognizes that work must change, that it must be driven by internal corporate realities and the marketplace. He understands that motivating workers to see meaning and purpose in their work comes at the same instant that work itself is becoming murkier, fraught with anxiety, and physically more demanding. He knows that managers must ensure that the effects of downsizing, reorganizing, and reengineering work processes somehow do not cripple their remaining staff's ability to work. And just as critically, they must motivate their employees to do more, adapt to change faster, and work with each other better. But he also knows there is a line between observing that it is raining and pissing down someone's back.

In Chapter One, I suggested that the polarization of the material and spiritual worlds creates settings in which both worlds are placed in jeopardy. The material world becomes more a struggle for basic survival, a world driven only by outer tangible realities. The spiritual world becomes a desperate, even neurotic desire to find an inner place of meaning that transcends the emptiness of outer realities. The idea of a soul wedding these two worlds together creates something new. The qualities of soul that wed together opposites are distinct from either the practical values of the material world or the transcendent values of the spirit world. Soul offers an elusive challenge.

The challenge is to find a third way, a path that takes us deeper into the realm of experience and reflection upon experience. The path of soul is indirect, circular, more tolerant of the flow of impressions, and infused with imagination. In contrast with spirit's call to look up toward higher abstractions and absolutes, soul can look down, taking in contradictory ideas and perceptions. And in contrast to submission to a marketplace that dictates a hard-edged attitude of survival, soul can be vulnerable and suffer.

Floyd's struggle represents the stirring of a soul brought into focus by contradictory experience. He understands both the need for change and the illusory aspects of embracing change. Floyd's image of Eastwood listening to Chief Dan George allowed him to circle back on his experience of the day's seminar. He could allow himself the imaginal connection between the words of senior management and the words of the Union army official. He could also recognize that he was not immune to what he found disquieting about his company's behavior; he too must be cautious of pissing down his own people's backs. Like all of us, Floyd must face how to proceed in a fragmented world.

In the final part of this book, I pursue the question of how to take up an organizational role without having to split apart the outer and inner worlds of experience. The richness and confusion of the soul can neither be harnessed by organizations nor ignored. We are humans, not cogs or transportable binary objects. By insisting we have souls, we open the door to an imaginal world that has both reality and creativity. We open a door to the struggle of contradictory impulses, in ourselves and in the workplace. The soul is rich in images and conversations. By attending to these pictures and dialogues in our mind, we cultivate the deeper regions of soul. And by attending to others from our own experience, we can begin to recognize the human condition from which we generate the organizational settings we share.

Part Three

. . . .

Journeying Toward Meaning, Coherence, and Wholeness

8

Taking Up Our Organizational Roles
How We Can Affirm Our Experience at Work

I recall one of my first consultations with a group of psychotherapists who were part of a not-for-profit community-counseling agency. They found themselves in conflict over every conceivable aspect of their work together. They could not agree on referral arrangements, on management of common office space, or on ways to maintain their shared kitchen. They could not even agree on the consultant that they wanted to work with. After a lengthy process and multiple interviews, they settled on me. I was told they had chosen me because of my background and experience in working with issues of authority, but they actually couldn't really agree on that either.

Before our first meeting together, I called the director of the agency. We agreed that he would begin the meeting with a question that would allow the members to introduce themselves to me: "What do you believe is the purpose of this organization?" I felt that, beyond introducing the members, the question would evoke some common themes that we could build on over the course of the consultation.

The question had barely left the director's mouth when conflict broke out. Members challenged why he should begin the meeting, why that question was necessary, why he was asking about the organization and not the purpose of the consultation. When he explained that he had talked briefly with me before the meeting, the members of the staff grew even more agitated. Who said he could talk with me before the meeting? Was he allying with the consultant and excluding them? Why should they talk about themselves when everyone knew he was the problem? Some members eyed me suspiciously, as if I had already betrayed them and there could be no forgiveness. One member explained to me that in the beginning of family therapy, you only talk with the whole family.

I was sitting in my worst nightmare. Issues of power, authority, shadow, dependency, and exclusion were coming at me like tennis balls shot out of one of those serving machines gone mad. I explained that one way to approach conflict was to address the purpose of the organization and the roles we play. I said I didn't view them as a family but as an organization with a purpose to serve the community. I told them I had talked with the director because he was the individual formally responsible for the organization. But just as critically, I said, they also had roles, formal and informal ones, that were crucial for the organization's effectiveness and their satisfaction. I wanted to hear about their roles and how they saw themselves in their organization.

One of the psychotherapists glared at me and stated in no uncertain terms, "I am a person, not a role." Heads nodded in agreement. The director slumped down in his chair, as if to say that he was once again defeated. Members began talking with each other about what the real problem in the organization was, ignoring both the director and me. I sat silent for what seemed a very long time, alternately wanting to interrupt, apologize, or simply shout curses. Finally, during a lull in the proceedings, I spoke out.

"Is this typical?" I asked. "Is this the way you work together, feeling angry, vulnerable, criticized, left out, without a common ground to stand on?" I noted, right or wrong, that the director's explanation of his action had been simply fuel for their angst. They seemed willing to carry on the conversation among themselves and quite selective about what would help them and what would not. "Is it possible," I asked them, "that you are willing to analyze what is wrong but not what you can do about it?" I told them I didn't know how I might help them.

The response from the group was tentative. Some thought I should know how to help them. Others said they were not angry and had not jumped on the director. One member acknowledged that this was an extreme example, albeit common, of how they worked together. They agreed they needed help, and a provisional truce was forged between me and the staff. They would be willing to talk about roles and purpose, and I would agree to listen to their feelings, to attend to them as whole persons.

I have regarded this early consultation as one of the most pivotal in focusing my attention on the tension between person and role. An organizational role, as it was for the psychotherapist who glared at me, is often associated with not being real. For her, role was possibly associated with a false face, like an actress in a play. As one person in the group said to me, "No one ever loved a role." From this perspective, there is a chasm between person and role that cannot be leaped. Yet finding one's role is tantamount to finding one's voice. Role relates to soul if we can begin to see how it shapes the person we are *as we act in the world*. Role helps us prioritize what matters.

In Part Two, we saw the dangers of falling under a false enchantment or simply being made to accommodate the efficiencies of increasingly mechanical and then technological systems. The person, split off from his or her own capacity to reflect and find meaning, becomes captive to the role defined by the workplace. The antidote to this state of affairs is to find a role that includes the whole person. Role can be a starting point from which to reflect on our own experience and take a new look at the organizational system of which we are part. The looking and reflecting creates new ways to change and cope.

Role, Experience, and Soul

The term *role* is used in writing about management and in everyday speech in a variety of ways. It may refer to a job description outlining a series of tasks, a position in a hierarchy found on an organizational chart, or even a set of overt and covert expectations related to our ideas about how a person should behave: a father with his children, a manager with her employees, a leader with his followers. Role takes on varied meanings based on its context. In organizations, we may hear about the need for role clarification; in the theater we might talk about role as a character in a play.

The origin of the English word *role* does come from the theater: the rolled-up parchment from which the actor read his lines. Role was something less than the whole person, words on a parchment that were simply read aloud with expressiveness. From this perspective, by definition, we are not being real when we take up role because we are acting out someone else's words and meaning. We assume a character to fit into someone else's drama.

In organizations, role has often been other-directed. The organization defines a role as discrete tasks that individuals must fit themselves to. I have seen job descriptions that go on for three single-spaced pages, as if capturing every possible behavior on the job ensures control over what the person will do. In fact, the opposite is true; the more functions that are added to the list, the less likely the individual is to fulfill the requirements. At risk is the coherence and meaning associated with work. Job descriptions of role echo Frederick Taylor's efficiency assumptions: break everything down into pieces and measure the result. If we reimagine what role means in the workplace of today, we can forge a connection to soul as a quality stirred to life by grappling with the often contradictory claims of what is inside the person and also what is outside in the demands of the workplace.

A more productive way to think of role, I have found, is as a *psychological stance*, an idea that we hold in our mind, rather than something written on a piece of paper, be it in the theater or in the workplace. Role is a mental construct that is fluid and constantly changing because the world around us is also dynamic and constantly changing. Finding and taking a role is a way to organize our behavior in relation to tasks and other people. The *things* we do are only the outer shell, the visible half of the unseen inner work that gives it meaning.

Role as a mental construct is associated with perceiving an underlying rationale for doing what we do. For example, a supervisor whose task is to give a staff writer specific editorial criticism realizes her role is better taken up by discussing the ideas behind the article rather than simply delineating the changes. Because the staff writer is new, the supervisor realizes her comments could easily be mistaken as a judgment of the writer's skills. Engaging the person on the ideas of the article allows them to be colleagues first, permitting the editorial changes to be an outcome of their common goals. The role, in contrast to being simply a task or signifying a hierarchical position, is an *idea* in the supervisor's mind.

Role, in this way, is related to soul because it is rooted in our ability to reflect, to sense what is most critical in the context of relationships. To take up an appropriate role, as did the supervisor in the example above, is to activate some part of our inner judgment in response to the demands that are placed upon us. She did not simply go over the changes because that was her job; she thought through the meaning behind the task. The work of finding and taking a role is akin to finding our voice, the inner voice that is the momentary synthesis of the competing demands that lie at the heart of experience. Role taking is an active rather than passive response to our environment. In taking up role, we find out something about our courage and creativity in how we respond to the opportunities and constraints of our world. We become active participants in our destiny.

In organizations, the inner work related to role is essential to survival. The challenges we face in the workplace of today can be seductive and intimidating. On the one hand, we can be swept away by the promise but not the reality of empowerment. We are led to believe we are in charge of our destiny, but the realities of the organization often prove otherwise. On the other hand, we can be overwhelmed by the multiple demands—the constant barrage of changing needs and expectations—that offer no clear guidelines or parameters as to where our work lies. Taking up a role consciously allows us to navigate the sheer cliffs of increasing expectations and the whirlpool of addictive work.

Attention to role can also act as a fire wall between the person and the workplace. Role allows us to define the parameters of our work, the aspects that are most meaningful and relevant to our position in the organization. But we can also understand the boundaries of our efforts, the limitations and distinctions between what we need to do and the expectations of others. When we locate ourselves within a role, we are protected from the psychological assault of others' expectations to be all things to all people because we know something about who we are and what the organization is attempting to do. We are not simply checking off tasks from our list of things to do. Nor are we absorbing others' endless expectations and demands.

The idea of finding and taking role can be thought of as something that happens internally. When I draw a graphic representation of this idea for clients, I make a stick figure of an individual. Inside the head I place a second stick figure, and other smaller stick figures nearby. I then draw a circle around the whole picture. I say the first stick figure represents the person, with an inner life and outer talents. The stick figure inside the head is our mental construct of our role, the image we have of the person we think we are in the context of a system (an organization, a family, etc.). The smaller stick figures represent others we have in our minds and our relations with them. Finally, what is within the circle represents the particular workplace, and the circle itself represents the boundary between that workplace and the larger environment. Role is contained in these interlocking concepts of the person, the role, and the system.

When we look at all these concepts together as a more complete picture, we are better able to think about role, because we are taking into account the person, the role and its relations with others, and the whole system in which action takes place. The dramatic motion implicit to this picture is that the image inside us is not static but constantly shifting. We can conceive not only of the current picture but also of others that may come after it. Unlike a job description, which carries a static concept even if we are constantly clarifying the arrangement of tasks, role is something we take on in the moment. It exists in the here and now. When we move a certain way, we influence what is outside us. When our environment changes, we move in response to the changes. It is not concrete or fixed, nor should it be taken too literally.

No one can give someone a role. Role taking is an internal choice that assumes the whole person is acting in response to others, a dance of constantly changing rhythms and beats. We may not be able to love a role, but we can learn to appreciate the discipline of the dance. To take up a role means first that we take account of the system we are in and our relations with others. We then take responsibility for ourselves in relationship: to others, to our work, to the system we are in, and to the larger environment that contains our system. The work of taking up role is often messy and chaotic, but ultimately it is something that, once accomplished, is easier to do again. The following anecdote illustrates what role taking can look like.

Experience, Awareness, and Change

Sitting in a room with three managers and the director of a department within a public utility company, I found my first impression was of their pale and worn look, as if the blood in their bodies must concentrate only on nourishing their essential organs. They had come to me because they felt they could barely survive. One manager was thinking of leaving; another was looking to transfer to an alternate location. They had been through a tremendous upheaval—reorganization, downsizing, changes in their scope of responsibility—and they had been told the changes were just beginning. They were worried about their jobs, about their responsibilities multiplying, about their stamina to carry on.

The leaders of their organization were talking about the need for customer focus and service, but the reality of their jobs seemed disconnected from such grand visions. They went to monthly teleconferences in which they heard about the esprit of employees at Disney and the customer focus at Nordstrom. One of the managers told me cynically that he's feeling goofy and doesn't shop at Nordstrom. They just wanted to know what their job was supposed to be.

I asked them to tell me about the experience of working. What is it like to wake up in the morning and think about coming to work? What is it like when they first come in? Who are they likely to talk to, or what they are likely to do? What is the flow of the day? Is it focused, choppy, hazy? What does it mean to feel goofy?

The conversation didn't begin easily, but slowly they warmed to it. One manager described waking up with a pit in her stomach, a tension that carried forward until she arrived. Another talked about the hectic nature of getting three kids to school and worrying about what she forgot to do. The third manager talked about really wanting to make the job work, emphasizing to me that he wanted to know his authority and the scope of his decision making.

As we began to talk more easily, images and metaphors arose that caught us all by surprise. The director said she felt plugged up inside and feared the organization was trying to give her an enema. The managers laughed at the absurd image of her running through the halls, not toward anything, but away from her fear of being given an enema. One of the managers said that working here "is like a permanent coronary: you can't catch your breath and your chest feels crushed." There were oohs and ahhs from the group as if she had hit a chord they all felt in their guts. There was an appreciation for her choice of metaphor, as when a vocalist has hit just the right note.

Later in the session, I asked them each to write down how they thought other members of their department saw them. I told them to write down the first thing that came to mind and to worry about reality—whatever that was—later. Their comments, written and then voiced aloud, had a remarkable similarity and overlap. They talked about being seen as gophers by their staff—get this, where's that, how come such and such is not available. One member said she thought she was seen as a foreman, telling people to get back to work, watch the time, obey the rules. Another commented that he was seen as dealing with what nobody else wanted to do, such as disciplining an employee or talking to someone with a problem in another department, or telling people bad news. "Oh no," said one of the managers mimicking a staff member on seeing her coming, "what's gone wrong now?"

As we discussed what these comments might be about, a manager acknowledged that part of the problem was that they were never around. They were constantly in meetings or responding to problems or answering phone mail. Sometimes they had fifteen messages before they even began their day. Their jobs were fragmented and everything seemed urgent. One manager said that by the end of the day it felt like a lifetime. There was silence, and all of a sudden the energy of our discussion faded. The reality of their experience had hit home and evoked a sense of hopelessness.

At this critical juncture, I made a mistake. I attempted to fill the sudden void with a motivational speech. I told them that as leaders, they needed to get hold of what they were doing and what they were about. If they careened from one thing to another, they could not hope to figure out what they needed to do. I picked up the slack in the energy by talking more forcefully and with greater optimism about what they could accomplish. In the middle of my comments, I got a funny feeling that I was losing them. I stopped and asked if

I was lecturing them. Three of the members shook their heads side to side, but the man who wanted to know about his authority was stone-faced. I asked him what he was thinking. He looked at me squarely and said, "I do think you're lecturing me and I resent it. You don't know what it's like for me."

I agreed I was lecturing them and I didn't think it would help very much. I was struck by how quickly I had picked up on the loss of energy and tried to fill in with a forced enthusiasm. My role was to be a resource to them, not another person filling them up with good ideas that go nowhere. I wondered out loud if this was how the organizational leaders or even the director who worked with them felt: combating despair with forced enthusiasm. Our experience of another person's pain can sometimes trigger grand visions of what could be. But you cannot give someone a role. I apologized. Yet, my mistake created an opportunity.

The director acknowledged that what had just happened also happened in their own staff meetings. Managers complained or became hopeless and she felt she had to solve the problems for everyone. "I respond by trying to be helpful just as you tried to be helpful by giving us a speech." The managers took notice of her comments and asked her more about when she thought this happened. They acknowledged they did the same with their staff. There was a dawning appreciation that they all got caught up in the dance. How did this happen?

In the course of several sessions together, there was further validation of their sense of fragmentation and lack of coherence. They each prepared a snapshot of their functions over the course of a typical week or month. Although there was nothing typical about their individual days, a pattern emerged about how they spent their time. A full third of their time was spent sitting in various meetings, one-fifth of their time was spent responding to messages, and a quarter was spent participating in interdepartmental continuous-improvement activities. Another fraction of their time was spent in solving things that went wrong on a particular day, and the remainder, a thin sliver, was spent interacting with their own staffs. There was no time to think, to pursue a purpose, or to reflect together with others.

For the director, the fragmentation of time was even more vivid. She was involved with other senior-level managers elsewhere in the organization to the point where she was only available to her managers in short group meetings and one-on-one sessions. These sessions invariably revolved around problems that could not really be addressed in an isolated fashion, so she was relegated to the role of listener and sympathizer. She too was frustrated.

The validation of their fragmented experience had a paradoxical effect on the group's thinking. Rather than lapse into the hopelessness of our first meeting, the director and her managers acknowledged that the roles they had were unacceptable to them. What was different was that they didn't view their plight as personal—who wouldn't be crazed in this kind of situation? The concept of role was beginning to act as a fire wall between their personal selves and the system they were in. They still expressed anxiety about their inertia, but they were not numb to it; nor did they blame others for it. Rather they began to see opportunities that might change the dance. And at the center of these changes was their own psychological stance. By working with their own experience, they gained perspective, and by plumbing the depth of their situation, they left with a new awareness of choice. Soul is stirred at just these moments when we face conflicts that demand new images of who we are and what we must do.

Assigned Roles and Work Roles

One first step in taking up a role as a constructive psychological stance is learning about how others might see us, and comparing that with our own experience of working. In the example of the public utility company, the managers were able to voice how they felt others viewed them: as gophers, foremen, and bearers of bad news. These *assigned* roles, if true, were critical clues to unraveling a mystery. Why did the staff seem so hostile and uncooperative? The answer, in part, was that they felt as if they worked on an assembly line with supervisors who had no real authority other than to watch over them and tell them more bad news. Comparing their perceptions of the staff with their own experience of anxiety, hollowness, and frenzy, the managers found there was a match. One of the managers noted that although their formal job descriptions had changed from supervisor to manager, staff still referred to them as supervisors. The role of *supervisor* had clear negative associations. In this department, the power of the assigned role held sway.

The assigned role is what others have determined is our place within the group. In this example, the assigned roles were related to status and personal characteristics. The assigned role, for purposes of definition, can also include discrete functional tasks such as responsibility for scheduling staff or ordering supplies. Although functional tasks are critical to organizational functioning, they can be replaced by automation, bundled in newly created positions, or managed by less-skilled professionals. The assigned role can bury a person in details that add little real value to the organization's effectiveness. As gophers, managers were seen as having little institutional authority over their areas. They could carry out inconsequential chores such as ordering supplies or filling out forms, but they were not viewed as having any real influence. They were seen as conduits for requests. As foremen—a role associated with surveillance and negative forms of discipline—they were perceived in an even more negative way. They could catch staff doing something wrong, but they could add no real value to operations. Even their attempts to praise people fell on deaf ears because staff did not really care about what their low-status managers felt about them. As gophers and foremen, they were stick figures with no real connection to either the work or the people.

The assigned role of bearer of bad news was problematic in a different way. When managers brought news of consolidation and new work processes, staff could ignore them as a way of ignoring the demands and new responsibilities of the changing workplace. It was easier to kill the messenger than to hear the message. Staff created barriers by distancing themselves from the message of change in the larger organization. They focused on the negative interpersonal skills of the managers or on the unreasonable requests of people higher up, rather than face the common problem of the organization. Staff would routinely say, "No one tells us anything around here." The managers colluded by acting defensively, by becoming aloof, disapproving, and even punitive.

The danger of the assigned role in organizations is that it can place us in a box from which we cannot escape. A manager tagged as a gopher or someone who never listens does not get the feedback he or she needs to change. From an operations perspective, the manager may not get the crucial feedback necessary for effective work flow—there is the sensation of vulnerability, that no one is watching your back. What goes wrong can ultimately get hung on the person in charge. Often, we call these accidents-waiting-to-happen "communication problems," but that simply makes them seem like interpersonal issues. The assigned role, often unspoken, has the potential to become destructive because feedback to or about the individual becomes narrower and prejudiced in a certain direction. The deeper issue is the inability to identify an effective *work role*, which is different from either a skill deficit in communication or a personality mismatch between individuals.

But when individuals can think about the distinction between their assigned roles and what they really need to do, they can begin to construct a work role that is relevant to their unique situation. The managers at the utility company could begin to see how the assigned roles of gopher, foreman, and messenger were interrelated in ways that made them appear inconsequential and punitive. Unless they could influence the perceptions of these unstated but negatively assigned roles, they could not hope to become effective. If they managed more often by "walking around," they might simply be seen as intensifying their surveillance. If they praised staff with more regularity, they might be viewed as being manipulative. If they held more meetings to discuss how work was changing, they might be viewed as wasting the staff's precious time. To find a psychological stance that was appropriate for the actual situation, they had to first identify work that was truly meaningful and relevant to the purposes of the larger organization.

Finding, Making, and Taking a Role

The essence of *finding* a role has to do with purpose. We must ask ourselves, where in the myriad of functions I have to perform is there meaning that has personal significance and meets organizational need? What lies underneath the frenzy of tasks that requires a strategy from me and that adds value to the discrete functions? For the managers, being in charge had meaning because they could see that no one else inside their area had as much access to information as they did. They were on the boundary between what was actually happening at the front lines of operations and the changes taking place in the larger organization. Information was currency if they learned how to use it.

This did not mean having to do everything. The opposite was true. As much as was conceivable, their staff also had to have the information necessary and the psychological stance appropriate to fulfill the many functions needed to run the department. Finding the role means finding what is needed in the moment, the purpose served by the potential inherent in all our actions.

In the case of the utility company, the director was working more and more outside the boundary of their department, which meant that the managers had to operate from the psychological stance of being in charge, rather than simply reporting their problems to the director. Individual meetings with the director, then, could not be devoted to airing their concerns but rather to asserting their plans. The managers' interactions with other departments had to become more strategic and purposeful rather than reactive and defensive, and their communication with their staff had to be timely and relevant. Staff wanted to know what was going on as it was happening, not after the fact.

To do this, the managers would have to take charge of their time spent in meetings and on the phone in order to assert themselves more fully. If that meant portioning out which managers went to which meetings and which messages were appropriate for them and which for others, then that was to be the challenge. It also meant that in each area of responsibility—fiscal, staffing, training, work flow—they had to have clear purposes as to what they were trying to achieve.

Making a role requires the inner work of reflection and creativity. Where are the ingredients that will make a difference: the place of activity, the groups we need to listen to, the people we should be talking to, the room in which we can think and plan? What is the stance of mindfulness that furthers one's intention? For example, in responding to a routine procedure, how is there an opportunity to rethink the activity and engage others in the same process? Managers who tell me that there is wasted effort in creating interdisciplinary teams and using quality tools for every old form that needs new processing are, I think, telling me that we have been seduced again by technique. We need individuals, as well as groups, who are clear about making roles that matter.

The making of the role involves carving out a space within one's mind about why the system you are in needs you. If you are forging new alliances in times of change, the organization needs you. If you are asking others to think for themselves when there is abject dependency, the organization needs you. If you are offering new ideas when everyone else is paralyzed by analysis, the organization needs you. You may not be liked for your efforts. You may not do it well. You may not be understood. But you are forging a role for yourself that is relevant.

The final aspect of role is *taking* it. When we take up our role in an organization, we are acting in alignment with the institutional authority of our position and the purposes of the organization. We know how to negotiate the boundaries of our decision making even if there are no formal guidelines. We take risks because we know something about how our system operates and how it needs to be challenged. We act with the assumption that each action creates the opportunity for new learning.

When I lectured the managers of the public utility company, I was out of role. But something new was created. We learned there could be mistakes and forgiveness. The director was afforded an opportunity to say something she had held back. The manager who was initially stone-faced but then confronted me with his truth learned that he could survive doing so. Taking up one's role, even when we don't quite get it right, affords others the opportunity to take up their own stance. We cannot give someone else a role, but we can model it and learn from the consequences.

Role taking requires using one's own personal power in the service of the task. Power and authority are different (as I discuss later on) because power is something personal—rooted in our personal expertise, our position within an organization, our history, our interpersonal savvy. Power can be used for personal gain and need not relate to the needs of others or the system we are in. Yet the recognition and use of personal power is essential to act in role.

I am speaking of power here not as domination of others but as the capacity to express one's inner self, one's talent, passion, skill. The soul loves power because without it we cannot effectively negotiate the interaction between inside and outside. Soulfulness requires both inner work—finding meaning and purpose—and outer work—seeking avenues for expression. Role taking also requires inner work—finding and making a role—as well as the outer work of acting in role. To do this we need connection to our own personal power. To take up role requires attention to the voice inside that must be heard. But we must know how to heed the voice.

The acceptance of our need to be heard can be a dangerous and exhilarating experience. When we heed the inner voice, we are acting from within rather than being controlled from without. There is a physical sensation of being in a place of power. Clients talk to me about the sense of purposefulness associated with *being in role*. The director at the public utility spoke to me once of how exciting it was when she stopped trying to fix everything and just listened with heightened attention. At one meeting of senior executives, she spoke up at just the right time and with information that was critical for the success of the project. "I was the only one who could have told them they were going off in the wrong direction, and it was scary but it wasn't. I knew I had to say it. I just knew." But being in role does not mean simply paying attention to thoughts and feelings inside oneself. Role taking requires attending to how one takes in what is outside as well.

The Organization in the Mind

The Grubb Institute is an international research and training organization based in London, with offices in Bryn Mawr, Pennsylvania. (Bruce Reed, founder of the institute, first introduced the concept of role reflected in this chapter.) The institute is dedicated to using systems thinking to study the structures and values of organizations. The title of the institute, named after Sir Kenneth Grubb, conjures up images of things that live in the earth rather than fancier names that might inspire thoughts of high-performing teams or visionary leadership. Yet the concept that role is a product of our digging around in the muck of our own imagination serves to underscore the institute's mission in an unintentional but synchronistic fashion.

When I attended a Grubb-sponsored conference at the College of Preachers on the grounds of the National Cathedral in Washington, D.C., I found one of our first activities deceptively simple. We were asked to draw a picture of our organization with ourselves in it.

"Do not draw an organizational chart," we were told; "use your imagination—be creative." I tore off a large sheet of flip-chart paper and grabbed some colored markers. I approached the task tentatively, sketching some abstract images on a notepad, trying to let whatever images were inside me flow out. I didn't believe I had artistic talent, and my images were rudimentary representations of what I hoped to portray. Thinking of one of my major client organizations that is actually an alliance between two separate legal entities, I drew two tornadoes, whirling coils with faces drawn inside the swirling lines. I placed myself outside looking toward the two interacting forces.

In preparing to discuss our pictures, we were given a series of questions to aid in our reflection: What is the emotional tone of the picture? Does the picture feel like a whole, or does it feel fragmented? Am I aware of any significant omission in the picture concerning myself and my feelings, my work relations, the context in which I work? Am I in the picture, and if so, where? The questions served to draw me deeper into the picture, obliging me to ask it questions, as if the picture contained clues I was not consciously aware of. I became a little dizzy staring at the whirling circles, as if I were being pulled into the eye of the storm.

When I presented, the feeling of dizziness was brought forward as "data," suggesting the price I pay to self-manage the chaos I sense in the system. One of the participants noted differences in the pattern of the two separate tornadoes, highlighting possible crucial differences in the cultures of the two organizational entities. There was no attempt to debate the accuracy of the picture in relation to the actual organization. The picture stood by itself, an artifact of what lay in my mind.

As we reviewed the drawings of other participants, a similar theme emerged regarding the unique way that each picture seemed to have its own independence. Many of the participants gained new perspectives on their drawings that were just the opposite of what they had intended. One minister in the group drew a boat with Christian oarsmen rowing across a channel to spread his ministry. He was shown calling out encouragement from the stern of the boat.

Another participant said that for him, the boat appeared as a ship, with galley slaves being chastised to row harder. The minister turned various shades of purple, but by the end of the conference he recognized there was an edge to his evangelical style that validated some element of this interpretation. For all of us, the drawings seemed to take on a life of their own the more we looked at them. We were encouraged to modify them at any time, and they were hung up throughout the length of the four-day conference.

One of the basic premises of the conference was that we take up our roles in relation to the *organization in the mind*. "In the mind" refers to the subconscious picture of the whole that we carry around inside us. It suggests that the individual, in role, holds a gestalt of the entire system: the structures, values, emotions, and purposes that constitute the whole system. Our behavior emerges from this background picture. We act, often without awareness, in relationship to an internalized image of our organization. If that organization is a tornado threatening to suck me inside, I may be quite tentative about the work I am willing to take on. If I think of myself as a benevolent crier on a ship sent by Christ, I may be unaware that others view me as dominating. The organization in my mind is the data from which I organize how I present myself and how I interpret others' behavior. What is critical to know is that the picture is born of our *experience*, rather than of the espoused values of the organization. From experience and reflection on experience, we construct meaning and our sense of belonging to the whole.

The organization in the mind, unfortunately, is often the last thing we pay attention to when navigating our way through organizational life. So often in organizations we are trying to figure out the motives of others, assess our job functions, address the expectations of bosses, subordinates, and peers. We lose ourselves, our own images, of what the organization means to us. The idea that within ourselves is a picture, fluid and ever-changing, creates an opportunity for deeper reflection and greater accountability. Yet this revolutionary way of looking at organizations carries with it responsibility and discomfort.

If we view it in this new way, the organization stops being a static object for study and becomes instead the context for discovering our own motives. We lose the distances between subject (self) and object (organization) and become part of a living organism that includes us. My picture of me looking at the two tornadoes does not represent me as a separate observer but rather a whole picture in which one individual *thinks* he is watching. The discomfort of this stance is that we cannot rationalize being at a safe distance, an innocent bystander, victim, voyeur, or consumer of a world created by others. We are participants and co-creators of a shared reality in which taking up role is tantamount to taking responsibility for one's part in the drama of organizational life.

The lesson of the drawings, leading to the awareness of an organization in the mind, is that you can better claim your role when you have the skill of shifting your perspective. Shifting perspective means moving your internal eye until you see more of the whole pattern. It is like the experience of learning to use a camera. When I first began, I was instructed to take pictures of the same tree in the same forest again and again. I would go out during early daylight and at twilight and after a rain and when the skies were overcast. Each image was different, sometimes subtly, sometimes dramatically. What mattered was the process and practice of taking perspective. Each time I went back to the forest, I was different, and so was the forest I was capturing for an instant.

Becoming aware of the organization in the mind is a tool for learning. When we form our own mental picture of our organization, we are on the way to claiming our role in relationship to the aims and values we believe our system stands for and the unique contribution we believe we are making. What is sad in organizations today is that we know that learning is a goal, but we still insist on preaching the organization's stated values and objectives. We still insist on individuals' passively internalizing what leaders say the organization is. We would still rather show a model of how learning occurs than actively respect that it is happening all the time. The concept of an organization in the mind allows us to appreciate that the route to learning runs through the deepening of our experience in role and our ability to express it to others. Soul, rather than being driven into the interior of the person, is stirred into action at the boundary of the relationship between self and others.

Experience, Learning, and Meaning

There is a poignant moment in the movie *Shadowlands,* in which Anthony Hopkins, playing C. S. Lewis, sits at his desk mourning the death of his wife, Joy. He is without a way to comprehend the loss that he feels and says to his brother: "Suffering is just suffering after all, no cause, no purpose, no pattern. Nothing, there is nothing to say, I know that now. I've just come up against a bit of experience . . . experience is a brutal teacher." After a pause, he speaks again: "But you learn. My god, you learn."

In the depth of despair, in that negative space within our souls to which no purpose or pattern seems evident, there still remains the fabric of our experience. Experience is not put in front of us in order for us to learn. Learning is something wrested from experience, even when experience is a brutal teacher. Lewis acknowledges the lack of meaning and purpose that can overwhelm our lives, but his pause speaks of his experience. From out of this pause comes something uniquely his own. Learning remains within our power—even after meaning has abandoned us—to cultivate experience, to draw from its hand the lessons it offers.

Experience and learning can be intertwined in this generative way if we recognize that no one can take away our experience of life. It is ours in the same way the soul has stood for something inviolate, the sacred legacy of being human. Toni Morrison, the Nobel Prize–winning author of *Sula, Beloved,* and *Song of Solomon,* voiced this sentiment when she reflected on one of the most difficult times in her life: "It was as though I had nothing left but my imagination. I had no will, no judgment, no perspective, no power, no authority, no self—just this brutal sense of irony, melancholy, and a trembling respect for words. I wrote like someone with a dirty habit. Compulsively. Slyly" (Holt, 1993, p. C-1).

In expressing her experience through imagination, a new kind of coherence was found, one deeper and suffused with emotion. Learning and experience become entwined as the journey takes us below our surface awareness. "I guess [writing] is like going underwater for me," Morrison once told an interviewer (Holt, 1993, p. C-1), and therein lies both the opportunity for discovery as well as the danger.

In organizations today, we face being assaulted by experience or cultivating it. When we honor the idea and fact that all individuals have their own experience, their own organization coded in images within their minds, we begin to recognize the daunting responsibility of building human systems that grow out of the *what is* of experience and the *what ought to be* of imagination. The tension of these two paths leads both individuals and groups into new learning. The cultivating of experience is a lesson relevant to modern organization. It is a lesson first learned at an individual level, as the following story illustrates.

Rachel Bridges was troubled. She had reached a point in her profession where little made sense and her job stood in jeopardy. Three months before, her entire staff had walked out during employee appreciation day in protest over conditions in their work area. Her supervisor had given her notice that over the next few months she must demonstrate a change if she was to continue with the organization. She was ambivalent herself about staying or quitting. I was offered as a resource to her, and she said she resented the conditions under which we were working together, but she was willing to give it a try.

As she told her story, a picture emerged of working six or seven days a week and staying late almost every weekday. She said she lives off "caffeine, cola power, and candy bars." The pressure of keeping up was finally wearing through her. Talking of her experience, she referred to a spiraling anxiety that made her less effective and more vulnerable: "I don't feel just disempowered, I feel disemboweled. My guts are hanging out there." What Rachel described was a feeling of emptiness and invisibility. "My staff see right through me."

In discussing some of the specific expectations of her managerial role, Rachel became animated and angry. "There was a reengineering project in my area that I was left out of completely, and now with the recommendations out, I'm supposed to jump on the bullet train and see it all gets done. They left out a few things like who was supposed to do all the work and what resources we have to do it." She said she was not out to blame anyone else, but she did not know what else to do. "I guess I have to stop trying to control. It's really about letting go, but I can't seem to do that."

Rachel brought up how foreign her job role seemed from who she really was: "In my soul, I'm open, sensitive, warm. I genuinely care about people." What was it about her role that seemed so foreign? How had the details and day-to-day crises separated her so completely from the person she knew herself to be? In responding to these questions, she reflected on how much she was simply being honest about how she felt. She let people see how upset she was and didn't try to hide her frustration and anger. In an odd sense, the way she took up her role was an honest reflection of her soul.

"How is role different?" she asked, beginning to explore her own answers. "Role is not really about me, is it? My role is to listen, to follow through, to clarify priorities, and to know what I'm talking about. These are the very things that give me trouble. When I'm under pressure, my hearing is the first thing to go. When I'm stressed, I never share with people what I'm doing or why something has to be done. It's so strange. I've felt personally assaulted, like it's my soul being attacked. Isn't it my role that's being harpooned? In a strange way that's a relief."

Reflective to begin with, Rachel now had new avenues to explore. Her images became more vivid as she reported that somehow she had to figure out how to let her "breast plate" drop without being stabbed through the heart. She acknowledged an ongoing fantasy, a belief that her staff wanted someone else and were disappointed that all they had was her. What would it mean to take up a new role, one that could give her some protection while still allowing her to lead and contribute?

In the months that followed, Rachel took her insights in new directions. She reported that her role had been premised on a system that was completely dysfunctional. At the heart of this insight was an awareness that she would not be needed if the place actually worked. On the one hand, her soul was traumatized daily by the trivial requests and annoying breakdowns that routinely came up. On the other hand, she wanted to feel needed. But the very things that made her feel needed were unpleasant: "There's this big gap between wanting to feel necessary, to know you matter, and being needed for all the wrong reasons. The gap is between *wanting* to matter—my soul needs—and *how* I matter—the trivial tasks of my role." She was not without humor and mimicked a sucking noise to indicate what it felt like to have this gap. The dissonance between role and soul had created a vacuum.

Rachel's increased capacity to be mindful of the system she was in allowed her to begin drawing pictures and writing out questions that seemed more appropriate to creating a new psychological role. She drew pictures with images (icons signifying heart, brain, knots, breast plates) and arrows diagramming both the emotional flow of her internal world and the process flow of work. The questions she wrote for herself were reminders of what her role must be about: "Do we have the right mix of people for the project? Do people know where they stand? Are people being asked to do things they know how to do?" She also noted system questions: "Is this system working in a way anything can get done? Do we have backup plans for things going wrong, and have we talked about them?" She had to remind herself that this wasn't a checklist but an internal role that was hers to take up. "I can't do all these things, and if they want me to, screw 'em. What I can do is pay attention and tell the truth and work with others to see what can be done. That's a huge relief even when I'm losing sleep over some new problem that's happening. I'm not responsible for everyone else."

One of the issues Rachel confronted through this process was how dissatisfied she was with one of the key people, outside her area, that she had to work with to get anything done. "Frankly, he's a jerk. He needs to feel in charge and in charge over me. He's opinionated and stubborn and doesn't want to hear what I have to say. He has a wall around him that goes on forever." She told a story about a time she tried to communicate with him about problems among her staff and he showed no interest.

Wrestling with her feelings, Rachel came to a temporary resolution. She didn't have to like him to work with him, and he didn't have to be concerned about her if it didn't affect their work together. "I envy people with boundaries," she said after a pause, "because that's at least one way you don't become overwhelmed with everyone's problems." In a roundabout way, she acknowledged that her work with others must be centered on outcomes. "If he doesn't view my staff as relevant to the work we're doing, then I have to show him why it matters or accept that it's OK. I can't dictate how he should be." Rachel had always wanted to be friends with people first before working on a task, but she was finding there needed to be alternative routes to relatedness. She noted on numerous occasions how much work did not get done because people, not liking each other, wrote each other off. "Maybe I need some boundaries of my own in order to relate."

Four months after she was put on probation, Rachel met with her supervisor about her performance. They had been meeting periodically, but this time it was to celebrate some of the changes that had been made. Rachel said her role was now less of an armor that kept others at a distance and more a coat that she could take on and off—"Maybe a coat with Kevlar inside, a lightweight armor that protects my heart." She gave as an example a staff member in her department who had filed a grievance about vacation time he believed was due him. Though she felt close to the employee and the action saddened her, she was able to focus on making the process a fair one, submitting her documentation without feeling personally attacked. "I told him that however it came out, I valued his work and looked forward to continuing our work together. I thought his jaw would drop." In addition, she was finding new ways to engage with and consult her staff rather than sitting alone in her office "doing all the planning."

In reviewing her changes, Rachel noted both personal differences and work-related ones. She had started to exercise and only occasionally worked six days a week. She also began to see how a self-imposed perfectionism had intruded on her ability to take on significant tasks, creating either avoidance or self-castigation. In a strange mirroring of her earlier image of disembowelment, she began to see the times she wielded the knife on herself. In doing so, she began to feel greater power over her own hand. Even with boundaries, those invisible markers she envied others having, she started to see that she had made progress: becoming less caught up in other people's problems and more able to set limits around what she tackled.

In regard to her work role, she outlined for the supervisor a distinction between her strategic role and what she called tactical priorities. Her strategic role within the department included oversight of operational systems, staff development, and financial performance—systems that needed constant retooling. Her strategic role outside the department included being a liaison with interdependent groups and functions. This amounted to building credibility with other managers and developing long-term commitments with individuals whose roles were also to keep the operation afloat. She found there were ways she could be needed for her creativity and resourcefulness rather than simply as someone to patch up the latest leak in the boat.

Her tactical priorities, in contrast, involved the self-discipline of taking up her role, managing the balance between work and personal life, and establishing clear boundaries with others. She was developing a way of paying attention to her own experience and cultivating that experience so that she could take charge of her immediate tasks. These were not rules, she said, only the beginnings of a map for navigating. "It's not like I got religion or anything."

Her supervisor wondered out loud if these changes could be learned by others or if one had to be in crisis to learn them. Rachel did not answer the question. She said she knew better now what she wanted to control and what she would never control. She hoped she would not need another crisis to remember what, in a sense, she had known from the start. "There's just some greater permeability now, less of a vacuum between my role and my soul."

Rachel's story alerts us to the need to create an internal sense of role amidst the complexity of the workplace. But the story also suggests a heightened awareness about the organizational systems of which we are a part. The next chapter explores how we can begin paying greater attention to the human system and organizational complexity out of which our role is constructed.

9

Viewing the Whole

A Way to Grapple with Contradictions

J ack Welch, the chief executive officer of GE, sent a stir through the corporate world when he said leaders who think they know what's going on just don't understand. The paradox implicit to his comment suggests that thinking you know is evidence that you don't, and that acting from a false assumption of knowing can be a dangerous obstacle in moving forward. The validity of his own comment came back to haunt Welch when one of GE's business units, Kidder Peabody, was shown to be reporting phantom profits. Welch's reputation as one of the most admired of CEOs was sullied when it was learned that Kidder Peabody's problems were part of a larger corporate culture that chased after the bottom line so avidly that executives typically did not know what was going on. But we must assume that they thought they did.

This is the dilemma that all of us face in an increasingly complex world fraught with ethical and moral contradictions. If we think we know, we don't, and if we think we don't know, we still have to act as if we do. This produces the leadership schizophrenia that so troubles us and creates conditions under which even the best-intentioned leaders may look away and hope that their rationale for how they want things will not be too sorely tested. Can we help but wonder why "positive thinking" is so seductive to those faced with complexity beyond comprehension?

In this chapter, I suggest a way to think about systems, about the whole, that allows for much greater tolerance for not knowing yet still allows action to be taken. Thinking about the whole is a discipline that takes into account empirical evidence and also subjective information involving feelings, intuition, and moral judgment. Issues of domination, surveillance, fragmentation, and illusion can be understood as aspects of a system that must be accounted for. Otherwise, our "knowing" becomes fragile. What we perceive as reality is only a half-truth.

Thinking About the Whole: Roles and Perspectives in Organizations

Imagine a shoe factory in New England that is known for its high-quality shoes and excellent craftsmanship. The employees of the factory have traditionally viewed it as an extension of their community. Many workers' parents and grandparents worked there, and the history of the factory's good times and bad are like a children's story told time and again. Along with the stories of changing economic cycles are tales of the social meaning that the factory holds among its employees. Company-sponsored dances and picnics are part of the lore of relationships that result in friendships, marriages, and community building that hold people together. Although modern times have frayed some of the commitments people have to each other, there is still a sense that the small town retains the familiarity and safety so valued by its inhabitants.

The new owners, a group of out-of-state investors, have affirmed their intent to keep the company well funded and capable of producing high-quality products. They have visited the factory and assured everyone that they value the high morale and familylike operations of the company. They profess their belief that well-paid workers and a good attitude are associated with the continued quality they value. Yet they also have a commitment to their shareholders and have vowed to produce the highest-quality products at the lowest possible costs. Increasing competition from both domestic and global markets has made them particularly sensitive to the changing modes of production necessary to stay profitable.

In the first year under new ownership, little of consequence changes. Some departments are merged and a few of the older employees leave with fairly reasonable severance packages. A mission statement is written, in cooperation with existing management, that calls for continued high quality at the lowest possible cost to customers.

But in the second year, the owners investigate new technology that will mean a changing skill mix that will upgrade some employee skills and pay but overall will require many fewer workers. Although they regret the short-term effects of their decision, they believe the long-term results will ensure the company's continued viability. The town is in an uproar. Almost every family will be affected or knows a family that will. Rumors are rampant that this is only the first of many future cuts and that the factory itself is being targeted to move to another state or even out of the country. Some of the rumors focus on the elimination of the company-sponsored picnics because a survey of workers had shown that a dwindling percentage of employees still value the activity. Employees feel helpless and call for a protest, a strike, or even sabotage of the new equipment.

The company owners are also concerned. They do not like hearing that the employees are upset and threatening action. They believe the past paternalistic practices of management fostered unrealistic expectations within a global economy and a dangerous insularity from the realities of business. They believe a few bad apples trapped in a romantic mind-set of small towns and company picnics are stirring up trouble and misrepresenting the majority of workers who care little about such things. Both sides prepare to do battle.

This imaginary company is an example of a system in upheaval. It illustrates the contradictions and moral dilemmas that are familiar to many who have had to face downsizing and dislocation. It also illustrates how different the same system might appear to individuals who occupy different roles.

For the employees of the company, the shoe factory is a social system as well as a work setting. Workers hold social, emotional, economic, and historical expectations that afford them a sense of continuity, familiarity, security, and self-esteem. They make something with their hands that they feel pride in. They earn a living that allows them to care for their children, and they participate in a community that affords them a link between past and future.

For the owners, the system is a business that has to sustain viability and profitability. They feel a fiduciary responsibility to install the latest technology, to stay abreast of competition, and to provide shareholder return on investment. For the shareholder, the system is part of a network of investments that promise a return on equity, calculated by its risk and potential earnings.

Each of these "system portraits" represents what might be within the mind of the individuals who take action within the organization as they see it. Each portrait overlaps the others in ways that hold the opportunity for cooperation and the common good but that can just as easily be the basis for all-out warfare.

The concept of multiple perspectives in organizational thinking means that each individual has a different mental picture that is influenced, but not determined by, the position he or she holds. No one can say that owners, workers, and shareholders should think in predetermined ways, only that they must answer to their own experience of the system. The organization in each person's mind is a function, at least in part, of his or her position within the system.

Thinking about organizations as composed of multiple perspectives does not imply a moral judgment or formula for deciding what is right. This is critical to understand for proponents of systems thinking, who tend to value it as a technology of conflict resolution or a means to arrive at an understanding that is somehow better because it is more complex. A systems outlook cannot justify organizational choices or impose a particular course of action. The domain of what makes up a system and the domain of what is the right thing to do are separate, and the boundary between them must be respected.

Systems thinking helps us account for behavior within groups that is on the surface polarized or, from a particular perspective, not rational. The worker who is willing to let the organization fail rather than have it change so it can be viable is acting from beliefs that most value the social system and economic arrangements that evolved with the business enterprise. The owner, whose actions may risk the failure of the entire enterprise, can believe sincerely in the necessity of change even if it is detrimental to a few. Both parties are willing to let the actual organization die so that the picture of the organization in their mind can live. Attending to and recognizing these multiple perspectives within the organization can reveal the emotional content that fuels the behavior of the parties involved.

In applying the concept of multiple perspectives to systems thinking and to taking up our roles, we must be prepared, without thinking we already know the solution, to struggle with competing pictures and contradictory forces. We will not understand all the elements that make up the picture, but we had better try to understand. To do less risks the arrogance of acting without knowledge or the paralysis that accompanies being forced to act without even a hypothesis for what is happening.

The paradox of knowing and not knowing propels us forward into inquiry, into wanting to appreciate how others see the same system. The value of such inquiry is what it reveals about the relationship between the human system of personal relationships and its external environment. Are individuals within a system aware of their external environment? Do they all interpret in similar ways what is outside the boundary of their system? Do they respond with different emotions? A systems perspective coupled with human curiosity and empathy allows us to interpret what is happening and act with the humility of knowing the limits of our knowing. The organization in the mind is a continually changing affair. We cannot possibly know what others think and feel, but what others report can influence our own picture of the system. In the case of the shoe factory, not being able to empathize with the varying perspectives risks polarization and inability to find common ground.

These internal pictures shape behavior as much as do external incentives, calls for excellence, or disciplinary processes. When we appreciate the nuance of each perspective, we begin to see a pattern emerge among the many perspectives that helps explain what before was unknowable. In the hypothetical shoe factory, employees cannot view their company as simply an equation between quality and cost. They hold an emotional connection to their past and a demand for a future that will serve the whole community. The owners, though aware of these needs, simply cannot account for them on an emotional level, and so they prefer to see a few bad apples and an outdated paternalistic mentality. To proceed beyond the limitations of our perspectives we need to step back far enough to see patterns emerge. And to do that, we need to appreciate how boundaries in our minds affect what we are able to picture.

Managing Boundaries Inside and Outside the Organization

The traditional view of organizations emphasizes the boundaries that seal them off from their environment. In this view, an organization is an island unto itself, and the traditional markers involve not the relationship with the environment but the internal boundaries. Examples of this kind of boundary include departments that are clearly separated from each other, vertical hierarchies in which everyone reports to the person above them, and discrete job tasks that have a beginning and an end. The boundaries are structural and external to the individual because they exist for everyone in the same way. One knows where one is in the hierarchy, what area or occupational title one has, and what job must be done. The boundaries offer consistency and continuity but are often rigid and unyielding. One does not challenge what appears objective and unapproachable.

In a systems view of organizations, one that accounts for multiple perspectives, the boundaries of an organization are not only more permeable with the larger environment but also more psychological. Rather than sealing off the worker from what is outside, the boundary between organization and environment is understood as where the learning occurs. The popular idea in corporate America of using focus groups made up of customers to inform workers of the experience of people using their products or services is an example of learning at this permeable boundary. The effect of the focus group is to shift the psychological boundary within the mind from one's own immediate work area to the end user who depends on the organization's collective efforts.

Boundaries, then, are not just external. They also exist within the mind of the individual. Taking up a role within an organization requires openness to making boundaries more permeable and sophistication as to how to manage one's own boundaries with others. In the previous chapter, Rachel Bridges demonstrated this skill by seeing her department's functions as part of a larger system while at the same time figuring out who was part of her network and how best to deal with them. Like the idea of role, boundaries allow us to reflect on where we begin and end without becoming excessively rigid.

The corporate world has zealously taken up half of this equation. There is an increasing emphasis on eliminating the internal and structural markers that have in the past determined how the workplace is understood. Jack Welch at GE carried this idea to an extreme, saying the "dream for the 1990s is a boundaryless company . . . where we knock down the walls that separate us from each other on the inside and from our key constituencies on the outside" (Hirschhorn and Gilmore, 1992, p. 104). Yet we may want to be cautious as to how far to take this idea of boundarylessness, lest we start to think we know and fall back into the paradox of not knowing. Boundaries are necessary in a system so that it can function. They are essential to psychological feelings of coherence and the maintenance of equilibrium because without them we are easily overwhelmed. Even when formally eliminated, boundaries do not simply disappear. Instead they become more subjective, lodged more in the organization in the mind rather than in an organizational chart. Imagine the feelings of someone who grows anxious in open spaces and is trapped in a glass-enclosed elevator riding up the side of a building. The person is unable to get out, but the world outside can get in. This is the danger of stressing the removal of boundaries in a system that has simply made them more invisible. Managing our boundaries, not simply eliminating them, is the new frontier for functioning in the workplace.

Organizational theorists Larry Hirschhorn and Thomas Gilmore have argued that the traditional organizational map individuals use to navigate for themselves no longer exists. In an article in the *Harvard Business Review*, they suggest that there are new boundaries that must be accounted for. These boundaries involve the psychological line between self and others as well as between self and work. They include how we manage authority, task, power, and identity. The article has drawings of a human head with the brain divided by these boundaries, which suggests an initial attempt at acknowledging the organization in the mind.

Managing our boundaries leads to questions about necessary tensions. The boundary questions about authority ask: How do we lead but remain open to criticism? How do we follow but still challenge superiors? The boundary questions involving task are: How do we depend on others we don't control? How do we specialize yet understand other people's jobs? Questions about power involve personal reward: What's in it for us? And questions about identity involve differentiation from others: Who is—and who isn't—us? The tensions raised by these questions involve defending one's interests without undermining the organization and feeling pride without devaluing others (Hirschhorn and Gilmore, 1992, p. 107). The discipline of taking these questions seriously changes the nature of viewing the organization as simply a place of domination and submission, or inclusion and exclusion, and substitutes instead a personal responsibility for managing one's own boundaries in relation to others. These questions obligate us simultaneously to respect our own subjective experience and still attend to others. The result, if pursued, is a greater permeability between self and others and between self and work.

In addition to their cognitive questions, Hirschhorn and Gilmore suggest an emotional link that ties these boundaries to our feelings. The organization in the mind is not simply an intellectual construct; it is also a way to appreciate emotional life. When the authority boundary is not being managed well, the necessary tensions between leading and following are torn apart, leading to rebellion, distrust, and passivity. When task is not understood and no one feels in charge, then shame, anxiety, and loss of confidence are triggered. When subgroups within a system have polarized, leading to a struggle for power, individuals may begin to feel powerless, exploited, and angry. When one's identity feels threatened, leading to fear of annihilation, individuals become deeply mistrustful and act contemptuously toward each other. These feelings, often thought to be purely individual matters, become recognizable as the results of violations of boundaries. A human system, unlike a mechanical one, operates fluidly across cognitive, emotional, and physical states. We cannot know the "reality" of such a system because each of us in it is in flux (as is the whole system), but we can identify patterns of behavior that suggest underlying coherence or turbulence. To do this, we need the skill of shifting our perspective.

Internal Focus: The Preserving System Perspective

Organizations face two challenges simultaneously. First, they are obligated to make boundaries more permeable, internally among departments and externally with their environment. Second, they are influenced more and more by how individuals manage ideas of role and boundaries in their minds. The more organizations face the first challenge, the more they must depend on the second. I believe this is why the quality efforts of the 1980s and the reengineering strategies of the 1990s have often failed; they emphasized eliminating or redrawing organizational boundaries without respecting the human capacity to cope or the tenacity of human systems to evolve at their own pace. Often, and frequently with good intentions, we have treated people as simply information processors to be engineered or gullible innocents who would buy in at the first offer of greater responsibility and a dash of group cohesion. "We may be dumb," a member of a redesign team told me once regarding his skepticism, "but we're not stupid."

One way to keep the underlying coherence or turbulence of an organization in mind is to imagine that there are two separate perspectives for seeing how human behavior is organized. In one, the organization exists without reference to its external environment, while the other emphasizes the interactions between the organization and its environment. Let us call the first perspective the *preserving system* because it functions "as if" its main purpose were to preserve existing patterns. The second strategy we shall call the *purposeful system* because of its focus on how the group as a whole accomplishes its objectives. These two perspectives are not incompatible, but they cannot be lumped together. Like the discovery within quantum physics that light is both wavelike and particlelike at the same time, preserving systems and purposeful systems exist simultaneously. The two strategies complement each other, but (as with light in quantum theory) they cannot both be observed at exactly the same moment. Both are necessary, and yet both can become destructive if either one is carried to an extreme.

Because of its internal focus, the preserving system is concerned with people and their feelings, their language, their customs, habits, and rituals. Management consultant Kate Regan tells groups to imagine themselves as anthropologists cutting through the underbrush and discovering, as if for the first time, an enclave of humans going about their activities. Who is grouped together? Who sits alone? Who seems to have power? Who is central to conversation?

If you wanted to bribe someone, what currency would you use? If you wanted to learn the truth, who would you want to interview? These questions are crucial to the preserving system perspective.

The preserving system was probably what Elton Mayo had in mind when he proposed using an anthropological perspective to study organizations. However, his ideas were quickly assimilated into a model that emphasized managing a worker's internal emotional state rather than respecting the unique human system created when people work together. The misplaced emphasis, premised more on the role of management to control, tended to interpret workers' needs for them rather than engage them in a dynamic discussion about their relations with work and fellow workers. The implicit challenge of a preserving system perspective is that there is an existing system of human relations outside the scope of direct managerial control.

The preserving system perspective gives lie to a straightforward view of behavior that attempts to manage resources toward a specified end. It draws attention to the limits of social engineering, specifically the limitations of treating human systems as a mechanism that can be directed by management. The control functions of management (planning, staffing, monitoring, goal setting) are relatively useless in this world; belief systems, existing power arrangements, unstated feelings, and inclusion and exclusion of members are more important. In other words, the preserving system perspective is about the meaning that members of an organization attribute to activities and events, rather than the activities or events themselves. Most of us who live in the system are unaware of the power of the preserving system because we are ourselves so immersed in it. In the hypothetical shoe factory, workers and owners dedicated to their own idea of preserving the organization face collective extinction. The power to impose new technology, a prerogative assumed by management, is set against an unwillingness to change, a prerogative assumed by workers.

The dramatic question at the core of the preserving system perspective is, What will we die for in order to keep alive the things that matter? It suggests a deeper underlying hypothesis about what matters most in a human system of interactions. Is it ideals such as freedom, free enterprise, equality? Is it qualities of human interaction such as self-interest, individual choice, status? Is it behaviors such as passivity, deference, dependency? The preserving system perspective alerts us to what is actually happening, not what is expected to happen or what should happen.

Many an attempt at social engineering, organizational intervention, and goal setting has foundered on the shoals of a tight and unyielding preserving system. When everyone is focused inward, without attending to what is happening outside in the environment or even internally with changes in the organization's management, structure, or policies, then concerns center on the preservation of the social rules, relations, and customs. Members of the organization worry about how to repel change, and how to distract attention from what is outside and direct it toward the inner workings of the system. New management, and their ideas on what should happen, come and go. What matters from this perspective is how the new people dress, their manners, their degree of intrusiveness into what is actually happening. New ideas are judged in reference to the old: "Oh, that was tried ten years ago." "The more things change around here, the more they stay the same." "That won't work because So-and-So won't buy it." These are statements of the preserving system at work, preserving what is known, honoring the often unarticulated and often unrecognized relational dynamics within the system.

Internal focus is not all bad, nor does it suggest that nothing can change. Nevertheless, the preserving system does not respond easily to rationality, external structure, or even new incentives. We might even think of it as the DNA of the system, the simple codes that give rise to immense complexity. The preserving system carries the genius as well as the resistance, the moral codes as well as the contradictions, the competence as well as the obsolescence. In the preserving system, the vitality to carry on regardless of the environment is a survival quality that must be regarded with respect. Efforts to change the "corporate culture" with pleas to work together better across departments, or superficial renditions of the "business case" for change, are simply not persuasive.

Leaders who attempt too dramatic a change are messing with a life form that can mutate unexpectedly and in unforeseen ways. Call it the Jurassic Park syndrome, when leaders regard the preserving system with contempt. The dinosaurs take over the park. One manager I work with reminds me, with no disrespect intended, that his staff are smart mice. If they are displeased, they will figure out how to get around any structural obstacles. He has learned to listen deeply to their concerns because he knows that real change won't happen by his orders. He has also learned, however, that this does not mean he must be passive or without goals. The preserving system's internal focus is only one perspective of how behavior flows in human systems.

The Purposeful System: Boundaries and the Environment

The purposeful system perspective is concerned with the aims and intentions of the system, what the people who constitute the system seek to do. Unlike the internal focus of the preserving system, attention to the boundary between the organization and the environment is central to the purposeful system. The questions implicit to this perspective are about meaning and relevance: What are we about? What does the environment in which we operate need us to do? To answer these questions requires more than a mission statement, more than a catalog of values or simple prescriptions such as increasing quality at the lowest possible cost.

In the hypothetical shoe factory, the positions associated with the various roles represent only a first look at how purpose is identified. Individuals have other ways to see their organizational system. The new owners, for example, might appreciate that competitiveness and shareholder return are strengthened if workers have some say over new technology. The workers might appreciate that a leaner employee base is inevitable and that they can influence how a transition is managed. Shareholders can regard return on equity as a long-term fiscal strategy rather than as an annual entitlement. Purpose is malleable, a mental construct that constantly evolves based on information and relationships. The purposeful perspective pays close attention to the complexity of the interactions and needs of all the stakeholders in the system.

The purposeful system perspective, like the preserving system perspective, is also based on survival, but survival that takes into account the environment rather than focusing on internal relations. The current debate over environmental constraints on how businesses use resources is an example of finding a deeper level of meaning regarding purpose. At the turn of the twentieth century, industrial titans like Carnegie, Ford, and Rockefeller could turn their attention exclusively toward production and empire building. Human as well as mineral resources were merely fuel for their notions of progress and the expansion of material goods. The organization in their minds was pretty much an extension of themselves and their appetite for dominating markets, controlling production, and influencing government policy. Although much of this picture remains the same today, information about ecological disaster and disintegrating communities demands attention. Leaders can choose to turn this information into opportunities for public relations, or they can ask themselves deeper questions about how their work relates to the survival of our own species and the planet.

The purposeful system perspective is analogous to piecing together a puzzle without the picture on the box that tells you what the finished design should look like. Sir Arthur Eddington, the theoretical physicist, once told a story comparing the fitting together of a jigsaw puzzle with the nature of scientific discovery: "One day you ask the scientist how he is getting on; he replies, 'Finely. I have very nearly finished this piece of blue sky.' Another day you ask how the sky is progressing and are told, 'I have added a lot more, but it was sea, not the sky; there's a boat floating on the top of it.' Perhaps next time it will have turned out to be a parasol upside down, but our friend is still enthusiastically delighted with the progress he is making" (Wilber, 1984, p. 205). Eddington is describing how a picture in our mind shifts with each new element that is added. If we remain open to new discovery, we may not need to disassemble the previous pieces, but we must be willing to revise our impression of what the whole puzzle (or purpose) will look like. There are times we may become absorbed with just a few pieces, but the trick is to remain open to new discovery and to delight in new pictures of the whole. In contrast to engineering a new system, purposeful thinking is responsive to how the whole is constructed, rather than simply defining the relationships among fragmentary pieces. Purposeful system thinking is therefore identified by how disciplined one is in creating a real dialogue about the nature of the work, its connection to one's own experience and to the organization's outcomes.

The purposeful system perspective recognizes a relationship between purpose and outcomes. What a system produces, both intentionally and unintentionally, is the scorecard for understanding how a system relates to its environment. The factory that produces large quantities of widgets, but widgets that are defective, is not attending to its purpose. The school system that is graduating large numbers of students but is unable to account for why these students cannot read or think is not reckoning with its purpose. The hospital that measures its success based on revenue alone but does not enhance the health of its members is not considering its purpose within the community. I once heard a group of ministers complaining furiously that their congregations were leaving them. They accounted for this as spiritual immaturity and flight from responsibility. What they had to face was their own responsibility to the deeper purpose of religion in society, the purpose of faith in a secular environment. The answers do not come easily. From a purposeful system perspective, the questions that continually propel discovery are, What is our system for? and, Is that purpose reflected in our outcomes?

Taking up a role in an organization is very much linked to these questions because they are what keeps the organization alive in each person's mind. It is more than simply deferring to the words of a mission statement or wishing that what we do has meaning because we say it does. It is a discipline of identifying how one's actions are related to organizational outcomes. To do that requires standing back enough to ask questions of our work and our role. Matthew Fox makes this connection in *The Reinvention of Work:* "Ask your work, 'Why are you working?' Ask your role, 'What role are we playing in the world?' Notice, let us not ask ourselves that question but our work and our role. Let work speak. Let work take responsibility for itself. Let work stand up and be counted. Give work its dignity of being, its nobility in being among us, for it is everywhere even when we may feel out of work or overworked" (Fox, 1994, p. 80). The purposeful system perspective takes as a given that we must be able to ask these questions to animate our work, to give our work its dignity and its soul. This is what is missing from the polarized perspectives in the shoe factory, where each side simply looks at how best to leverage its own position.

Attending to the Whole

Preserving and purposeful perspectives cannot be observed simultaneously. We are condemned, by the nature of being a participant observer, to attend to each state separately. However, by appreciating that these two perspectives can exist simultaneously, we can extend our own observational powers. When we attend to the feeling states, rituals, power dynamics, and habits of organizational life, we are engaging in the preserving system perspective. When we attend to the organization's aims in the community, the allocation of resources, and the revised boundaries in our mind, we are participating in the purposeful system perspective. Our capacity to shift perspective, to honor and engage both, is a mark of our capacity to take up role. We must be alert to the tendency to view one perspective as good and the other as bad. Both are necessary.

When we try to hold opposing ideas together at once, there is a necessary tension that can either fracture understanding or generate greater flexibility. A key function, therefore, of holding together the preserving and purposeful perspectives is to alert the individual to the differences and tensions between desired outcomes and actual events. By holding both these twin realities, we can better bend with the organization we are in and respond to it and each other in creative ways. But most important, we can take up a role with purpose without going crazy.

I have seen absolute delight on the faces of managers who begin to recognize how their efforts at fostering a new vision do not account for the way things are. One manager confessed to a nagging doubt that while her staff was outwardly agreeable to being involved in her vision, they secretly felt she would fail to bring about change. They subtly sent her the message that things could never change and that they resented any changes asked of them. They would tell her how hard she was trying and how she should not be discouraged, but they also seemed resigned to maintaining their behavior exactly as before. Rather than simply labeling their behavior as resistance, she began to appreciate the genius of their strategy, keeping her at a distance while maintaining the habits they were accustomed to. She began to feel less crazy and less incompetent in understanding how both their agreement and their reluctance could be a mutual reality. She could see that the need to preserve what they knew and the desire to change were not mutually exclusive realities.

In another example, I worked with a manager who felt whiplashed by one crisis after another. Each time, it seemed that one group had it out for another group within her organization. Everyone blamed everyone else for the problems, and each group articulated an absolute helplessness to do anything about it. Donning the role of anthropologist, we came up with three rules that seemed to describe everyone's behavior. (These behavioral rules may be viewed as the unconscious patterns that preserved the system; I use *unconscious* here as meaning behavior so familiar it was below conscious awareness.) First, avoid conflict. Second, point out problems. Third, accept no responsibility for the problems pointed out.

From this perspective, we began to construct a set of behaviors that would respond to these conditions. Bring out conflicts before they erupt, and ask people how they might want to respond to them. Second, acknowledge the problems that are voiced but demand to know what people individually can do about them. Third, identify individuals most likely to model new behavior and support their attempts to do so. Finally, bring forward information about how their work affects others, including quantifying which outcomes are going well and which poorly.

Most critically, the manager had to present herself as supporting her staff as they worked out problems with each other, rather than fixing their problems for them. From this psychological stance, she felt more prepared to tackle the sometimes intractable concerns presented to her.

Taking up a purposeful role and demanding the same of others runs the danger of the self-imposed expectation to be at all times clear and certain. The skill of practicing not knowing, while still having purpose, involves the ability to lead others (and oneself) to a deeper understanding of the nature of the problem and the solution. Not being clear acknowledges a respect for what one is bound to leave out. Niels Bohr, the quantum physicist, demonstrated this skill with ample creativity and consternation. Historian of science Barbara Lovett Cline wrote: "As soon as [Bohr] completed a sentence he would see what it failed to say and begin to change it, trying to put, in that one sentence, different points of view and the connections and interactions among them. It was not perfect clarity he sought but a flexible and deep understanding. The idea could be made to seem clear but then, he felt, one's understanding of it necessarily would be shallow" (Cline, [1965] 1987, p. 214).

Bohr would chide himself to "Work, finish, publish!" But just as consistently, he would hand over the paper to a colleague and ask, "How can this be improved?" It is this practice of disciplined "not knowing" that propels one to grapple with the shifting sands of the preserving and purposeful perspectives and the role one is taking up.

In grappling with contradictions, the soul is stirred into being. Soul resides in the tension between apparent opposites, born from our own experience and reflection on experience. Soul is paradoxical in its essence. What kills soul in organizations is the wish to cleave the paradox in half, to ignore one side or to ignore the tension between the two sides. The coexistence of preserving and purposeful perspectives is one example of this tension.

To think about the whole, we are obliged to hold paradox together. We can be neither solely visionary nor exclusively pragmatic. We must deal with the power of individuals and groups to insist on continuity as well as the human desire to change. In doing so, we are confronted with our own role in the larger scheme of things. And in staring into this pool of self-reflection, we may be aided by understanding the difference between personal power and how we take up our authority in larger systems.

Roles, Power, and Authority

Amanda Block, a manager caught in a turf war stirred up by a reorganization, was battling over changes in the reporting structure that would reassign members from the operations division to her technical division. The head of the operations division stonewalled and then flatly rejected the proposed changes. "I'm fighting within the system instead of about the system," she told me. She realized that the technical and operations divisions had historically been at war and the reorganization had just become a new context for the fight to continue: "We have simply blamed each other for the failures and canceled out each other's positions. For every five things that they fail to do for us, they point out five things we don't do for them. I thought the fight over reporting relationships was the battle that would finally solve the problem. Now, I'm not so sure. My role in this is not to just win the battle, as I've thought, but to address the failures of our collective efforts. And to do that I need to form some kind of relationship with the other division head, who, by the way, I can't stand."

I wondered out loud if there was something valuable about the fight, some underlying incentive to keep things at a standoff. At first, she could not think of anything other than egos and a need for power. But after a moment she recounted how she had had good relations with the head of operation's predecessor, but their good relationship alone had had little impact on the problems. The battles within the system continued. "Maybe there is a fear that neither side understands the other well enough to work together without one side dictating to the other. Maybe keeping the fight going prevents a premature solution that wouldn't work. I never thought about it that way."

In this case, the value of the preserving system may have been associated with staying inwardly focused and holding to the familiar as a preventive strategy against reallocating power through a change in the reporting structure. Without faith in a shared belief about the nature of the problems or of ways to address them, the two divisions simply stared each other down. Amanda was so focused on addressing the deficiencies of her division that she had not seen how she might have been set up to fight with the head of the other division. She assumed the new reorganization design authorized her to move forward but did not account for the intricate web of existing arrangements. Her new awareness seemed to lessen the animosity she felt toward the other division head, depersonalizing the nature of their charged relationship.

As this example illustrates, in organizations today there is a great deal of struggle about how to get things done without the formal authority to demand compliance. This is understandable, given the high degree of interdependence and fluidity that marks present-day organizational life. The erosion of external boundaries makes any notion of clear and consistent chains of command obsolete if not simply foolish. Even under a traditional hierarchy, such as the military, officers will say that there is still no way of preventing "a crate from falling off the back of a truck." In other words, giving an order and having it followed, even when positional roles are clear, can often still be a dicey affair.

In organizational theory, much has been written about the difference between power and authority—the hope being that understanding the difference will somehow help one be influential as opposed to irrelevant. I propose a way of deepening our understanding of the difference between power and authority, a distinction that focuses on one's relationship to role and task.

The simplest definition of authority is the ability to make decisions that guide the actions of others. Authority in organizations is associated with the right to command, act, enforce rules, and—in areas of appropriate jurisdiction—have the last word. When employees complain they have responsibility with no authority, they are pointing out the limitations of their position in the organization to elicit compliance. Amanda felt she had the responsibility of overseeing the change in reporting structure but no clear authority to see that it got done. Authority is distinct from personal power because it is rooted in the shared beliefs of how a system must operate, whether that be a hierarchical relationship in an organization or a clan structure based on hereditary relationships. Authority is not personal in the sense that the ability to issue commands and the willingness to comply are *not* based on how one feels about the particular people involved. Authority depends on the animating breath of credibility in the system and is therefore communal in nature because its power is located in its members' shared beliefs.

Authority is an aspect of power but limited to the particular context from which it draws meaning. A military official has authority by virtue of the shared beliefs in a chain of command; a religious figure has authority by shared acceptance of his or her relationship to divinity, and a board member by a shared belief in the legal requirements of incorporation. The fraying of authority develops whenever the shared beliefs that hold people together are challenged or clarity about jurisdiction is blurred. The authority of a professor is hindered by a diminishing faith in the value of learning. The authority of police officers is hindered by a loss of faith in their truly standing for justice, and managers lose authority when multiple jurisdictions blur faith in a coherent reporting structure.

Power, on the other hand, derives from an array of more personal and individualistic attributes. Power can be associated with persuasion as well as intimidation, the skillful use of language as well as brute force, reputation as well as fear. Power can derive from personal relationships separate from collective aims, and from an ability to resist regardless of organizational imperatives. Power is more individualistic than communal; it can be located in the control over ideas as well as over material resources, in access to information as well as in hard currency. To be effective, power needs an instrument, whether an idea or a gun. In the absence of shared beliefs, power tends toward the coercive. As we have seen in Parts One and Two, ideas of normality, efficiency, and even workplace harmony have become instruments of overt and subtle coercion, rather than truly communal in the sense of shared values.

We need both authority and power to act in the world, to get things done, to move forward toward objectives. The taking up of a role in our mind requires awareness of the communal nature of authority and the individual nature of power. Both can be constructive and nurturing, and both can contain virulent shadows.

The challenge of finding and then taking up a role is fraught with the difficulties of seeing how the whole system operates in relation to power and authority. Thinking about how to take up her authority in role, Amanda had to contemplate where her jurisdiction began and ended and where the boundaries between her division and operations blurred. Her insight that she needed to have some form of relationship with the head of operations was not premised on liking each other but rather was based on having to develop some common ground, a shared belief, about how to proceed. In this way they could both examine existing arrangements and ask questions about the purpose of their collective efforts.

"I'm learning," Amanda told me, "that taking up role is more impersonal and more visual than I had known. I have to see myself against the background of all these other systems that exist. I have to see the picture of the organization in my own mind to appreciate how different someone else's picture might be. And when I do that, something changes. I don't know exactly what, but I know that I'm released from the burden of my own assumptions. I'm freed somehow to explore what else is happening around me."

Amanda's session with me ended with no clear resolution, but a road had been hacked out of the wilderness of personal opinions, perspectives, and assumptions. On this road was a foreshadowing of what it might look like to share a collective aim, to pursue a common goal. We attend to the whole by nurturing the whole person who *feels* the whole organization inside.

How does one account for the whole without disowning one's own emotional experience? How does one stay on track amidst the "pinches" of organizational interaction? How can we move from personal experience to organizational purpose and shared aims? To answer these questions requires not simply personal skills in such areas as negotiating and dispute resolution but also a way to distinguish role from the morass of organizational tasks. By wrestling with the limitations of her task to dictate a new reporting structure, Amanda discovered a new way to look upon authority that was more communal and interactional in nature. How can all of us keep in mind the distinction between person/role and simply performing organizational tasks? How can all of us respect both power and authority?

Navigating the Turbulence of Complex Systems

My experience has taught me that organizations that fail to distinguish the tension between power and authority often swing wildly between excessively personal and individualistic behaviors on the one hand and impersonal and rigid corporate requirements on the other. We look for a redesign to foster compliance, as if authority does not have to be located in people, or we depend too much on personal relationships to override the blurriness of boundaries regarding task and jurisdiction. For example, an organization based primarily on personal relationships among members tends to generate a kind of power that fosters an atmosphere of inclusion and exclusion, a need for control and fear of being controlled, and an inclination toward dependency alongside a dread of becoming dependent. The perception of power focuses the attention of group members inward because it is so much about their relations among themselves. The perception of power becomes a currency that often drives the relationships among members: who has certain knowledge, or a particular viewpoint, or a higher position can be the basis for how individuals align themselves with each other.

Relationships may be the cement of working effectively together, but the cement can harden and rigidify. Relationships in organizations can actually work against necessary outcomes, as members become more absorbed with each other than with what the work is. The tendency for relationships to become an end in themselves can become highly destructive, fostering an unrealistic view that everyone should get along while inadvertently encouraging a setting where there is less ability to do the work. In relationship-based systems that revolve around power—the qualities, competencies, and loyalties of individuals—the tasks implicit to work become subordinate to the relations among the members of the group. The limitations of a preserving system perspective are most pronounced when one is immersed in organizations based primarily on the good will of personal relationships.

An alternative to overdependence on personal relationships as a way to get things done occurs when a person in role is propelled by the integration of power and authority. In this context, authority is the alignment of person/role with organizational purpose. Authority is taken up when a person responds to the question of what the environment needs, not just the demands of the members in the system. When Amanda reflected on the outcomes necessary for both divisions, she began to consider how each group lacked knowledge about the other. She could also see a value in the internal focus of her organization as necessary to prevent premature solutions. In this way, she was able to make use of the shifting perspectives and also see that she was not simply an individual caught in an interpersonal conflict. She was then better positioned to use her personal power in service of the authority vested in her role.

Authority drives relatedness. Rather than forming relationships based solely on positional hierarchy or liking or disliking a person, relatedness is a discipline of pursuing a shared aim with others. From this relatedness members can foster the capacity to marshal forces on behalf of the system, its tasks, and its purpose within society. Relatedness is a natural extension of reflecting on role and authority. We realize we cannot accomplish what the system needs by ourselves. Amanda realized she could not achieve her desired outcome by simply stating her expectations or forcing someone higher up to make a decision for them. There was something missing—shared purpose—that hindered how these two divisions accomplished their work. Relatedness requires some baseline of shared purpose that allows individuals to negotiate with each other outside the domain of just personal power.

The skill of taking up authority within a role not only drives relatedness with others but also demands personal reflection. In role, our responsibility is not tied to who we like or dislike or what we would like to do or not do, but to the necessary tensions implicit in leading and following, dependency and autonomy, getting a job done and contributing to a work environment that allows others to feel accomplished. From out of these tensions arises a more fully human person, able to take charge and to listen, capable of seeing what is outside the system and of responding to the internal group dynamics. What is born from the fire of these internal tensions is an individual who can recognize his or her own frailty and the frailty of others. "We're all crazy," the head of a human resource department told me recently, "we just have to recognize when."

We are people in roles, and we take up our authority with some measure of our own personal power. I have known managers who understood their role with some depth but could not find their personal power. They could not find a way to act from their whole being. We need a sense of our own power and person to give life to a role. Power, though it is easily misused, is an essential ingredient to managing the internal tensions associated with role. We must hunt for our own power, that connective spark between what lies within and what is demanded of us from without. Power is the grace that permits relationship to our environment. When it remains connected with authority, power is a raw energy that propels individuals within organizations forward. We begin to seek not only survival but the rationale for why our organization should continue.

10

A Path with Soul

Joining Our Inner and Outer Worlds

*The seat of the soul is there where the inner world
and the outer world meet. Where they overlap, it is in
every point of the overlap.*

Novalis (Cousineau, 1994)

This final chapter returns us to the theme of soul as a quality stirred into being through reflection on experience and action in the world. To care for the soul within us and outside in the world, we need to recognize that soul is not our possession, but rather the points of overlap where interior experience and the outer world are joined. In the stories that have been woven through this book, there has been an underlying premise that neither self-reflection nor external analysis alone can gain access to the deeper regions of soul. We are continuously challenged by the overlapping nature of both inner and outer worlds. Psychologist James Hillman has written that we need a depth psychology of extraversion, a way of reestablishing the heartfelt connection to the world. He means to awaken us to the idea that reflection, fantasy, and analysis need not be exclusively self-oriented but rather can be joined with the analysis, fantasies, and reflections of the world around us. The greater part of the soul, he reminds us, is outside the body.

We need some markers in our journey back and forth between the inner and outer worlds. In the workplace, we need to take up roles relevant to functioning, but we also need to take up roles as citizens and participants in a reality beyond the confines of a single

,

organization. And in seeking the meaning of these roles, we come face to face with the daunting challenges of moral choice and human responsibility. A response to these challenges suggests that the journey can be furthered by respect for uncertainty, inclination for dialogue, and regard for paradox and for the interconnectivity of all life. What these responses have in common is respect for wonder and the many-faceted aspects of soul. Uncertainty, dialogue, and paradox evoke the ambiguity of experience and the responsibility for each of us to pursue an individual journey in a world animated with soul.

The Unknowable, the Invisible, and the Uncertain

The time has come again for the idea that we are all interconnected in known and unknown ways. We see it expressed in the ecological movement, where we find out that the plight of a rain forest has a relationship to the air we breathe. We sense it in the coincidences that mark our lives with meaning. We hear about it from advances in science, particularly quantum physics. And we are trying to find analogies to what we are learning and apply them to human systems and organizational environments. Margaret Wheatley captures the spirit of this inquiry by describing a central lesson drawn from areas as diverse as biology, chemistry, and physics, as well as theories of evolution and chaos:

> In new science, the underlying currents are a movement toward holism, toward understanding the system as a system and giving primary value to the relationships that exist among seemingly discrete parts. Donnella Meadows, a systems thinker, quotes an ancient Sufi teaching that captures this shift in focus: "You think because you understand one you must understand two, because one and one makes two. But you must also understand *and*." When we view systems from this perspective, we enter

an entirely new landscape of connections, of phenom-
ena that cannot be reduced to simple cause and effect,
and of the constant flux of dynamic processes [Wheat-
ley, 1992, p. 9].

The *and* is the point of overlap; it indicates a unity of relationship. Caring for the soul suggests an appreciation for *and*. But entering into what Wheatley calls a new "landscape of connections" can
be disruptive because it may challenge the validity of what is
known. From this perspective, soul seeking, soul searching, caring
for soul may disorient and disrupt, a trickster waiting at every turn.
What is left of our world when one and one no longer make two?
What is left is a deeper principle about the resiliency of human consciousness, an opportunity to establish new frameworks that somehow can account for the *and* as well as the *one*. What is left is a
search for deeper underlying patterns to understand physical as well
as human behavior.

The discoveries of quantum physics are one example of ideas
helping to shape an appreciation for deeper underlying patterns.
The quantum principle of "indeterminacy" or "uncertainty," for
instance, emerged from the collaboration of Werner Heisenberg and
Niels Bohr. They could not find a way to account for the dual
nature of an electron behaving as a wave and as a particle. "Can
nature possibly be as absurd as it seems to us in these atomic experiments?" wondered Heisenberg as he walked alone in near despair.
Bohr too was exhausted, and they both sought peace from each
other; their differences had drained the creativity from their discussions. Each needed a chance to collect his own thoughts. And
in their separate worlds, they came, in overlapping fashion, to a resolution of their problem.

Heisenberg discovered what was to become a fundamental
premise of quantum physics, a mathematical relationship involving the measurement of energy at a specific instant of time. At the
root of this relationship was uncertainty. If you begin with an exact

measurement of an electron's position, you cannot be certain of its momentum. If you are certain of its momentum, you cannot know its exact position. And if you cannot know both momentum and position at the same time, you cannot analyze the causal development of its movement. Unlike the laws of classical physics that allowed for seemingly exact prediction of movement in large bodies, the subatomic world escaped prediction. And it escaped prediction because of unity in a relationship: position and momentum could not be separated. To know one meant its companion could not be known. They are, said Heisenberg in comparing his insight to the tiny figures in a miniature house that respond to humidity, "like the man and woman in the weather house. If one comes out, the other goes in" (Cline, [1965] 1987, p. 207).

Bohr's contribution to this inseparable unity introduced yet another facet of relationship. He was interested in the meaning, the use of language and logic, behind the mathematical formulas. He came to believe that in the subatomic realm the act of looking itself influences what will be seen. Physicist John Wheeler more recently observed that the idea of a universe separated from the observer by "a six inch slab of plate glass" is thus shattered (Peat, 1987, p. 4). The stance of science, in which it observes a reality "out there," is challenged. We participate in the universe, and our very participation creates uncertainty. We cannot separate the tools of observation—whether mechanical device or our own consciousness—from the thing we are observing. Just as position and momentum are inseparable, so too may be the observer and the observed. We are subject to uncertainty, and we help create it.

The idea that uncertainty underpinned the search for knowledge, however, disturbed Albert Einstein, one of the founders of quantum theory, who held a reverence for an underlying continuity in nature. Einstein argued that God does not play dice with the universe. His actual words, taken from a letter to a colleague, were: "Quantum mechanics is certainly imposing. But an inner voice tells me that it is not yet the real thing. The theory says a lot, but it does not really bring us any closer to the secret of the Old One. I, at any rate, am convinced that He does not throw dice" (Clark, 1971, p. 340). Bohr's reply to Einstein, less well known but also arising from an inner voice, was just as revealing: "Stop telling God what to do" (Calder, [1979] 1980, p. 235).

The tension that arises from these two views continues to perplex those who ponder the nature of reality and its implications in day-to-day living. For Einstein, statistical probability alone represented an assault on his faith that the workings of nature could be comprehensible and objective, could be understood with the right framework. For Einstein, there was a pull toward a recognizable harmony in nature that could be known. The secrets of the "Old One" gave meaning and urgency to our quest for knowledge. Humility was an outcome of recognizing our deficiency of understanding. For Bohr, uncertainty was a principle that represented not a deficiency in understanding, but a richer appreciation for the limitation of our quest for final understanding. Quantum relationships opened doors to new ways of appreciating unities of relationship without having to explain them as separate entities with causal connection. Uncertainty offered a humility that arises from appreciating that our own desire to frame the question partially obstructs the answer. To borrow an image from Nietzsche, reality is reflected in a mirror and our own face obstructs the view.

The tension of these two views cannot be resolved, any more than physics can resolve the wave/particle duality that suggests the properties of one cannot be more primary than the other. But the relationship of two seemingly contradictory views does form a whole of its own. Relationship evokes wholeness when our point of view is at the boundary.

The implication for organizations is profound. We enter into groups with a high regard for uncertainty even as we try to understand and assess the causal nature of our actions. We still try to arrange the discrete variables that inform structure, but we are, in a more heightened way, also attending to the relationship among variables. The "wave" function of groups (shared values, common assumptions, joint goals) is complementary with the "particle" nature of groups (individual tasks, self-interest, subgroup agendas). They cannot be acted on separately. If there is a large disturbance in one set of functions, then we can expect to see it manifested in the other. If there is an inability to gain satisfaction at the individual level, then we might expect these dissatisfactions to show up as a breakdown in the group. We are all part of the group dance; we cannot solve the problem through isolated analysis or avoid the group by becoming more insulated from its behavior.

This way of looking at group behavior is very different from the usual remedies proposed to "fix" organizational problems. Team building, for example, an extension of the human relations approach to organizations, attempts to emphasize personal relationships and group adhesion. But translating what being a team player means in a particular context defies any set of rules or principles that can be devised because there is no way to predict all the variables. The concept of team building breaks down with the uncertainty inherent in human systems. We cannot foresee when the assertion of one individual or the changing demands of the workplace will break down the intent of working together.

Reengineering, a reworking of Taylor's approach to creating a science of management, offers the potential to view sets of relationships rather than fix isolated problems, but uncertainty again asserts itself. We cannot reengineer in a vacuum; the dance of the system continues and influences the meaning attributed to every phase of the new design. The existing relationships and the permeability of the organization with its environment randomly shape its capacity to sustain change. In the time it has taken to write these last few pages, one of my clients received a death threat, another was informed of lost funding, and a third had to replace a quarter of her staff. Uncertainty is an essential feature of organizational life, and there is no model for change design or set of organizational precepts that can eliminate its influence. Reengineering as a model never promised to eliminate uncertainty and randomness, but all too often the *idea* of reengineering did. There was offered an illusory hope that change could be brought about in an incremental, causal, controlled fashion.

Uncertainty and Synchronicity

Our attempts to understand organizational behavior and implicitly control where it is heading must include indeterminacy and uncertainty. The failure of a model to work in one setting when it worked in another should come as a relief, not a burden. We are released from the collective illusion that given the right prescription, a cure will be forthcoming. We are freed from the straitjacket of individual expectations that we could make it work if we were just smart enough, or if we just stayed more up-to-date on the latest management tips, or just worked ourselves closer to exhaustion. Instead, a respect for uncertainty suggests qualities of alertness, an attention to multiple relationships, and a certain calmness in the face of happenstance. We are reminded by the daily events of our lives that we are not captains of our own souls, but neither are we utterly without direction or meaning. We stay tenuously at the boundary of believing a greater force does not play dice with our lives; but neither can we dictate what the gods should do.

Respecting uncertainty places us at the points of overlap between inner meaning and outer events. Coincidences that appear to be random patterns, thrown out by pure chance, take on a meaning in experience. A colleague, Mark, who was reluctant to submit a manuscript to a particular publishing house was convinced by a friend to allow him to submit the manuscript on Mark's behalf. The manuscript was lost, and the friend offered to submit a second copy to an alternative editor. This manuscript was rejected, but Mark formed a relationship with the editor that resulted in a later book contract. For Mark, the random events formed a pattern leading, in this case, to a relationship with an editor and the challenge of writing a book different from the one he reluctantly submitted. The meaning was that the particular chain of events led to a desired outcome, but at the same time it mirrored Mark's intense ambivalence about writing a new book. The lost manuscript, the persistence of a friend in submitting a second copy, the rejection of the first manuscript, the connection made with the editor all led inexorably to a choice Mark had put off for years.

Carl Jung, in collaboration with the quantum physicist Wolfgang Pauli, introduced the term *synchronicity* to describe external acausal events that mirror internal processes. As author F. David Peat wrote in exploring the implications of quantum theories: "While the conventional laws of physics do not heed human desires or the need for meaning—apples fall whether we will them to or not—synchronicities act as mirrors to the inner processes of mind and take the form of outer manifestations of interior transformations" (Peat, 1987, p. 24). The recognition of relationship between inner processes and outer events received unexpected popular attention in James Redfield's 1993 book *The Celestine Prophecy*, which promoted the idea that coincidences relate deeply to our personal odyssey in life. Whether we believe we understand the cause of these acausal events is not the point. In uncertainty is a glimpse of soul, if we know how to pay attention. We create meaning from the patterns that reach us, tuning in to what the philosopher Martin Buber called the "sphere of the between."

In organizations, assessing meaning from randomness is one way of attending to the overlapping sphere of self and others. All the planning in the world cannot determine how things turn out. Randomness plays tricks with the details of our plans. The outcome of a critical meeting is influenced when a member cannot show up or a location becomes inaccessible because of a rainstorm. A report deadline is met, but the envelope that carries the report is routed to the wrong department. A tightly structured implementation plan is made irrelevant by the loss of funding. A carefully crafted long-range plan is made obsolete by new initiatives from competitors. In myriad ways, randomness asserts itself into the details of our efforts.

One way to look at this is to affix blame, to find the culprit, to plan harder, to attempt to gain greater control over the details. The word *control*, in fact, originates from a medieval method of checking the details of accounts using a duplicate register (*contra rotulus*, "against the roll"). Another way is suggested by respect for uncertainty. We can look for patterns, attempt to find an opportunity in the new patterns that emerge, seek to recalibrate our own intentions, and forge relationships that incorporate randomness rather than condemn it. We do not have to abandon planning or individual accountability but instead can link them with a richer perspective that tolerates both a causal connection between events and an appreciation for the dice being thrown. The soul is in the details, but so too is the devil.

There is a Zen parable that captures the mysterious connection between attending to our own consciousness and the external events that enfold us. A respected teacher was asked by members of a village if he could come and bring rain to their dry fields. They had tried many different approaches, including soliciting the help of a number of rainmakers, but still no rain came. When the teacher agreed to come, he asked only that he be given a small house and a garden he could tend. Day in, day out, he tended his small garden, neither performing incantations nor asking anything further of the villagers. After a while, rain began to fall on the parched earth. When asked how he could achieve such a miracle, he answered humbly that when he came to the village, he sensed disharmony within himself. Each day by tending his garden, he returned a little more to himself. As to the rain falling, he could not say. The garden is a wonderful metaphor because it suggests that if there is a safe place for something to grow, then harmony may be restored elsewhere.

To care for the soul suggests a return to the self, but a self that interacts intimately with the world around us. Every day we enter situations that are inherently uncertain but still marked by underlying patterns. These patterns may be emotional fields, dry because there is little nourishment or turbulent because of unresolved feelings of anger, disappointment, or frenzy. When we come in contact with each other, some aspect of the underlying field affects us. Like the teacher in the story, we can come to recognize the disharmony in ourselves and begin to make a place where the particulars can be tended. Yet to embrace the idea that our own consciousness is influenced by and influences what is around us, we must honor the overlap of self and other. We must look for the unity of what happens and how it happens as inseparable from each other, without forcing a causal link to explain each occurrence.

One lesson I draw from this in organizations is an orientation toward goal setting and shared outcomes that lives in the here and now rather than in a romanticized future. Goal setting does not always account for the way things are, becoming instead simply wishful thinking, that is, the belief that envisioning goals will cause them to happen. When we work with others more in the here and now, our attention is drawn to the immediate link between how something happens and what we wish will happen in the future. We become less susceptible to abstract goals that separate the experience of doing from a desired but detached future. We become more attentive to the here and now of relationship among people and processes. In this context, outcome is a self-limiting process that continually asks, What can be achieved with others, now? My goals, for example, may be to establish teamwork, or design a process for organizational learning, or identify a vision for the next five years, but these are abstract concepts. Outcome relates more to the particulars of what can be realistically achieved. Attending to outcomes obliges us to hold the twin realities of what is hoped for and what is. The question becomes not simply "What are our goals?" or "What happened in the past?" but "What are the next steps we should take? What can we do that has continuity with where we are coming from and where we are going?"

An outcome orientation speaks to the question of how we can work with others without either imposing a rigid sequence of instructions or wallowing in group paralysis. When individuals can assert viable outcomes and groups can participate in creating shared outcomes, the details follow naturally rather than being forced. Uncertainty is accepted as part of moving forward together rather than becoming an enemy that must be annihilated. The wear and tear of working in a group that cannot tolerate uncertainty is exhausting. By contrast, working with those who share a sense of desired and feasible outcomes can be energizing. All of us are familiar with groups in which every unforeseen event creates chaos, while in other groups the unforeseeable does not hinder moving forward, creating instead opportunities for new learning and new ways of approaching a situation. Members of the organization are propelled by questions regarding actions to be taken rather than how they can control the unforeseeable.

An outcome orientation and a respect for uncertainty are associated because, taken together, they hold the middle between causality and chaos. Sometimes what we want to accomplish actually gets done, and sometimes outcomes we didn't anticipate take over. Our own consciousness holds these two potentials from warring with each other. We learn, for example, that delegating may involve losing control over the details but still allows us to influence an outcome. But to influence the outcome we must attend to the particulars of the relationship, not just the details of the task. In a world that accounts for uncertainty, it is relationship with others, not control over the discrete parts, that influences causality.

When we become aware that different realities can occur simultaneously, we gain a capacity both to shift our own attention and to rely on the realities of others. We become aware that different people in different contexts help us *see* a reality we determine together. We honor the fact that data, about the group and its purpose, are spread out among the participants. Rather than holding

on tightly to just that portion of events we observe, we open ourselves to the multiplicity of perception, deepening our own experience of outward events. Each individual is a mirror of the whole,
but simultaneously each individual can account for only a portion
of what is happening. We need dialogue with each other that
evokes a greater whole.

An Inclination for Dialogue and Deep Listening

Martin Buber told a powerful story of his own experience with dialogue. On Easter Sunday of 1941, there was a gathering of men from
throughout Europe, apprehensive of the catastrophe brought on by
world war. They sought in some way to establish a supranational
authority that could avert calamity. The gravity of their task and
the honesty and unreserved quality of their conversations created
a heightened sense of being with each other. In the midst of a plan
to make their initial ideas public, a Christian member of the group
lodged a protest that too many Jews were being nominated. He
asked whether nations would be receptive if Jews were in too great
a proportion. Buber, not unreceptive to the argument but bristling
at the covert implication, rose to protest.

In the middle of his reply, Buber wandered off course and found
himself lecturing his Christian colleague that it was the Jews who
better understood Jesus. It was the Jews who could know him from
within, who could understand Jesus in a fashion that was inaccessible to those who submitted to him. Buber wrote: "'In a way that
remains inaccessible to you'—so I directly addressed the former clergyman. He stood up, I stood up, we looked into the heart of one
another's eyes. 'It is gone,' he said, and before everyone we gave one
another the kiss of brotherhood. The discussion of the situation
between Jews and Christians had been transformed into a bond
between the Christian and the Jew. In this transformation dialogue
was fulfilled. Opinions were gone, in a bodily way the factual took
place" (Buber, [1947] 1965, pp. 5–6).

What can we make of this extraordinary interaction? What might it mean that "In this transformation dialogue was fulfilled"? How could telling a former clergyman on Easter that he did not understand Jesus be a prelude to dialogue? Yet in the clashing of their opinions, opinions were obliterated. In the midst of what was sure to be polarization within the group, a bond was formed between two individuals that extended into the group itself. How could this be?

At the core of this story, I believe, lies an image of overlapping regions. The context for the story is of individuals who have come together to speak the truth, who respect the essential purpose of their quest to avert catastrophe. In this situation, the forces threatening to split the world apart—nationalism, ethnic and religious division, economic superiority—reappear in microcosm, in the form of what proportion of Jews are acceptable to promote ideas of peace. How could it be otherwise if this group takes its daunting challenge seriously? How could this group not share a permeable boundary with the fragmentation let loose in the wider world?

In protesting the clergyman's protest, Buber establishes the first prerequisite of dialogue: *before a conversation of two must be the assertion of one*. To meet at the boundary with another does not mean leaving one's own ground, nor does it mean being swallowed up by the ideas of the other. We cannot exchange our individual perceptions in order to don the cloak of group perception. We cannot ignore our own deeply ingrained worldview by adopting a false mask of base agreement with others.

The problem is not the conflict between the individual and the group; it is instead that beliefs inherent in individualism and collectivism destroy real dialogue in equal but opposite ways. When Buber asserted that Christians were excluded from Christ's teaching, he was confronting his colleague's assertion that Jews, in too great a proportion, must be excluded. At this juncture, the two "looked into the heart of one another's eyes," and the invisible boundary that kept them from exchange dissolved. This, I suspect,

was what it meant when in the heat of argument the former clergyman said, "It is gone." What was gone was the distance that kept
them from meeting at the boundary. What was gone was the insularity of opinion that separated and isolated one individual from
permeability with another. In its place were the two, gazing together
at mere opinions.

"All real living is meeting," wrote Buber. And from this simple
formula we find a passage to perceiving soul as something not within
but between. Within the space between inner and outer, relationship takes on animation. Dialogue, from *dia* and *logos*, means literally *across the meaning of the word*, a journey across and back
between the inner coherence of the one and the other. The journey is about thought itself, how thought puts form to our speech
and behavior. When we have dialogue, we meet at the crossing
between the forms of each other's thought. We pace up and down
our own side of the crossing, until there is a moment of connection.

Quoting Friedrich Heinrich Jacobi, Buber poetically evokes the
moment of meeting the other: "I open eye or ear, or stretch forth
my hand, and feel in the same moment inseparably: Thou and I, I
and Thou." At these moments, "The I is impossible without the
Thou" (Buber, [1947] 1965, p. 209). Caring for the soul is an assertion that there is no self and no true perception of other without
the trip from inside to outside and back again. We meet at the
boundary of our whole selves and realize, during moments of grace,
that we are not apart from others. We touch each other through our
senses, by sight, hearing, smell, feel, taste, and intuition, and we
know a fleeting unity. The unity is as enduring a truth as separateness. This is how Buber can say that when opinions dissipate, one
experiences the factual in a bodily way. The physical nature of connection is present, even without touch.

The more one experiences dialogue, however, the more one
senses its ethereal quality. We are doomed, by the nature of our separate identity, to notice how fleeting unity is to human consciousness. We cannot go back to tribal times, when unity was an

assumption that required less attention. To participate in dialogue requires a graciousness toward its coming and going, to connection and separation. To live too long in a perception of unity would be to invite the merger with another rather than the meeting at the boundary. Caring for the soul is an assertion of sending and receiving, a submission to a unity greater than self, but not a merger that obliterates self. Amanda Block, in the last chapter, faced this challenge implicit in dialogue; she had to perceive a common purpose with an individual she disliked. Dialogue suggests she had to find a way through their differences without losing herself.

Central to dialogue is the skill of deep listening, becoming mindful of our own capacity to receive another's message. When we become personally aware not simply of another's words but of his or her seeking to address us, we begin to *tune in* to the sphere of the between. What is it they are trying to say with their hands, their eyes, their breath? What is it we are asserting by our own physical nature, by our own opinions, by our own assumptions? To seek the between is not to lose oneself but rather to have a heightened sense of oneself in relation. Deep listening is an experience of more than just catching the words of another. It is an invitation to attend to one's own depths. In a line edited from his original manuscript of *I and Thou*, Buber offered an image: "Thus the fisherman gets his catch. But the find is for the diver" (Buber, [1923] 1970, p. 55).

In the experience of listening, truly listening, we discover ourselves to be the diver, not the fisherman. We find we are no longer entertaining the other with our cleverness or intelligence but entertaining thought itself—our own and the thought we are listening to. Ideas, images, fragments of sensation sweep through the mind: "Oh, now, that's an idea. Where did that come from? Now, whose thought was that, mine or the other?" Like Alice in Wonderland, we follow thought down its rabbit hole because that is where the pictures and conversation take form. (Alice begins her journey after peeping at her sister's book and finding it boring; she declares ". . . what is the use of a book without pictures or conversations?") Down underneath, in the labyrinth, the deeper assumptions that give form to thought can be glimpsed. Down underneath are the varied manifestations of soul that are shared across human consciousness. Deep listening is where the overlapping regions lie, the sphere of the between.

Associated with this principle of deep listening is our capacity for play. Play is the stuff of learning, the innocence associated with seeing new things with old eyes and old sounds with new ears. In play, there is greater receptivity when coming across the boundary and finding new forms of thought that seem upside down and inside out. In play is the freedom for improvisation, so critical to dealing with uncertainty and addressing others in the spirit of dialogue. In play we entertain thoughts and ideas as guests in our home, not as intruders threatening our need for certainty. In organizations I have found that only when some degree of play is validated do groups find traction to move forward. The individual who tentatively suggests they are "playing" with an idea, and is welcomed for that perspective, allows others in the group to also experience some measure of freedom to follow thought down into the rabbit hole.

The principles of listening and play give rise to an ability to suspend certainty, to hold out opinions, ideas, and assumptions, and view them as manifestations of how we are thinking. *Thinking* is used here to signify not only conscious intellect but also feelings, intentions, emotions, and desires. This suspension of certainty leads to new avenues of inquiry, the ability to ask new questions. In Chapter Eight, when Rachel Bridges asked how role was different from soul, she was leading herself into new areas for exploration. She was able to suspend her sense of alienation and engage her imagination. Her image of herself as empty and invisible gave way to a picture of herself as resourceful and creative. Suspending certainty, however, is not simply about our ability to look at an idea in new ways; it is the discipline of looking at ourselves having an idea. Rachel began to recognize she was the author of the images she articulated, the interpreter and artist at the boundary of the internal world she felt and the external environment with which she interacted. With this awareness, she could take up more personal authority in how to proceed, no longer the victim of separation between an internal world and an external one.

The capacity to suspend certainty does not in itself change external reality, but it does offer an alternative way to look upon ourselves and our experiences in relation. We can experience ourselves as part of a larger unity in which our own thought stands at a shared boundary with others. In Buber's story, the transformation from conflict to dialogue took place when individuals transcended their own personal biographies—their separate histories, opinions, life experiences—and were joined together at the boundary they shared, "a bond *between* the Christian and the Jew" (emphasis mine). Caring with the soul suggests we search for the betweenness, not a merger that obliterates identity but a suspension of our own assumptions long enough to open a door to shared meaning. "The I is impossible without the Thou."

How can the principles of dialogue remain relevant today and in organizations? How can we care for the soul amidst the constant pull to separation and self-interest? How can we link what appears to be a metaphysical concept of overriding unity with the rock-hard nature of separate reality? I think a place to begin is by noting where the soul's absence is most felt.

Communication, Information, and Dialogue

In organizations, one of the most common pronouncements is that there are problems with *communication*. The word has come to mean almost anything: staff lacking in morale, resistance to change, an inability to follow the simplest directions. Communication is on the top of everyone's list of things to do, but somehow it just doesn't get done. Managers repeat over and over, to themselves and to anyone who will listen, that they have communicated. They have sent out memos, presentations have been made, and expectations have been stated. The implicit assumption is that people just don't listen.

Dialogue suggests something else. If an individual cannot find a shared boundary, a place where information moves across and back, then communication has not taken place. The sender has no receiver for his or her message. The person receiving may not even be aware of what is being sent. Both wander up and down their own side of the crossing, oblivious or outright hostile to the other. One individual says, "I've already told them," and the other says, "No one tells me anything here." Both are correct. The first person has said the words, but the second person only hears the sounds. There is no form that holds the sounds together, no journey across the meaning of the word. "Always get a receipt," a colleague of mine says about communication. What he means is always attend to how a person responds: a question, his or her body language, a sense of connection to the sender. Ironically, enthusiasm and agreement are not sure signs that information has been received. These behaviors can often have more to do with relations of power and a wish to be liked. Dialogue takes place when both parties can assert their differences and then discover a crossing between. The key is in how each informs the other.

To *inform* is to put "form in." When we talk at a deeper level of conversation, the form behind our ideas can be discerned. We understand each other in a more profound way because the feelings, intentions, and desires of the other can be glimpsed. We no longer say to ourselves, "I've told him what he needs to know," but rather, "I know better what he feels and thinks about what I've said." Sending and receiving information become less separated from each other. The unity of I and Thou is reflected in the unity of talking and listening, an art of conversation more than a technique of imposing information on someone else. From the perspective of dialogue, the exchange of information is about a shift from the stance of individual opinion to a stance of connection. The outcome is that we feel heard and we can hear the other.

In the workplace, we are drowning in information but have too little time to make sense of it together. Information pours in over fax lines, computer modems, phone lines, and interoffice mail. We have the technology to put information out in vast quantities but not the human interaction to put "form in." Without a capacity for meaningful human dialogue, the information age will split, chunk, and cluster bits of information just as we once broke down mechanical parts for assembly. The ability to hold onto the whole, to create coherence, happens in relation with others. Information processed by machines electronically or conversations held at long distances over phone lines omit the sensory information, feelings, intuitions, and context for human judgments to be made. A manager I work with once complained of a conference call in which five people in five different locations attempted to arrive at a critical decision with just thirty minutes to talk. She found herself yelling at the group that no one even understood what question they were trying to answer. In the middle of her harangue, she stopped and realized she was screaming at a phone. She felt foolish and confused. "I can't see any of you," she finally said, "I can't get a picture of what you really think. I have no sense what you are all feeling or what you believe is important." The art of conversation, critical to constructing meaning out of disparate pieces of information, is fragmented by the very technology meant to serve human needs for communication.

Dialogue reminds us, particularly during those times we feel under pressure, of what is most important about communication. Like the manager screaming at the phone on her desk, we need to stop and become aware of the absurdity of pretending that communication is taking place just because we are hearing the content of each other's words. Dialogue suggests a deeper level of connection that allows for the underlying motivations, assumptions, and beliefs to rise up out of our words.

Caring for the soul asks us to look below and through the visible world in order to see what truly matters. The inclination for dialogue reminds us that the true life of meeting another is hidden and invisible, like a root that lies under the ground. But from that root

grows the plant, and from dialogue emerges the blossoming of a connection with an other. We activate the energies of the soul when
we become mindful of what grows in hidden places. We become
better prepared to meet the visible world knowing that there are
hidden roots below.

The Soul of the World:
A Place of Meaningful Paradox

Soul holds the middle among opposing forces, between conscious
and unconscious processes, between the individual and the group,
between the material and the spiritual. Soul is a place of meaningful paradox. Buber discovered an underlying unity through confrontation with another. Heisenberg and Bohr found a new way of
seeing physical reality by exhausting each other's perceptions. The
recognition of paradox, what seems at the surface contradictory, can
be the opening for new discoveries.

In a world infused with soul, there is recognition that paradox
rules. The recognition releases for a moment the bonds of separateness, received opinion, and dogma. We cannot know two because we know one. We must contemplate *and*, the relationship at
the boundary of what is known. T. S. Eliot wrote:

> At the still point of the turning world. Neither flesh nor
>   fleshless;
> Neither from nor towards; at the still point, there the dance
>   is,
> But neither arrest nor movement. And do not call it fixity,
> Where past and future are gathered. Neither movement
>   from nor towards,
> Neither ascent nor decline. Except for the point, the still
>   point,
>
> [Eliot, 1943, p. 15]

Eliot's verse might well be an ode to quantum physics, but I think it works also as a contemplative riddle about the elusive quality of soul: the essential paradoxes that lie at the still point. At the still point, separation no longer rules, categories of knowledge disappear, motion is no longer causal. Time itself is gathered together, and past and present lose their separateness. We are drawn into a landscape in which soul cannot be held onto inside us but instead must be perceived through our senses and our imagination. Soul draws our attention outward, to the soul's beauty and its pain. We are in the land of the butterfly, where soul perches on the still point between the known and the unknowable.

The world is infused with soul. We do not have to carry the full weight of soulmaking in ourselves. We do not have to possess soul, but simply recognize how soul possesses us. Soul, at once personal and individual, is also a window to the world around us. Soul is outside as much as it is inside, if we can respect soul's unique markings on everything we touch.

We should be careful, therefore, when we talk of only a particular quality of the soul (such as love) as having a central place, or a particular aspect of an organization (such as customer focus) as being the "soul" of a business. These are visions of the soul as internal and romanticized. Soul is not only an individual's or a group's best intentions. More often, soul appears to us first as our wounds, as the pathologies that show themselves when soul is ignored. Caring for the soul means becoming attentive to how soul is missing or present in the world around us—the soul spark that lives in the other and must be accounted for.

The notion that soul lives outside us is a tricky concept for those of us who have been raised with clear distinctions between what is human and what animal, and between what is animate and what inanimate. Can a moose have a soul? Can a rock? Can a building? In ancient times the idea of *anima mundi* described the feeling for a "world soul" that incorporated the whole of nature. In all things was animation, soul addressing us through its own nature. Buber's first inkling of otherness was evoked as a child, in friendship with a horse on his grandfather's estate. In *I and Thou*, he has a remarkable passage that touches on an exchange of glances and an imaginary conversation between himself and a house cat. The cat asks: "Can it be that you mean me? Do you actually want that I should not merely do tricks for you? Do I concern you? Am I there for you? Am I there?" (Buber, [1923] 1970, p. 145) The mystery and grandeur of soul lies in suspension of a world solely *there* for human utility. At the still point, the whole of nature takes on a spark of life, addressing us in much the same manner as Buber's cat. At the still point, we see not merely a world of things doing tricks for us, but a world ensouled, asking: "Do I concern you? Am I there," separate from you?

The challenge of our times is that we will adapt ourselves to a world that ignores soul, draining our natural resources and exhausting our human energies. The more we search for our own soul, the less we will be able to find it among the rubble left of the world around us. The soul that is flattened to fit our own image of surface goodness rebels. The world soul that is uncared for turns angry, whether it be manifested in ecological crisis or in collective human crisis, embodied in our cities, our institutions, our businesses, and our communities. The question of caring for the soul is not "What is the solution?" but "Where do I start to heal the wounds that surround me and that are in me?" From this stance comes the beginning of solutions.

To proceed forward with this question in mind, we must quiet down enough to hear what beckons and what it makes sense for us to do. In each of the many roles we play—employee, employer, father, wife, volunteer, activist—there are myriad opportunities for service, for caring with attention to soul. But we must be prepared to grapple with paradox, to ask of ourselves and others what animates our actions. The concept of anima mundi, that soul is alive in the world, has a very down-to-earth implication for organizations and for all of us who live and work in them. What we do has consequence. The fate of the world hangs on the thread of our individual and collective consciousness. We may wrestle at times with the inflation and deflation that accompany such a responsibility, but to deny responsibility is to take flight from what the world asks of us. In serving, there lies a dual purpose: to offer help to another and to attend to our own need for learning and growth. In helping another, we extend the hand of soul reaching out; in attending to our own learning, we take another step on our own journey. The two purposes, taken together, contain the self-importance of doing good while still permitting good action to be taken.

To care for the soul begins with a glance outside ourselves and a glance that is returned. "Can it be that you mean me? Do you actually want that I should not merely do tricks for you? Do I concern you? Am I there for you? Am I there?"

We are transformed not by caring for our own soul in isolation but by entering into a dialogue with something outside ourselves. It may, at times, be work we care about, or someone we care about, or something we feel needs attention. But whatever it is, we must meet it at the boundary and know it as something alive, animated by its own powers—a spark of soul addressing us.

References

. . . .

Adams, H. *The Education of Henry Adams: An Autobiography.* Boston: Houghton Mifflin, 1961. (Originally published 1918.)

Baida, P. *Poor Richard's Legacy: American Business Values from Benjamin Franklin to Michael Milken.* New York: William Morrow, 1990.

Bell, D. *The End of Ideology: On the Exhaustion of Political Ideas in the Fifties.* New York: Collier, 1961. (Originally published by Free Press, 1960.)

Bellah, R. *Habits of the Heart: Individualism and Commitment in American Life.* Berkeley: University of California Press, 1985.

Bentham, J. *The Works of Jeremy Bentham.* Vol. 4. London: Simpkin, Marshall, 1843.

Boorstin, D. *The Americans: The Democratic Experience.* New York: Vintage Books, 1974. (Originally published by Random House, 1973.)

Bowles, S., and Gintis, H. *Schooling in Capitalist America: Educational Reform and the Contradictions of Economic Life.* New York: Basic Books, 1976.

Braverman, H. *Labor and Monopoly Capital: The Degradation of Work in the Twentieth Century.* New York: Monthly Review Press, 1974.

Brown, J. *The Social Psychology of Industry: Human Relations in the Factory.* New York: Penguin Books, 1954.

Buber, M. *Between Man and Man.* (R. Smith, trans.). New York: Macmillan, 1965. (Originally published 1947.)

Buber, M. *I and Thou.* (W. Kaufmann, trans.). New York: Charles Scribner's Sons, 1970. (Originally published 1923.)

Calder, N. *Einstein's Universe: Relativity Made Plain—The Amazing Achievement of Albert Einstein and What It Means Today.* New York: Penguin Books, 1980. (Originally published by Viking, 1979.)

Champy, J. *Reengineering Management: The Mandate for New Leadership*. New York: HarperBusiness, 1995.

Clark, R. *Einstein: The Life and Times*. New York: World Publishing, 1971.

Cline, B. L. *Men Who Made a New Physics: Physicists and the Quantum Theory*. Chicago: University of Chicago Press, 1987. (Originally published 1965.)

Copley, F. B. *Frederick W. Taylor: Father of Scientific Management*. 2 vols. New York: Harper & Row, 1923.

Coupland, D. *Microserfs*. New York: ReganBooks, 1995.

Cousineau, P. (ed.). *The Soul of the World: A Modern Book of Hours*. New York: HarperSanFrancisco, 1993.

Cousineau, P. (ed.). *Soul, An Archaeology: Readings from Socrates to Ray Charles*. New York: HarperSanFrancisco, 1994.

Drucker, P. *The Practice of Management*. New York: Harper & Row, 1954.

Eiseley, L. *The Immense Journey: An Imaginative Naturalist Explores the Mysteries of Man and Nature*. New York: Random House, 1957.

Eliot, T. S. *Four Quartets*. New York: Harcourt, Brace, & World, 1943.

Fassel, D. *Working Ourselves to Death: The High Cost of Workaholism and the Rewards of Recovery*. New York: HarperSanFrancisco, 1990.

Foucault, M. *Madness and Civilization: A History of Insanity in the Age of Reason*. (R. Howard, trans.). New York: Vintage Books, 1965.

Foucault, M. *Power/Knowledge: Selected Interviews and Other Writings 1972–1977*. (C. Gordon, ed.). (C. Gordon, L. Marshall, J. Mepham, K. Soper, trans.). New York: Pantheon, 1980.

Fox, M. *The Reinvention of Work: A New Vision of Livelihood for Our Time*. New York: HarperSanFrancisco, 1994.

Genasci, L. "New Workplace Issue: Forced Overtime." *San Francisco Examiner*, Oct. 2, 1994, p. 28.

Giedion, S. *Mechanization Takes Command: A Contribution to Anonymous History*. New York: W. W. Norton, 1969. (Originally published 1948.)

Golding, W. "Why Boys Become Vicious." *San Francisco Examiner*, Feb. 28, 1993, p. D-1.

Hampden-Turner, C. *Radical Man: The Process of Psycho-Social Development*. Cambridge, Mass.: Schenkman, 1970.

Hillman, J. *The Thought of the Heart and the Soul of the World*. Dallas: Spring Publications, 1993.

Hirschhorn, L., and Gilmore, T. "The New Boundaries of the 'Boundaryless' Company." *Harvard Business Review*, 1992, 70(3), 104–115.

Holt, P. "Morrison's Poetic Force Earns Nobel." *San Francisco Chronicle*, Oct. 8, 1993, p. C-1.

Howard, R. *Brave New Workplace: America's Corporate Utopias—How They Create Inequalities and Social Conflict in Our Working Lives*. New York: Penguin Books, 1985.

Jung, C. *Modern Man in Search of a Soul*. (W. S. Dell, C. F. Baynes, trans.). New York: Harcourt Brace Jovanovich, 1933.

Jung, C. *Psychology and Religion*. New Haven, Conn.: Yale University Press, 1938.

Jung, C. *Psychology and Alchemy*. (R.F.C. Hull, trans.). Princeton, N.J.: Princeton University Press, 1953 (new material copyright ©1968 by Bollingen Foundation).

Jung, C. *The Psychology of the Transference*. (R.F.C. Hull, trans.). Princeton, N.J.: Princeton University Press, 1954.

Jung, C. *The Archetypes and the Collective Unconscious*. (R.F.C. Hull, trans.). Bollingen Series xx. Princeton, N.J.: Princeton University Press, 1959.

Jung, C. *Memories, Dreams, Reflections*. (R. Winston, C. Winston, trans.). New York: Vintage Books, 1965. (Originally published 1961.)

Kendall, D. "Renovation of the Heart." *San Francisco Chronicle*, Oct. 24, 1993, p. 12.

Knox, B. (ed.). *Classical Literature*. New York: W. W. Norton, 1993.

Lewis, S. *Babbitt*. New York: Harcourt Brace, 1922.

Madrigal, A. "What Is This Thing Called Love?" *Sunday San Francisco Chronicle*, June 26, 1994, Review p. 7.

Mayo, E. *The Human Problems of an Industrial Civilization*. New York: Viking Press, 1933.

Miller, J. *The Passion of Michel Foucault*. New York: Simon & Schuster, 1993.

Needleman, J. *Lost Christianity*. Garden City, N.Y.: Doubleday, 1980.

O'Shaughnessy, E. "The New Establishment." *Vanity Fair*, Oct. 1994, pp. 214–240.

Peat, F. D. *Synchronicity: The Bridge Between Matter and Mind*. New York: Bantam Books, 1987.

Peters, T. J., and Waterman, R. H., Jr. *In Search of Excellence: Lessons from America's Best-Run Companies*. New York: Harper & Row, 1982.

Redfield, J. *The Celestine Prophecy: An Adventure*. New York: Warner Books, 1993.

Robinson, D. (ed.). *Significant Contributions to the History of Psychology. Series C: Medical Psychology. Vol. III: P. Pinel, H. Mandsky*. Washington, D.C.: University Publications of America, 1977.

Roethlisberger, F. J., and Dickson, W. J. *Management and the Worker: An Account of a Research Program Conducted by the Western Electric Company, Hawthorne Works, Chicago*. Cambridge, Mass.: Harvard University Press, 1964. (Originally published 1939.)

Rosenzweig, R., Brier, S., and Brown, J. *Who Built America?: From the Centennial Celebration of 1876 to the Great War of 1914*. New York: American Social History Productions; Los Angeles: Voyager (distributor of CD-ROM), 1993.

Schor, J. B. *The Overworked American: The Unexpected Decline of Leisure*. New York: Basic Books, 1991.

Schwartz, J. "World at a Loss for Words." *San Francisco Chronicle*, March 3, 1994, p. 3.

Singer, J. *A Gnostic Book of Hours: Keys to Inner Wisdom*. New York: HarperSanFrancisco, 1992.

Smith, L. "Stamina: Who Has It, Why You Need It, How You Get It." *Fortune*, Nov. 28, 1994, pp. 127–139.

Taylor, F. W. *The Principles of Scientific Management*. New York: W. W. Norton, 1967. (Originally published 1911.)

Thiele, L. P. *Friedrich Nietzsche and the Politics of the Soul: A Study of Heroic Individualism*. Princeton, N.J.: Princeton University Press, 1990.

Tocqueville, A. de. *Democracy in America*. (J. P. Mayer and M. Lerner, eds.; G. Lawrence, trans.). New York: HarperPerennial, 1969. (Originally published 1840.)

Tolman, W. *Social Engineering*. New York: McGraw Hill, 1909.

Tully, S. "Are You Paid Enough?" *Fortune*, June 26, 1995, pp. 66–76.

von Hoffman, N. *Capitalist Fools: Tales of American Business, from Carnegie to Forbes to the Milken Gang*. New York: Doubleday, 1992.

Weiner, B. "Bergman Harnessed His Demons to the Chariots of Art." *San Francisco Chronicle*, Jan. 24, 1994, p. 4.

Weisbord, M. *Productive Workplaces: Organizing and Managing for Dignity, Meaning, and Community*. San Francisco: Jossey-Bass, 1987.

Wheatley, M. J. *Leadership and the New Science: Learning About Organization from an Orderly Universe*. San Francisco: Berrett-Koehler, 1992.

Whyte, W. H., Jr. *The Organization Man*. New York: Simon & Schuster, 1956.

Wiesel, E. *Souls on Fire: Portraits and Legends of Hasidic Masters*. (M. Wiesel, trans.). New York: Summit Books, 1972.

Wilber, K. (ed.). *Quantum Questions: Mystical Writings of the World's Great Physicists*. Boston: Shambhala, 1984.

Woodcock, G. *Anarchism: A History of Libertarian Ideas and Movements*. New York: World Publishing, 1962.

Zilboorg, G, and Henry, G. W. *A History of Medical Psychology*. New York.: W. W. Norton, 1941.

Zuboff, S. *In the Age of the Smart Machine: The Future of Work and Power*. New York: Basic Books, 1988.

Index

The Author

. . . .

Alan Briskin is the founder and owner of Alan Briskin & Associates, an Oakland, California organizational development consulting practice that helps business leaders, executives, and managers actively engaged with navigating change, defining work roles, and redesigning their work settings. His consulting clients have included organizations in the fields of accounting, banking, education, healthcare, insurance, high technology, software, law, manufacturing, media, mental health, criminal justice, and religion. He also consults to other management consultants in their work with organizations in the areas of change, leadership, and the development of learning organizations and to individuals who wish to enhance their professional and personal satisfaction with work roles.

His long-standing interest in the dynamics of the workplace began with his work in his family's business in the garment district of Manhattan and continued through a varied educational and professional career. He received his undergraduate degree in education from Goddard College (1974) and his M.A. and Ph.D. in organizational psychology from the Wright Institute in Berkeley, California. (1984). He has worked as a delivery man and assembler, been a director of education for a residential treatment center, a jobs counselor in a state prison, taught as an adjunct faculty in management and organizational behavior at both undergraduate and graduate levels, and designed and facilitated a leadership program for residents of Contra Costa County, California.

A former director of the Center for Organizational Studies, he is a professional associate of The Grubb Institute, an international research and training institute based in London, England. He has written articles in the areas of leadership, organizational behavior, and the history of management practices. This is his first book.

Berrett-Koehler Publishers

BERRETT-KOEHLER is an independent publisher of books, periodicals, and other publications at the leading edge of new thinking and innovative practice on work, business, management, leadership, stewardship, career development, human resources, entrepreneurship, and global sustainability.

Since the company's founding in 1992, we have been committed to supporting the movement toward a more enlightened world of work by publishing books, periodicals, and other publications that help us to integrate our values with our work and work lives, and to create more humane and effective organizations.

We have chosen to focus on the areas of work, business, and organizations, because these are central elements in many people's lives today. Furthermore, the work world is going through tumultuous changes, from the decline of job security to the rise of new structures for organizing people and work. We believe that change is needed at all levels—individual, organizational, community, and global—and our publications address each of these levels.

We seek to create new lenses for understanding organizations, to legitimize topics that people care deeply about but that current business orthodoxy censors or considers secondary to bottom-line concerns, and to uncover new meaning, means, and ends for our work and work lives.

See next page for other books from Berrett-Koehler Publishers

*Other leading-edge business books
from Berrett-Koehler Publishers*

Reawakening the Spirit in Work
The Power of Dharmic Management

Jack Hawley

HAWLEY RESPONDS directly to a widespread desire for spirituality at work, offering a practical vision of work permeated with "dharma"—deep integrity fusing spirit, character, human values, and decency. Through real-life examples, He shows how people can create improved workplaces and more resilient, effective, and successful organizations. He shows how leaders and managers who are motivated by a spiritual vision will liberate the best in people, and explains why all leadership is spiritual.

Hardcover, 224 pages, 5/95 • ISBN 1-881052-22-2 CIP
Item no. 52222-225 $24.95

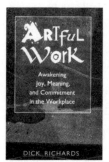

Artful Work
Awakening Joy, Meaning, and Commitment in the Workplace

Dick Richards

DICK RICHARDS applies the assumptions of artists about work and life to the challenges facing people and organizations in today's rapidly changing world. He reminds us that all work can be artful, and that artfulness is the key to passion and commitment. Readers will learn to take an inspired approach to their work, renewing their experience of it as a creative, participative, and purposeful endeavor.

Hardcover, 144 pages, 3/95 • ISBN 1-881052-63-X CIP
Item no. 5263X-225 $25.00

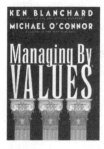

Managing By Values
Ken Blanchard and Michael O'Connor

BASED ON over twenty-five years of research and application, *Managing By Values* provides a practical game plan for defining, clarifying, and communicating an organization's values and insuring that it's practices are in line with those values throughout the organization.

Hardcover, 140 pages, 1/97 • ISBN 1-57675-007-8 CIP
Item no. 50078-225 $20.00

Available at your favorite bookstore, or call (800) 929-2929

The Power of Purpose
Creating Meaning in Your Life and Work
Richard J. Leider

WE ALL POSSESS a unique ability to do the work we were made for. Concise and easy to read, and including numerous stories of people living on purpose, *The Power of Purpose* is a remarkable tool to help you find your calling, an original guide to discovering the work you love to do.

Hardcover, 170 pages, 9/97 • ISBN 1-57675-021-3 CIP
Item no. 50213-225 $20.00

Repacking Your Bags
Lighten Your Load for the Rest of Your Life
Richard J. Leider and David A. Shapiro

LEARN HOW TO climb out from under the many burdens you're carrying and find the fulfillment that's missing in your life. A simple yet elegant process teaches you to balance the demands of work, love, and place in order to create and live your own vision of success.

Paperback, 234 pages, 2/96 • ISBN 1-881052-87-7 CIP
Item no. 52877-225 $14.95

Hardcover, 1/95 • ISBN 1-881052-67-2 CIP • **Item no. 52672-225 $21.95**

Your Signature Path
Gaining New Perspectives on Life and Work
Geoffrey M. Bellman

YOUR SIGNATURE PATH explores the uniqueness of the mark each of us makes in the world. Bestselling author Geoffrey M. Bellman offers thought-provoking insights and practical tools for evaluating who you are, what you are doing, and where you want your path to lead.

Hardcover, 200 pages, 10/96 • ISBN 1-57675-004-3 CIP
Item no. 50043-225 $24.95

Available at your favorite bookstore, or call (800) 929-2929

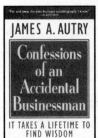

Confessions of an Accidental Businessman

It Takes a Lifetime to Find Wisdom

James A. Autry

IN *CONFESSIONS OF AN ACCIDENTAL BUSINESSMAN*, best-selling author James Autry blends candid and engaging autobiography with practical and realistic lessons in management and leadership. Reflecting on his thirty-two years in business, Autry shares a lifetime of hard-earned wisdom about the art of business leadership, as well as the art of living a balanced life.

Hardcover, 250 pages, 10/96 • ISBN 1-57675-003 CIP
Item no. 75003-225 $24.95

A Simpler Way

Margaret J. Wheatley and Myron Kellner-Rogers

A *SIMPLER WAY* is the widely awaited new book from Margaret J. Wheatley, author of the best-selling *Leadership and the New Science*. Here, Wheatley and coauthor Myron Kellner-Rogers explore the primary question, "How could we organize human endeavor if we developed different understandings of how life organizes itself?" They draw on the work of scientists, philosophers, poets, novelists, spiritual teachers, colleagues, audiences, and each other in search of new ways of understanding life and how organizing activities occur. *A Simpler Way* presents a profoundly different world view that changes how we live our lives and how we can create organizations that thrive.

Hardcover, 168 pages, 9/96 • ISBN 1-881052-95-8 • **Item no. 52958-225 $27.95**

301 Ways to Have Fun at Work

Dave Hemsath and Leslie Yerkes
Illustrated by Dan McQuillen

IN THIS ENTERTAINING and comprehensive guide, Hemsath and Yerkes show readers how to have fun at work—everyday. Written for anyone who works in any type of organization, *301 Ways to Have Fun at Work* provides more than 300 ideas for creating a dynamic, fun-filled work environment.

Paperback, 300 pages, 6/97 • ISBN 1-57675-019-1 CIP
Item no. 50191-225 $14.95

Available at your favorite bookstore, or call (800) 929-2929